BUSINESS REENGINEERING

—— THE SURVIVAL GUIDE ——

Selected titles from the YOURDON PRESS COMPUTING SERIES
Ed Yourdon, *Advisor*

BUSINESS REENGINEERING
— THE SURVIVAL GUIDE —

Dorine C. Andrews
Susan K. Stalick

YOURDON PRESS
Prentice Hall Building
Englewood Cliffs, NJ 07632

Library of Congress Cataloging-In-Publication Data

```
Andrews, Dorine C.
    Business Reengineering: the survival guide
    / Dorine C. Andrews, Susan K. Stalick.
       p.308  cm. — (Yourdon Press computing series)
    Includes bibliographical references and index.
    ISBN 0-13-014853-9
    1. Organizational change--Management.
    I. Stalick, Susan K.  II. Title.  III. Series.
HD58.A7  1994                               93-43618
658.4'063—dc20                                   CIP
```

Editorial/production supervision: BooksCraft, Inc., Indianapolis, IN
Jacket design: Lundgren Graphics, Ltd.
Jacket art: Stockworks, stock illustration © Eric C. Westbrook
Interior design: Robert Coalson
Acquisitions editor: Paul Becker
Manufacturing manager: Alexis R. Heydt

© 1994 by P T R Prentice Hall
Prentice-Hall, Inc.
A Simon & Schuster Company
Englewood Cliffs, New Jersey 07632

The publisher offers discounts on this book when ordered in
bulk quantities. For more information contact: Corporate
Sales Department, PTR Prentice Hall, 113 Sylvan Avenue,
Englewood Cliffs, NJ 07632, Phone: 201-592-2863, FAX:
201-592-2249

Printed in the United States of America
10 9 8 7 6 5 4 3 2

ISBN 0-13-014853-9

ISBN 0-13-014853-9

90000

9 780130 148537

Prentice-Hall International (UK) Limited, *London*
Prentice-Hall of Australia Pty. Limited, *Sydney*
Prentice-Hall Canada Inc., *Toronto*
Prentice-Hall Hispanoamericana, S.A., *Mexico*
Prentice-Hall of India Private Limited, *New Delhi*
Prentice-Hall of Japan, Inc., *Tokyo*
Simon & Schuster Asia Pte. Ltd., *Singapore*
Editora Prentice-Hall do Brasil, Ltda., *Rio de Janeiro*

CONTENTS

CHAPTER 3: Know Where You Are Going   41

CHAPTER 6: Move with Purpose   153

Contents

PREFACE

Some call it organization restructuring. Others talk about process re-design. If they don't know the buzz words, people may talk about working smarter or even reinventing government. We call it business reengineering. It means radically changing how people work—changing business policies and controls, systems and technology, organizational relationships and business practices, and reward programs.

Is business reengineering something really new? Isn't it old wine in new bottles? The answer to both these questions is yes and no. What business reengineering is trying to accomplish (i.e. making organizations more effective) is certainly not new. Nor are many of the techniques employed by business reengineers new. Four key assumptions distinguish business reengineering from other organizational changes strategies. They are:

1. Radical change can only occur when old ways of thinking and operating are destroyed.
2. Concrete results must be realized quickly.
3. Information technology plays a key role in any organizational change effort.
4. Any change affects *all* parts of the organization; therefore, a successful change effort must address and integrate people, technology, structure, and management philosophy.

This book is about making business reengineering happen in your organization. It is a practical guide for business professionals, information systems experts, managers, and executives who have been charged with making change. Everything you are about to read has been tried and tested.

Everywhere we have worked, we have been impressed by the project teams who have attempted reengineering. Their commitment, creativity, and willingness to learn and challenge the status quo continually exceed our expectations. The same cannot be said for many of their organizational leaders. The commitment to business reengineering must come from the top of the organization. And any business executive will *tell* you this. However, what executives say at the beginning of a business reengineering effort and what they do when faced with the uncomfortable reality of radical change often differ. Therefore, we make a special plea to executives to take the time to read this book. Their understanding of what reengineering is, how to make it successful, and of their role in the change process is greatly needed. In our experience, executive leadership is the single most important reengineering success factor, and yet it is outside the control of most project teams.

Business reengineering requires an interdisciplinary and collaborative approach. No one person can make a reengineering project succeed. It demands a team of people with a wide range of skills and knowledge, who can communicate across the organization and support each other in the struggle to change their organizations.

Business reengineering also requires courage. You must stand up to people and force them to confront issues they have previously been unwilling to face. In the midst of crisis you must remain calm, committed, and focused on the future.

Business reengineering is not about compromise or trade-offs. It is about creating a new reality that radically shifts the organization. That kind of shift is fraught with risks that cannot and should not be ignored. But, the risks can be managed.

So what is a "street-smart" business reengineer? It is someone who has the confidence, skills, knowledge, and tools to anticipate and act appropriately in any situation. Street-smart business reengineers are like experienced travelers. They are savvy folks with practical know-how. But, unlike experienced travelers who acquire street smarts through experience, most of us don't have the time to learn the tricks of the trade through trial and error. Therefore, this book provides basic "street smarts" for business reengineers.

As you travel through the pages of this book, here is what you will find:
- Chapter 1, "Know Where You Are," describes situations that are good opportunities for business reengineering, explains how to document them, and demonstrates how to develop a business case for project funding.
- Chapter 2, "Lighting the Way," reviews the basic principles for quality business reengineering—principles for process re-design, for organization transformation, and for continuous process and

project improvement. These principles provide a baseline for evaluating project quality.

- Chapter 3, "Know Where You Are Going," provides a guide for creating the vision for your reengineering project, a picture of the future organization.

- Chapter 4, "Don't Walk Alone," shows how to create a team structure that will involve the right people throughout the life of the project. It is different from traditional project team structures, introducing new roles and providing the means to expand and contract team membership as needed. This team structure ensures that project decisions are made by "insiders," those who will live in the reengineered environment. Business reengineering designs cannot be implemented by "them." They must be implemented by "us."

- Every savvy traveler has a map for guidance, whether it's on paper or in his head. In chapter 5, "Prepare for the Journey," we provide a map for business reengineers—a life cycle methodology for the reengineering project. Beginning with the first "twinkle" of an idea, this methodology provides a step-by-step approach for getting the job done as effectively and efficiently as possible. Each of the eight steps has clearly defined outcomes, activities, accountabilities, and decisions. There are even tips and techniques for approaching the work in each step.

- Much of the project work is based in on facilitation techniques. In chapter 6, "Move with Purpose," readers will learn the basics of quality facilitation along with guidelines for its use throughout a business reengineering project. Business reengineering cannot be dictated or commanded. Reengineering succeeds because of innovative thinking and consensus-building by people who understand the business and people who understand the processes and technologies.

- Lest you think reengineering is simple, chapter 7, "The Road Is Not Smooth, Watch for Danger," describes obstacles and problems you may encounter and how to overcome them. Organization and change issues become much more significant in business reengineering than in any other type of project.

Therefore, street-smart business reengineers must be politically savvy and persistently committed.

- And, in the end, with your reengineering completed, chapter 8, "Form the Neighborhood Watch," tells how to transition to a continuous process improvement mode so reengineering will never have to be done again.

After some 25 years of working with a variety of business and government organizations, we believe that radical change comes to an organization only with the structure and skills to make it happen. The natural inertia of an organization and the active resistance of individual people defeat many. Commitment and enthusiasm are critical, but they are not enough. Business reengineering takes "street-smarts." It is not work for the naive or the arrogant.

We wish to thank the many people who contributed their experience and ideas to the creation of this book. Special thanks go to all of those people who have worked with us on projects over the past several years as the knowledge in this book was created and tested. And many thanks for the tireless efforts of our production support team who included Karie Newmyer, Debbie Lawless, and Nancy Campbell.

Dorine Andrews
Susan Stalick

BUSINESS REENGINEERING

— THE SURVIVAL GUIDE —

CHAPTER 1

KNOW WHERE YOU ARE

Business reengineering is the act of radically changing how the work is done. To quote MIT's Michael Hammer, "The job of business reengineering is to rip the guts out of an organization and reassemble them in the context of today's changing business world." Why would we need to do this? Isn't this an insane way to bring change to a business? It is like sitting on your porch day after day and watching your neighborhood decay around you. Eventually conditions become so bad that simple repairs won't work. You must demolish entire buildings and build new ones and invest large amounts of money in new streets, lighting, and sidewalks. Sounds exorbitant, doesn't it? But this is exactly the situation in many organizations today! Organizations have allowed themselves to deteriorate, lose focus, and become bureaucratic and archaic in their operations. They patch, fix, and make do. We are famous for making something out of nothing, squeezing the most out of the least, making do with less. In the short run this can work. We can deliver those quarterly results. However, what works in the short run can be disastrous in the longer run. One reason for not having a long-term future focus is that not everyone recognizes the problems or understands their implications. Sometimes people feel threatened by the prospect of change. In one company, a reengineering project team unknowingly recommended eliminating a process that was created and installed by its vice president. The vice president's reaction was, "That process is just fine. The problem is that people have misused it. Your job is to fix the process, not get rid of it." So, people become defensive. Others see the problems as too overwhelming so "we just learn to work around it." In some organizations, power and status are derived from being able to fight the problem rather than solve it. People are rewarded for doing without or working "lean and mean."

The Dimensions of Business Reengineering

In our culture of quick fixes and silver-bullet solutions, many executives miscalculate what it takes to reengineer a business successfully. Early reengineering projects have been limited in scope with a minimum of affected "hard" processes and cross-organizational involvement, such as invoicing/billing or warehouse management processes. But today people are reengineering multiple business units, departments, and divisions that are involved with "soft" processes like planning, product development, and support servicing. In reality, this type of reengineering is more difficult because of the ambiguous scope and potential power conflicts associated with change. It requires more resources than most executives are willing to commit.

Such reengineering takes time. And the larger the project, the more time is required. Street-smart business reengineers understand that business reengineering requires infrastructure changes and cultural transformation in addition to process, organization, and technology changes.

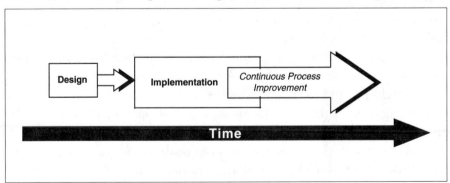

Figure 1.1 The Business Reengineering Continuum

Furthermore, once the "radical" changes are made, they must install continuous process improvement practices in the business operation to prevent future deterioration and ensure preventative maintenance (Figure 1.1).

There are nine dimensions to business reengineering that we divide into three layers (Figure 1.2). The first of these—the most visible and most concrete—is the physical/technical layer. Within this layer are the dimensions of process, technology, and organization structures. These dimensions provide the organization's operational foundation. The second layer, the infrastructure layer, consists of the reward structure, measurement systems, and management methods. These support the physical/technical operational layer. The third layer is the least visible and most difficult to change. These dimensions are organizational culture, political power, and individual belief systems. By understanding each of these layers and their dimensions, street-smart business reengineers can formulate a successful project strategy.

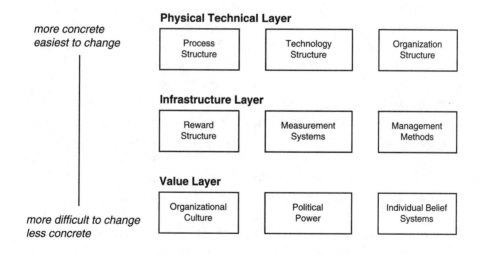

Figure 1.2   The Dimensions of Business Reengineering

The Physical/Technical Dimensions

This is where many business reengineers mistakenly focus their efforts. This is because the physical/technical dimensions are what people can easily see and do. However, if this layer is the only focus, business reengineering is doomed to fail. Also within this layer, if the three dimensions of process structure, technology structure, and organization structure are out of balance, many operational problems can occur.

The *process structure* consists of the business processes, their outcomes, and the policies, practices and procedures that support the processes. Process structure defines what, when, and how work is performed. Processes can be triggered by internal events, timing cycles, or external stimuli. Processes produce the business outcomes—the business products and services. Some processes demand considerable control and rigidity, such as processes for operating a nuclear plant. Other processes allow a more flexible approach. For example, a customer complaint-handling process could allow the customer service reps to decide how to solve the customers' problems. Processes are grouped into work flows, information flows, and time flows to show their interdependencies. They can be decomposed into smaller processes of tasks and steps, which can take an infinite variety of forms. The true purpose of process is to produce a "quality" outcome in a timely, predictable manner. Processes, in and of themselves, are meaningless—it is the outcomes that are important.

Some processes originate by design; others emerge informally to meet real or perceived organizational needs. If all processes were purposefully designed and maintained to meet evolving business needs with the outcomes clearly in mind, reengineering would be unnecessary. Unfortunately, this is not the case. Many of the processes performed in our businesses today emerge informally and spontaneously or become inadequate because they are not changed as business needs change. Therefore, we can often find multiple organization units duplicating the work of a single process or no organization unit performing a whole process. We can find processes that are undocumented, inconsistently applied, and personality dependent.

The *technology structure* consists of the automated communication, networking, and computer systems used to support the process structure. It includes the data, applications, communications, platforms, and related technologies. Supported by local and wide area networks, imaging systems, and mobile communications networks, we can communicate with just about anyone in any location at any time. Developers using relational database products and advanced development software languages and tools can deliver technology much faster and more cheaply. Optical scanning devices, bar codes, smart cards, and other new technologies eliminate time-consuming and error-producing data entry.

The sensible application of technology depends on the competent integration of technology with work processes. Historically, we too often have relied on technology to solve business problems. Overlaying technology on ineffective business processes only aggravates the underlying problems. People then blame the technology. And then the technology is not used effectively or is even abandoned.

The *organization structure* defines who performs, manages, and is accountable for each business process. Organization includes the job structure, reporting and work-group relationships, accountabilities, job content, and skill/knowledge requirements. When process and organization structures are out of alignment, there are gaps in accountability. Too often, executives trying to improve the organization change only the organization's structure, adding to, rather than reducing, confusion.

The recent focus on organization structure design has been to use innovations such as nonhierarchical reporting relationships, fluid organizations, broader job accountabilities, and self-managing teams. In addition to providing new options, it also raises new issues concerning managerial and supervisory roles and process management responsibilities.

The Infrastructure Dimensions

The interpretation of policies and procedures heavily influences how the physical/technical dimensions perform on a day-to-day basis. Therefore, if the physical/technical dimensions change, the infrastructure dimensions must also change because they reinforce desired operational behavior. Without proper reinforcement, performance in the reengineered environment will deteriorate. Without new skills, managerial support, adequate incentives, and feedback, people will return to the old, comfortable ways of working.

The *reward structure* regulates behavior. Rewards may be formal or informal, financial or recognition based. Ideally, well-designed jobs provide a work environment that is rewarding in and of itself. Such jobs motivate people to think and take action, to excel, and to meet performance goals. Often, however, there are disconnects between the desired behaviors and behaviors that are actually rewarded. Changing reward structures can pose difficult problems, since the reward processes, policies, and practices are often seen as outside the scope of a business reengineering project. Yet, reward structures can be crucial to reinforcing new behavior.

The *measurement systems* define the feedback processes that provide information on process performance. Good measurement systems provide actionable information, which enables people to improve process performance within their sphere of control and accountability. However, measurement systems must deliver appropriate information. Too much information will be ignored; incomplete information generates faulty decisions. Measurements should uncover the need for change and reduce the randomness and unpredictability of process performance. Measurements should be made available directly and simultaneously to process performers and managers.

Management methods consist of the practices and techniques used to supervise, develop, and support the people who perform the business processes. They are the primary reinforcers of an employee's day-to-day performance. How are people treated? Do they participate in business decision making? Does management support their personal growth and development? These and other aspects of management strongly affect process performance. This dimension is too often one of the most neglected in reengineering because it is seen as outside the project scope. But, unless managers and supervisors understand and learn how to support the new environment, the benefits will quickly erode.

The Value Dimensions

These almost invisible dimensions define the organization's culture and drive behavior. It is from these dimensions that leadership and improvement philosophies must emerge. If these dimensions are not aligned to reinforce behavior supportive of the reengineered operation, even the best business reengineering design will not outlast its initial implementation. There will be nothing to reduce the natural resistance and reaction to change.

Organizational culture consists of the unspoken, collective rules and beliefs of the organization. We can discern this dimension through the organization's language, symbols, myths, and rituals. The culture defines what is important to the organization more forcefully than any memo from the CEO. For example, one organization could not have a meeting without an overhead projector and a set of overheads for even the most informal presentation. Each page had to be landscape printed and framed. We asked several people why this was so. The answer was always the same: "I really don't know. It's just the way it's done around here. Just try having a meeting without one and see what happens." The older the culture, the more embedded the beliefs and values and the more difficult change becomes. But changing embedded corporate values is perhaps the most powerful form of change. After 40 years, one automobile manufacturer closed its plush headquarters and moved its executives to plant sites. That sent a very strong message to all that the days of kings and peasants were over.

With *political power*, individuals manipulate and shape the actions and behaviors of others. Both formal and informal leaders use power to promulgate and reinforce culture. Political power can originate from formal authority or personal power. The former is acquired through the position held in the organization, and the latter through expertise, knowledge, or connections. If reengineering the physical/technical dimensions upsets the existing power balance, resistance can be fierce. The threat of a loss of power can provoke a dramatic, often confrontational or subversive, response. In one organization, the vice presidents, when faced with the actual streamlining of the business organizations and the potential dispersal of headquarters control to the field locations, bluntly refused to accept a reengineering project team's radical vision. Then, when the team returned with a more simplified, incremental approach, these same vice presidents rejected the second solution as not radical enough. You may never know why funding was turned down and your team was transferred to Siberia; then again you may. To ignore power issues is to ignore a reality of organizational life.

Individual belief systems are the attitudes and mental models that individuals apply to themselves, those they work with, and the work itself. People at all levels in the organization have mental models and beliefs that shape their attitudes toward others and their behavior on the job. Cultural characteristics like impatience, skepticism, openness, control, rigidity, or flexibility find their origins within individual mental models. For example, if employees believe that management can't be trusted, or that nothing will change, empowering these employees to take action and make decisions will take more than an announcement. Skepticism and caution must be overcome. In one organization, it took over a year to convince people that they were really empowered.

Aligning the value dimensions to support the reengineered organization requires organization executives to demonstrate leadership. Many business reengineering projects require fundamental changes in the values held by executives, as well as the rest of the organization. In such cases, project leadership is difficult to develop. Executives resist change as much as anyone. To tell executives that their beliefs are obstructing change is like telling the emperor that he has no clothes. This explains why many organizations do not reengineer until conditions become so bad that the leader's existing beliefs finally give way or a new executive is put in place.

When is Reengineering the Answer?

For the past 50 years, theorists and practitioners from many different disciplines have been working to improve business quality and productivity, and we're learning which reengineering efforts yield the most benefits. Emerging priorities for reengineering focus on changing customer relationships (either internal or external to the organization) and repositioning the organization in the marketplace. Studies have shown that cost reduction alone is not a sufficient focus for obtaining results. In fact, when the objective is only to reduce costs (for example, automating to reduce head count), failure is often the result. The right reengineering opportunities are situations in which a combination of these benefits can be achieved:

- Increase the organization's ability to customize products and services while retaining mass-production economics
- Increase customer satisfaction with products and services so they prefer your products and services over those of your competitors
- Make it easy and pleasant for customers to do business with your organization
- Break organizational boundaries, bringing customers into the information channels through communication, networking, and computer technologies
- Decrease response time to customers, eliminate errors and

complaints, and reduce product and service development and manufacturing cycle time

- Process more customer requests and higher volumes from each customer, and deliver "value-driven" prices to customers without reducing profitability
- Improve the quality of work life and individual capabilities for contribution so that people experience ownership of their work and of customers and see their contribution to the organization
- Improve the sharing and utilization of organization knowledge so the organization does not become/remain dependent on the expertise of a few people

To identify the right opportunities for business reengineering, the first step is to survey the current environment—that is, to collect hard data and identify the organization's actual problems. Reengineering based on gut feelings does not sell. You can use the diagnostic tool in appendix A to systematically capture the problems and their root causes. These are warning signs of trouble that indicate the need for reengineering:

- **The explosion of chaos and bureaucracy.** In most organizations, work processes were not designed—they evolved out of the chaos of doing business. Small groups start out working informally and communicating easily and quickly. As the successful organization grows, informal work patterns break under stress. The organization develops a process and rule set to fix the mistake or prevent it from happening again. This phenomenon repeats itself until the maze of overlapping and sometimes contradictory processes make work difficult for all but the most seasoned employees. Procedures become completely habitualized. New, untrained employees with no access to accurate procedural references therefore make mistakes that veterans do not. And veterans can do the wrong thing for years without any awareness of the mistake. For example, a team of headquarters accountants visiting a field billing office found clerks misapplying account codes to expense vouchers. The team asked a clerk why she was using the wrong account. She replied, "Listen, I've been doing this job for 20 years, and you're not going to tell me I'm doing it wrong."
- **Thinking for customers.** Too many organizations design processes based on the assumption that they know what's best for

customers. The organization becomes inflexible, often driving frustrated customers to competitors or regulatory commissions. Only the "rules" count, and employees who take the initiative to help customers may even be punished for bypassing official procedures. In one utility company, sales reps could quote only exact prices—even when customers wanted only estimates. If a sales rep said, "The monthly price is about $14.00," the measurement personnel monitoring the call would deduct points from the sales rep's performance rating.

- **Automation of existing bureaucracy.** The 1970s and 1980s brought the proliferation of computers in business. Too often, however, the result was automation of existing manual procedures. Paper flows became information flows, paper files became electronic files, and so on. Computerization reinforced bureaucracy rather than breaking through it. Limitations of the technology, inexperience, and fear of disrupting the work place all contributed to this initial response to computerization. For example, in an insurance company's claims department, automation created paper printouts to replace handwritten claim files. Paper continued to move from one desk to another as the claim was processed. Even more wasteful are the legions of organizations that simply duplicated existing processes, maintaining both paper and electronic forms of data.

- **Bottlenecks and disconnects in critical cross-organizational work processes.** Many businesses have organizational units, suppliers, and distributors that operate as isolated "smoke-stack" environments. Although each unit is part of the manufacturing stream, each operates as if it has no relationship to the other units. Much time is spent in costly and cumbersome processes preparing work for processing, resolving problems and errors, and tracking the work in progress, thus creating duplicate and inaccurate data. In one large automobile manufacturing company, each division reentered information about incoming work into its own systems and sent paper with the outgoing work. Part numbers were different in each division, and supplier and distributor numbering systems did not correspond to any of the divisions' part-numbering systems.

- **Elusiveness of accountability.** Most of our organizations are structured by function (sales, manufacturing, engineering, maintenance, human resources, information systems, and so on), but essential business processes (for example, planning, product design and development, order management, product management, customer service and support) cut across the functions. This makes it difficult, if not impossible, to establish accountability for a complete business process. Consequently, these processes—the heart and soul of our organizations—either splinter into smaller subprocesses or are replicated many times over. Responsiveness and timeliness are lost as downstream processes suffer from upstream inaccuracies, incompleteness, and lateness. Follow-up and follow-through become organizational nightmares. For example, in one manufacturing organization, the sales promotion planning process was broken into five subprocesses, each assigned to a different group. If any plans or budgets were late, inaccurate, or incomplete, customers' programs could not be updated in time to avoid invoicing errors and deductions. Over a five-year period, the number of changes in plans and budgets after processing deadlines increased from 10 to 57 percent as the process deteriorated from lack of management, measurement, and accountability.
- **Chaos of downsizing.** Downsizing an organization's work force leaves survivors demoralized, the work environment inadequately staffed, and people with inadequate skills performing the work. Tasks can no longer be processed within their current configuration. Work is dropped, problems remain unsolved, and planning becomes nonexistent as survivors scramble to fight the emerging crises. Instead of focusing on what is essential, people stick with what they know and are comfortable with. For example, a large government organization downsized its headquarters staff by 40 percent. A headquarters process traditionally supported by four people became the responsibility of one person, who worked 16 hours a day for 6 months before demanding a transfer to a field location.
- **The turmoil of integration and merger.** The integration or merger of organizations creates a new organizational entity with

11

work processes that often duplicate or conflict with each other. For example, the purchase of four companies gave the new company four different sets of policies, procedures, and formula options for processing customer orders. In a five-year period, over $80 million would be wasted supporting these overlapping and redundant operations. Integrating the customer order management process created massive difficulties as three of the companies tried to adopt the order management system of the fourth company. Field work loads tripled, errors increased 50 percent, and over 100 additional clerical people were hired to prepare inputs and correct errors.

Even if business processes appear to function effectively, customers (either internal or external) may find the products and support services less than satisfactory. "Perceived" poor quality by the customer has the same result as "actual" poor quality and means that the processes used to design, develop, and support the products and services are suspect. The situations you're likely to find during diagnosis include:

- **Lack of a "big-picture" concept and poor communication.** A fragmented, "over-the-wall," linear approach to product or service design, development, and support processes can create costly mistakes and provide ample opportunity for different groups to blame each other.
- **Inattention to detail.** Ignoring the customer in the rush to bring a product to market can lead to miscalculations of how the product will actually be used. For example, an information systems (IS) department trying to understand its customers' needs created a form to gather customer requests. The form was so lengthy and difficult to use that both customers and IS programmers chose to communicate on the phone instead. Soon, the organization's managers had no idea what was going on.
- **Designer arrogance and customer exclusion.** When designers presume they know what the customer needs, the results can be costly and even embarrassing. In a telephone company, a group of male engineers designed a telephone targeted to women who stayed home during the day. The designers assumed that a woman would want to lie in bed while chatting with her friends, so the phone was very lightweight with a smooth bottom. Customers

complained that the phones kept falling off the table when they tried to dial. It had to be redesigned.

- **Focus on correction, not error prevention.** When product designs are based on inadequate or inaccurate information, the result is usually a dissatisfied customer. It's been our experience and studies consistently show that approximately 75 percent of changes demanded by customers after a computer system installation are due to a mismatch between system specifications and customer expectations.

- **Measurement problems.** The lack of measurement data or the measurement of the wrong data impedes product and service design, development, and support. Because of one organization's rapid growth, seven or more product groups were working directly with customers, thus circumventing the one measured, formal customer contact and support group.

- **Focus only on external customers.** When customer relations training targets only employees who work directly with external customers (for example, sales and support representatives), then internal work units become disconnected from customers. This can dramatically affect their ability to service and support customers. In one company, a salesperson promised an important customer a specific configuration for a product by a certain date. But when the salesperson talked with production scheduling, he was told by the production manager, "You're no more important than the next sales guy. We've got our own problems and we're not going to change the schedule right before a union negotiation."

Creating the Business Case

Street-smart business reengineers know that, it is critical to create a business case that, as Vaughn Merlyn put it so succinctly, "creates massive discomfort with the status quo." The initial business case must sell executives on the *value of the change*. Don't let anyone fool you—reengineering takes lots of time and money. Decision makers will not sponsor reengineering projects without a realistic estimate of the financial return on their investment. Reengineering advocates must show what it costs to continue the status quo—added expenses and lost revenue, lost customers, and lost sales. In other words, the business case must show that

13

the cost of not changing is too high. The initial business case must elicit sufficient executive commitment to create a design for the reengineered business operation and a plan for its implementation.

In addition to fixing specific, current problems, business reengineering should move the organization toward achieving its long-term goals in the marketplace and position it for future change. If your organization's executives don't have a set of clearly articulated long-term goals and vision for the organization, movement may be difficult. Without a vision, the organization's executives won't want to spend the money.

Although creating a new design is easy and can start with a clean slate, reengineering implementations are difficult and messy. Implementation requires working with the current environment, with all its problems and complexities, multiple technologies and cultural encumbrances, habits, and belief systems. It's like trying to live in your house during a major renovation. Not only does it cost more than you planned, but the dust gets into your toothbrush as well as your cupboards. You can't find anything for months because all the closets and shelves have to be emptied. So it won't be worth it unless the transformation is extraordinary.

Street-smart business reengineers don't ask people to put up with inconvenient and stressful changes to their work lives without good reason. They deliver a business case that makes two points:

- **The necessity for change.** Business reengineers should base the business case on quantitative data that translates "what everyone already knows" into facts and numbers. They should use both point-in-time data and trend data to support analyses of revenues, customer complaints, direct and indirect processing costs, rates of absenteeism, volumes of back orders, and costs to correct errors and delays in deliveries. They should use quantitative data to evaluate strategic industry trends, the economy, customer preferences and buying patterns, and other market research.
- **The alternative to change.** Business reengineers who want to effect change use hard and soft data to paint a picture of the future if the organization doesn't change. They use current data to project today's bottom line into tomorrow.

Once the facts are on the table, street-smart business reengineers get a commitment to:
- Frame the project so it is fully defined and understood

- Create a reengineered vision of the business, its values, and goals
- Build a detailed process redesign of the business operations
- Plan the implementation
- Conduct a proof of concept (if needed)

Only then will savvy business reengineers ask for the "big bucks" for implementation.

Critical Success Factors for Business Reengineering Projects

In our experience, few business reengineering projects can deliver everything they promise. So, a business reengineering project can be the most challenging assignment one undertakes. To be successful requires a strategy that incorporates these critical success factors:

- **A business focus—a focus on all dimensions.** Business reengineering is much more than process redesign. And it is much more than the introduction of new technologies or restructuring of the organization. Success depends on integrating all three— process, technology, and organization, plus supporting that integration with new infrastructure and values.
- **A methodology and project approach.** Any reengineering effort requires discipline and structure. The methodology must be systematic and fact focused. It is much more than merely shifting organization structure or changing a few job positions. The methodology must require people to "team up" for the long-term benefit and health of the total organization and compel the project team to epitomize the behavior and culture envisioned for the new environment. It also must deliver clearly detailed, executable, and trackable plans for action and implementation. A winning business reengineering methodology must articulate how to secure funding, manage power struggles, and sell the new ideas.

  Using any other approach for business reengineering guarantees that the effort will get lost in the quicksand of daily work and crises. Without discipline, structure, and a project approach, there will always be something more important to do. With a project approach, people can charge their time and be held accountable for measurable results.
- **Time.** Business reengineering takes time. The initial design work

may take only six to eight weeks. Implementing the new design, testing the alternatives, and supporting the change is an iterative process that may take two years or more. Reinforcing new behaviors and values is an ongoing process. Executives must be able to stick with the program, even when the pace of progress seems to be two steps forward and one step back.

- **Partnership participation.** Business reengineering is not done by three or four experts. It is accomplished only as the result of efforts by people from all over the organization. Executives, managers, and professionals must champion the project—all are key to problem definition as well as solution development and implementation. Ownership and "buy-in" of reengineering project decisions are critical to success. Those who have lived with the problems are closest to the solutions, not to mention having to live with the results. Business people must work in partnership with IS professionals, outside business experts, and others who can contribute to the most effective solution.

   Creating an effective partnership requires flexible, trained teams. The reengineering project should not establish additional permanent organizational structures. Initial reengineering efforts should be led by a temporary cross-organizational, multilevel, and cross-functional team that reports directly to an executive sponsor. Different team members are needed at different times for different tasks. As the team completes one phase of the project, some members will return to their normal jobs, others will continue reengineering, and new recruits will enlist.

   A key to successful teamwork is training. Bringing people together and expecting them to function intuitively as an effective team is unrealistic and bound to fail. People need to be taught how to perform as a team. Behavioral, managerial, and leadership skills are more important than technical skills—facilitation skills are critical for team survival and progress.

- **Visible, active leadership.** This is the most important of all the critical success factors. Executives and managers *must* demonstrate long-term commitment to business reengineering—in terms of dollars, people, and executive visibility. Most executives and managers underestimate the effect of their own behavior.

16

Employees become cynical about empowerment when their leader overrides their first empowered decision or punishes them for showing initiative. Leaders must be careful not to use negative reinforcement—positive reinforcement is much more effective. However, most managers and executives do not receive skills training in leadership. We seldom teach managers how to lead. Studies show that training budgets allocate 80 percent of their resources to technical training and only 20 percent to leadership training. Therefore, it is critical that we help our executives to demonstrate this leadership.

The leadership begins when managers move from an event or crisis management style to a process management style that energizes the organization and encourages a learning-oriented rather than blame-oriented approach. It is the job of the executive leaders and middle managers to:

— Enable people to step back and evaluate how the work is performed. This may mean changing work priorities.
— Resist the temptation to silence dissident voices.
— Simplify problem solving.
— Listen instead of dictate and demand.
— Remove barriers and obstacles to performance.
— Reward and encourage ideas.
— Allow people to have fun at their work.

Business reengineering begins the process of transforming a dysfunctional organization into a learning, productive, quality-focused, customer driven organization. Business reengineering must be customer driven. The organization that defines its quality, values, and future internally will not remain competitive in a global economy.

Conventional boundaries among customers, producers, suppliers, and distributors become irrelevant when quality is defined in terms of added value, cost sensitivity, responsiveness, and functionality. It is no longer adequate to fix the picture that is within the frame. We have to change the frame too.

Business reengineering must enable people to handle more change successfully. The rate of change today is unprecedented. People born into a world whose fastest form of transportation was a train now see people breaking the sound barrier and leaving the earth's atmosphere. The electronic equipment industry produces a new product every 6 to 18 months. At least two news networks change their broadcast programming every 30 minutes and scan the world for news every 2 minutes. And change isn't slowing down—in fact, futurists say it is accelerating. Organizations that wait years to change their antiquated operations will not survive.

CHAPTER 2

LIGHTING THE WAY

A healthy neighborhood has a solid foundation of functional and attractive buildings, roads, lighting, parks, and sidewalks. When you walk down the street, the whole environment tells you, "This is a safe, pleasant, and stimulating place to live and work." There is a good balance of residential and commercial properties so people can shop and work right in the neighborhood. There are playhouses, movie theaters, and restaurants for evening entertainment, and tennis courts, school playgrounds, and parks for daytime recreation and sports. Some structures may be old, while others may be newer. As new structures are built or enhanced, well-designed building and zoning standards ensure that the vision of the neighborhood remains intact and each structure is of quality, durable construction.

Are there any standards by which street-smart business reengineers can judge the quality and durability of their reengineering design for an organization? Are there standards that can guide their work to ensure its success and their own survival? For over 50 years, theorists and practitioners from many different disciplines have tried to light the way with such guidelines and principles. Industrial engineers and operations research

19

specialists manipulate business structures and technical processes with motion studies and efficiency mathematics. Human relations experts and industrial psychologists design different managerial, compensation, and performance-measurement systems. Others, like organizational development (OD) experts, focus their transformation efforts on business culture, values, and belief systems. Information systems professionals, armed with new modeling techniques and advanced computer technologies, have become the newest crusaders for business change. The real answer to reengineering, however, is a set of interdisciplinary and systematic principles that address all facets of organizational change. For reengineering change to be successful, three questions must be answered:

- How do we develop effective reengineering designs?
- How can we ensure a successful implementation?
- How can we ensure continued application, productivity, and effectiveness after the reengineering?

These questions can be answered through three sets of interlocking principles: process redesign, transformation, and continuous process improvement (Figure 2.1).

Business Process Redesign Principles

What distinguishes an effective business operation from a mediocre or ineffective one? Is there one right way to organize people and delegate

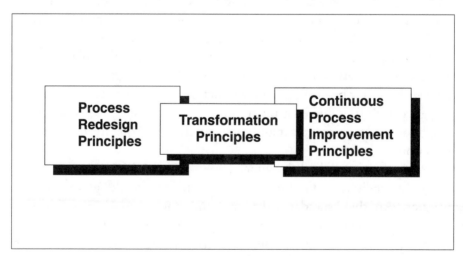

Figure 2.1   The Principles of Business Reengineering

authority? Is there a surefire way to guarantee that the right products get to the right customers at the right time? How can we incorporate technology into people's jobs without making them feel like automatons? Since the early 1980s, a growing body of evidence has supported several explicit principles that can create work processes that are efficient for the organization, as well as intrinsically rewarding to those who perform the jobs. Seven principles for business process redesign are presented below. These principles can serve both as a guide to the redesign of work and as the criteria against which to measure the redesigned processes for quality and effectiveness. Combined with piloting and/or simulation testing, these guidelines will ensure an effective physical/technical component of the reengineered business operation.

The power of these principles was demonstrated dramatically within an insurance company claims-processing operation. Claims were received and checked for completeness by one unit. On a daily basis, the unit supervisor would batch and summarize the verified claims before sending them to another unit for research. After research, the claims would be checked, summarized, and forwarded to the approval unit. If any information was missing or new questions arose, the entire process had to be repeated. A customer trying to ascertain claim status would be told that it was "pending approval." Processing took three to six weeks. A business reengineering project structured the verification, research, and approval units into market-segment customer-support units. Each unit was completely responsible for processing the customer claims assigned to it. All claims could be processed—there was no exception handling outside the units. Using a single-source computer database, the units scanned all claims and assigned them to representatives who had access to all information necessary to verify, research, and approve a claim. When a customer called to check claim status, the information was immediately available to the claims representative or another unit member. Work could easily shift from one unit to another when emergencies arose. Standards and guidelines for payments were clear. New business policies and practices required limited supervisory involvement, review, or approval. Such work was delegated to supervisors by the work units as they deemed necessary. Processing time was reduced to five days. Unit performance (and the performance of each person within the unit) could be measured by the number of claims processed, the processing time per claim, and the costs associated with the claim. Customer satisfaction could now be related to a unit or an individual. Two supervisory positions were eliminated and the same staff could handle 40 percent more volume. This example dramatically illustrates the value derived when these seven process redesign principles are followed (Figure 2.2).

- • Organize Work Around Outcomes

- • Provide Direct Access to Customers

- • Harness Technology

- • Control Through Policies, Practices, and Feedback

- • Enable Interdependent and Simultaneous Work

- • Give Decision-making Power to Workers

- • Build in Feedback Channels

Figure 2.2   Business Process Redesign Principles

Organize Work Around Outcomes

Organizing work around outcomes (for example, a processed claim) rather than tasks (verifying claim information) enables people to measure the direct impact of their work on the organization. This, in turn, provides managers with the means to hold individuals and teams accountable. Work designed around outcomes means business processes are grouped together to eliminate the need for "handoffs" and excessive checking. It allows designers to combine individual tasks, eliminate exception handling, subsume information processing into the work itself, and minimize or eliminate unnecessary intermediary outcomes and supervisory reviews. When work is organized around outcomes, jobs become *vertically loaded,* meaning that people can act on information that they generate themselves. This compression of work significantly reduces cycle times and improves responsiveness—two important goals for business reengineers.

Provide Direct Access to Customers

Providing direct access to customers, whether internal or external to the organization, is the second principle of business process redesign. Work groups can now be held accountable for their behavior. Direct access allows for timely and accurate responses to customer inquiries. In many traditional operations, working with customers is considered a management function. In one IS organization, for example, a customer group prepares a request for services, which is then sent to its IS management counterpart. The service request is then distributed to the development group, which communicates with the customer only through the IS manager. As a result, the final product often does not meet customer expectations. The principle of direct access to customers eliminates this common mismatch between customer expectations and product development. People at the working level have the authority to establish and maintain customer relationships without intermediaries. They work cross-functionally and cross-organizationally with peer groups and up and down the hierarchy. If an IS project team wanted to contact the sales vice president for an interview, it would do so directly, without asking permission or going through its manager.

Let's look at another example that demonstrates the power of working directly with people. A certain utility company requires a vice president's approval signature for any purchase over $1,000,000. Within the company, the need for such a purchase was identified and documented as a purchase request by the manager of a substation. In the traditional operation, the purchase request passed over at least five desks before it reached the vice president for signature. This took over six weeks. Why? Each manager in the chain of command wanted to know what was going to their boss before it went, just in case any questions were asked. Were their signatures required on the purchase request? No. In the reengineered process, the purchase request was generated and approved in the same manner, but it was electronically transmitted to the vice president with a letter of explanation and budget allocation numbers applied. At the same time, copies were transmitted to each intermediary manager for information purposes. This simple reengineering solution reduced the time required to approve purchasing requests from six weeks to less than one week.

Harness Technology

Today's technology can provide universal access to information. Previous examples demonstrate how automation changes information access by eliminating the screening and power brokering that traditionally surrounds information. Technology allows people to act independently, bound by neither time nor place. Using notebook computers and data and telecommunication networks, a salesperson can check inventory in a warehouse in Asia from a customer's office in Iowa and set delivery dates without checking with headquarters. Harnessing technology means providing access to the right information at the right time. Rapid technological changes, however, mean business reengineers must have a handle on the future. They must be able to anticipate information needs and answer the question, "Where does technology provide the most return on investment while still allowing flexibility for future changes?"

Control Through Policies, Practices, and Feedback

Without review cycles, approval chains, and barriers to communication, how do you maintain operational and financial control? The answer is by instituting clear, well-documented policies and practices on which to base decision making, followed by training in applying those policies and practices, and a solid feedback process that clearly identifies errors and potential problems. Feedback can take the form of periodic measurements or an audit process that randomly checks compliance with policy and practices. In one retail organization, for example, sales clerks could follow these guidelines to discount a product "on the spot" for a dissatisfied customer.

1. The customer returns a defective product that is now out of stock.

2. An available product would please the customer.

3. The product is in the same price range.

4. The discounted price for the replacement product is not lower than the price paid for the original.

Comparing inventory to transaction records and inspecting returned products on an audit basis provides sufficient feedback to managers on guideline adherence. Customers are delighted with the responsiveness to their needs.

Enable Interdependent and Simultaneous Work

When people have access to information and can communicate cross-functionally and cross-organizationally, then work can be performed simultaneously instead of linearly (Figure 2.3). People can work in teams, with teams being held accountable and rewarded for the final outcome. Individuals are rewarded only when the team achieves its objectives. In the U.S. automobile industry, it used to require at least five years to take a vehicle from concept to showroom. Each work unit, such as design, engineering, manufacturing, assembly, marketing, and sales, functioned independently and in sequence. For example, a vehicle concept required approval before it went to engineering, and manufacturing was not consulted until all the engineering work was complete. This over-the-wall approach not only took time, it also created complexities and problems that increased the final cost of the vehicle. In the reengineered environment, both cycle time and cost of manufacturing are significantly reduced. The vehicle team is now able to anticipate downstream problems and complexities early in the cycle before incurring unnecessary costs. Although each unit is responsible for different subprocesses, an

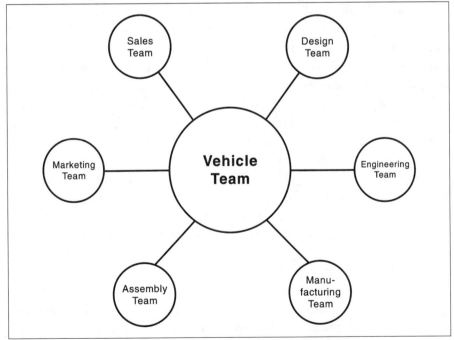

Figure 2.3   Interdependent, Simultaneous Work Teams

integrated team performs information sharing, planning, and problem solving. These work units are often colocated and linked by 24-hour electronic conferencing technology, increasing their ability to work simultaneously.

Give Decision-Making Power to Workers

Access to accurate information and a clear understanding of policies and practices empowers people to make informed, competent decisions. No longer bound by cumbersome approval processes and outmoded bureaucracies, people can act quickly, responding to customer needs as they arise. A new atmosphere of trust and optimism replaces the fear and pessimism that has prevailed in too many organizations for too long.

When business reengineers force decision-making power downward in their organizations, the results become apparent almost immediately. As workers develop their ability and willingness to make significant decisions, the role of management shifts from supervisor to coach, from boss to facilitator, and from tactician to strategist. The underlying assumption in the reengineered environment is that "people will act with integrity."

People with direct decision-making power can act quickly, without intermediary approval levels or bureaucracies of specialty work. Some banks have empowered customer representatives to approve loan requests within one hour over the telephone. In a traditional environment, the normal process takes four or more weeks. How can this happen? It's easy when people have access to the information they need to make decisions, have clear guidelines and boundaries for decision making, and have been taught to identify exception cases and ask for help when necessary. This creates a new managerial environment. As the need for control, review, supervision, and approvals disappears, new organization roles and processes can be added. The manager can now become a futurist, a planner, an obstacle remover, a subject matter expert, a process facilitator, an employee coach, a technical advisor, and an interteam coordinator.

Build in Feedback Channels

All business operations need to know how well they are meeting their goals. If measurement, assessment, and change capabilities are not designed into the processes, then they must be added. When this occurs, the people who perform the work may see this part of their job as different from the "real" work—an extra burden that has nothing to do with getting the job done. And, when they are not held accountable for measurement, assessment, and change implementation, the problem becomes worse. The only logical way to avoid these problems is to construct business processes in which measurement, assessment, and change become part of the process itself. This means that individuals and teams receive direct and immediate feedback from customers and others with whom they interact, not indirectly through managers or at the end of the process, when it is too late to change. How should this happen? Here is an example. An automobile dealership, as part of its customer service process, calls a customer any time that input from the customer can add to the quality of the work being done. For example, the customer will be called when:

• The car needs additional work
• The car will not be ready on time
• The car is ready to be picked up

Then, within five days after the work is done, the customer receives a last call. The caller asks the customer 10 questions regarding the service he received and obtains specific examples of customer satisfaction or dissatisfaction. This information goes simultaneously to the service group and to its managers. This means the group can make immediate improvements to prevent problems from recurring.

Transformation Principles

Reengineering a business operation means changing its culture. People must begin to act and think in new, perhaps uncomfortable, ways. Existing work processes are profoundly modified or have given way to entirely new ways of working. There are new relationships and accountabilities established, and new technologies have replaced old ones. There's a whole lot of learning *and* unlearning to do. With significant changes occurring rapidly, one after another, in short time spans, there is tremendous ambiguity. As one person put it, "There is weeping and wailing in the wilderness." This transition period may last months or several years. Kubler-Ross, Bridges, Atkinson, Beer, Senge, Moss, Kanter, and other change experts tell us that implementing change is much harder than designing the change. This is because resistance is highest during implementation, when people begin to face what the change means for them at a very personal level. That is why it is so critical to involve those who will be responsible for making the change work in the reengineering process. Without their support, the reengineering effort will fail.

Street-smart business reengineers use the following seven transformation principles to guide their project strategy, structure, and process (Figure 2.4).

- Assumptions and Biases Shape Behavior

- People Believe What You Do, Not What You Say

- Involvement Breeds Acceptance

- Just Don't Do Something, Sit There

- Change the Foundation First

- Change Takes Time, but Not That Much

- Progress is Not Linear, nor Is It Smooth

Figure 2.4   Transformation Principles

Assumptions and Biases Shape Behavior

Behavior cannot change until the underlying causes of the behavior are addressed. These are the biases, beliefs, and assumptions that determine an individual's mental model and in turn, his or her behavior. At the very least, we must acknowledge the power of these mental models before transformation can begin. As Peter Senge so aptly states,

> . . . new images fail to get put into practice because they conflict with deeply held internal images of how the world works, images that limit us to familiar ways of thinking and acting.

If unrecognized and unmanaged, these familiar ways of thinking and acting will be the death knell. For every reengineering project begun, there will be at least two that will not succeed because of this failure to anticipate the power of biases and assumptions. Reengineering must change the way people think as much as it changes the way the business operates.

28

This includes the executives who chartered the reengineering in the first place. In project after project we hear:

- It can't be done.
- We can't talk to our customers.
- It costs too much; it takes too long.
- No one wants to change.
- They never do what they say.
- We don't have time to do this.

And on, and on, and on. These are biases and assumptions that are "true" in every sense of the word.

There are a variety of techniques that reengineers can use successfully to bring to the surface and manage biases and assumptions. Several are referenced in Peter Senge's book, *The Fifth Discipline.* We have also used the Hartman Value Profile, a unique instrument that mathematically measures thinking structure, as well as a variety of simple exercises that force people to recognize that their perspective may not be the only perspective with validity.

People Believe What You Do, Not What You Say

The past is rich in failed attempts at change. When changes are announced, many sit skeptically mumbling under their breaths, "I'll believe it when I see it." In many cases, their skepticism is justified. Leaders may give lip service to an idea or change but take little or no action. It is a lot easier for a leader to say "you are empowered" than to actually let go of the decision making. To stop organizational hostilities, blaming, and power grabbing, the project team needs to demonstrate that cooperative action is easier, more rewarding, and more productive. Executive sponsors and project team members must demonstrate the behaviors that will be valued in the reengineered environment. For example, if teamwork and empowerment are important values in the reengineered environment, then teams composed of stakeholders in the reengineered business processes should be empowered to make decisions and take action. Having outside experts or headquarters groups reengineer behind closed doors sends out signals of distrust, thus invalidating the organization's value system.

But, modeling behavior is not enough—there must also be consistent follow-through. Too many leaders display initial enthusiasm and commitment to change and then discontinue funding for implementation. They become fearful of the required investment or diverted by other matters and changed priorities, or a new crisis grabs their attention. Shrewd business reengineers must carefully strategize to build long-term executive commitment. The team must be careful not to promise too much too quickly, thereby destroying its credibility. Instead, the team members must be willing to speak the truth, challenge deceit, and act with integrity.

Involvement Breeds Acceptance

It is an old principle of selling, that "people must own before they buy." This means, for example, that a person won't buy a car until he can envision himself driving it. Before we buy, we test-drive the car, look under the hood, study the specifications, compare it to other cars, negotiate a price that we can live with, and make sure we get what we want. People won't accept the reengineering until they can see themselves living and working in the reengineered environment. Street-smart business reengineers involve those most affected by the change in its design and implementation. This involvement not only delivers a better, more easily implemented solution; it also minimizes resistance to the change. Involvement alleviates much of the pain associated with change, allowing us to move more quickly from denial to acceptance.

When people are involved in designing and planning new business operations, it is difficult to deny what is happening. The project team for one business reengineering project included a core group from headquarters, champions from each of six divisions, and subject-matter experts. Their participation in redesigning a key business process cemented their commitment to its implementation in their own business units. They came to believe that the changes were absolutely required if the organization was to survive. Their competitors were moving ahead of them in the marketplace, and their complex business processes precluded customer responsiveness. These problems diverted financial and personnel resources that were needed elsewhere in the organization. The champions decided to take a proactive role in making the changes a reality. They believed in the benefits of the changes that were coming, were adamant about seeing the changes through, and helped each other overcome the inevitable implementation obstacles. And they steadfastly resisted dilution of the changes at implementation time. Not everyone from a large organization can be involved in designing and implementing change. But involving key individuals in the project from its inception helps ensure organizationwide commitment.

Just Don't Do Something, Sit There

Like the bounty hunter in the days of the wild west, business managers have a tendency to "shoot first and ask questions later" when facing an operational crisis. The obvious problem with this approach is that sometimes the wrong person gets shot. In the old days, that put the bounty hunter in a lot of trouble with the law. It does the same for business managers. Rather than solving the original problem, hasty action often exacerbates it or even sets off a negative chain reaction. This reactive behavior is typical in most business organizations. For example, one organization we work with was attempting to integrate five divisions into a single product-processing management system. This was extremely problematic since each organization had its own existing systems and methods for managing the products. When the second and third divisions were brought into the new system, the project fell three months behind schedule. Management reacted by increasing implementation resources and pressuring the project team to move faster, after which the project fell an additional two months behind. The problem turned out to have nothing to do with a lack of resources or how the project team was working; it was an underlying mistaken assumption about the integration. The first division to change to the new system had an existing system very much like the new one. Under pressure to achieve implementation faster, the project team had assumed that all the divisions could adapt to the new system as easily as the first one. By acting without thinking first, the project team ran straight into a brick wall that cost several people their jobs. Its first mistake was not thinking through the assumptions; the second mistake was not planning for every contingency; and the third mistake was using coercion rather than eliciting buy-in. These mistakes are typical of those made by project teams and executives who act before they think. They not only create project delays and unnecessary pressures, but they also encourage an "us vs. them" atmosphere in which the original purpose of the project and the customer-service focus are lost. Street-smart business reengineers bring in people from all affected organizations to help them think through their implementation before the team acts.

31

Change the Foundation First

Which should be the first processes to change once implementation begins? Should they be those that are easiest to change? Should they be those that will provide the biggest benefit? The decision is not an easy one. Many changes are interdependent, and the biggest improvements often require the biggest investments. It may be difficult to obtain that kind of funding early in an implementation in a risk-averse, cautious culture. A guiding principle to follow during the first phase of implementation is to create a foundation—that is, a common-knowledge base and view of the problem and its solution.

This foundation is best achieved through introducing a common language and a set of business practices to support the language. Let's look at several examples to demonstrate the point. In one multidivision company, each division had its own training group operating independently. There was no consistent process for collecting, analyzing, and displaying information to measure training effectiveness or the company's return on investment. The first step in this reengineering effort was to create a common language for talking about training and a set of measures to evaluate training effectiveness. Each training group could measure and compare itself to other groups or to the total training function. The common language was reflected in a logical data model that was constructed at sessions attended by representatives from all the training groups. This data model was used to select a training information software package, which was installed throughout the company. Later phases of the reengineering project simplified and integrated the division training groups.

Another company developed a common language to define structures and incentives for motivating their customers to promote the company's products to consumers. Until that time, each business unit had its own language. A common worksheet was developed, and everyone involved with the customer was trained in the new language and its benefits. Now, all promotions are measured accurately and consistently, and there is common feedback for improving the processes that created and managed the incentives. This forms the basis for later reengineering phases for designing and installing a common database to support the business units.

Change Takes Time, but Not That Much

Transformation is a process, not a single event. How long should the implementation of a reengineering design take? It doesn't happen overnight. Systems must be built, processes overhauled, reference materials developed, and people trained. But to delay until everything is ready and then implement everything at once can be devastating. Buy-in is best achieved through incremental implementation, allowing verification of benefits and refinement of the solution. Big-bang implementation concentrates all the risks and disregards the typical business need for short-term results. From the beginning of a reengineering project, change should occur every six to nine months. Modularizing the reengineering design reduces risk and forces detailed planning of each implementation phase. Some may claim that evolutionary implementation of a radical reengineering design is impossible and creates too much disruption for too long. However, for projects that affect processes across multiple organizations with complex technology and differing business practices, a moderate amount of disruption over a long period of time is preferable to a massive disruption that sends the organization into total chaos.

Progress Is Not Linear, nor Is It Smooth

A linear approach to transforming an organization is one in which each change follows logically upon its predecessor and each module of change is orderly and functions independently of other changes. Unfortunately, reengineering an operating environment is a very disorderly process! For every three steps forward, there may be one or two steps back. For almost any change, and certainly for radical change, the learning process generally results in negative progress toward the goals before a turnaround occurs and positive progress is made (Figure 2.5).

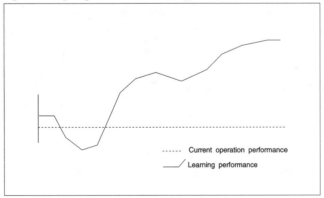

Figure 2.5   The Learning-Curve Effect

Integrating new technology into current systems and communications architecture may be extremely difficult, requiring interim solutions until the conversion is complete. In many cases, short-term fixes to existing systems are made in parallel with new development efforts even when plans are being made to replace the existing system. And at some point, people (even project team members) will ask, "Why did we decide to do all this?" The reasons for the business reengineering and its benefits must remain highly visible throughout the project. Otherwise, project team members may become frustrated midstream after the initial process redesign work is completed. They want to go out and "do it," feeling that "if I'm not actively changing the environment, then I'm not really working." But reengineering requires systematic, one-step-at-a-time changes to the infrastructure and belief systems as well as to the direct business operation. This means that much of the work must be done behind the scenes before a new operation process can be rolled out. Patience, timing, and persistence are critical to a successful transition. Progress will occur in spurts, with plateaus and even regression as the new skills and practices of learners take effect.

Another factor that can contribute to bumpy progress is pressure to back off from or weaken the reengineering design. This may occur at any point in the project and can have several causes. In some cases, people become overwhelmed by the extent of change. Some may lack the will to change; others may be skeptical of their organization's ability to change. Others just don't want to make a long-term investment. Even though the money they spend now will pay off later, they want results *now*. It is particularly problematic if these views are held by the organization's leaders. Sometimes a project director and team must recommend stopping the project rather than proceeding with inadequate funding and limited resources. A reasoned decision to stop is better than a failed implementation.

Continuous Process Improvement Principles

Even in an ideally reengineered business environment, time will age the operation just as weather and use take a toll on a building structure. Maintenance is critical. Unless assessment and improvement techniques become part of the operation, the positive effects of the reengineering will gradually deteriorate.

Any or all components of the reengineering can be affected. Time and complacency are the culprits when external forces and unforeseen events alter the environment. People must have the skills, time, and authority to maintain the reengineered business processes. The six principles outlined in Figure 2.6 provide guidance for continued productivity and success. Without continuous process improvement, the reengineering project team may win the battle but lose the war.

- Improvement is Everyone's Responsibility

- Improvement is Always Desirable

- Pay Attention to Detail

- Quality Requires Systemic Work

- Create an Ongoing Exchange and Sharing of Information

- Quality is Driven by Individuals, Not Organizations

Figure 2.6   Continuous Process Improvement Principles

Improvement Is Everyone's Responsibility

When the business reengineering project team completes the implementation, the team disbands. The business operation has no group to blame or go to for help any longer. Establishing a separate quality or process improvement group will only reinforce the idea that solving problems is someone else's responsibility. Instead, each manager and each unit must be accountable for continuous improvement in these seven areas:

- Communication
- Quality
- Error reduction
- Productivity
- Customer satisfaction
- Cost reduction
- Worker satisfaction and enjoyment

For example, one work unit sent documentation to everyone involved in the product development process. It took a lot of time and paper, but they were proud of their ability to create and distribute the documentation. Eventually, however, they asked their key customers (the recipients of the documentation) for suggestions on improving the process. The customers responded with, "Stop sending everything to everyone. Most people don't need it all. Some do." So they surveyed all customers and created a new documentation distribution system. Some people received only a cover letter and a notation to "Call if you need more detailed documentation." A second group received the entire document. The result—reduced reproduction time, increased customer satisfaction, and reduced reproduction and distribution costs. The work unit plans to survey customers every six months to maintain a responsive and efficient distribution process. The unit members made quality improvement part of their job—they didn't wait for complaints or directives from management.

Improvement Is Always Desirable

People who think they're doing the job as well as it can be done can become complacent. Look at what happened to IBM from 1985 to 1993. Once denial set in, innovation became "the way we've always done it." A successful, healthy work unit, whether it consists of a large corporation or only two people, should constantly strive to improve what it does with the resources it has. Focusing on customers and improvements keeps the unit's mode of operations proactive and anticipatory rather than reactive. For example, one training group developed a new job reference manual with a supporting training program. It was an excellent program, the best in the business. However, the training group asked each class for ideas on how to make the materials better. Two things happened. First, the class consistently rated the instructor and class as excellent. Second, the suggestions from one class resulted in a significant simplification to the reference manual, making learning easier for everyone. And the process continues with small improvements reflected in quarterly updates to the materials. Maximum customer satisfaction is achieved at minimal cost.

In order to make improvements like this, people must be heard and given the power to implement improvements. When their ideas are ignored, people shut down and give up. They disassociate from the job and make do with poor quality. Business reengineering projects must address management style, reward programs, and measurement systems to correct this. Street-smart business reengineers create an environment where ideas for improvement are heard, where people can make changes, and where they are rewarded for speaking out. If these values are not part of the reengineered environment, history will repeat itself within two or three years.

Pay Attention to Detail

This principle applies to both the reengineering and the postimplementation process improvement environment. Improvements are lasting only when people attend to the lowest level of detail. Conceptual designs cannot become detailed process designs or be successfully implemented without such attention. Let's look at one business reengineering project. A team of line managers and workers redesigned its worker's compensation management operation. The team hired a consultant to write the reference manual for the operation, which would document all new business practices and procedures. This would enable new workers to join the operation and receive formal training. When the consultant began to translate the design document into reference procedures and decisions, she found many gaps and points of confusion. The consultant held a series of meetings with the team to clarify the design and add the detail required to complete the reference manual. This step was essential to the implementation. Without a reference manual and training, people would have quickly fallen back into the old work patterns.

From a process-improvement perspective, inattention to the lowest level of detail can be disastrous. Four astronauts died because small O-rings were not tested—workers, supervisors, and managers assumed the equipment was good. It was a fatal assumption. Although results are not usually fatal, ignoring details precludes improvement. Only when the automobile industry examined exactly how it designed and engineered vehicles did it discover time delays and cost increases.

Work processes must provide detailed feedback data before the problem turns into a crisis. *We should use data to anticipate need, not react to a crisis.* Without accurate and timely data, improvements aren't made in time and customer needs are ignored.

Quality Requires Systemic Work

Many problematic situations are beyond the control of any one person or work unit. The reengineering project team should have uncovered and addressed these problem conditions during the process redesign work. In some instances, however, the root cause of the problem lies outside the scope of the project. In one state, a complaint about a child-care center prompts an immediate and intensive investigation by a government agency. Recommendations for action (closing, fining, or censuring the center) are forwarded to the court for approval. The problem is that the court does not take proactive measures to prevent child endangerment—it acts only after the occurrence of actual abuse or an accident. This type of systemic problem could not be corrected by the investigating agency—the government body must enact legislation to enable the court to act. In another example of a problem with a systemic root cause, a business work group learned that it could be more responsive to its customers by establishing flextime, enabling people to stagger their hours to ensure continual coverage during traditional shift changes. But the union contract prevented any single work unit from varying standard work hours. A violation could result in the work group manager being fined and the participating employees suspended. Improving the environment and customer responsiveness required a systemic change—a change in the union contract and supporting business policy.

When such situations arise, people must have the skills to identify and analyze the problem, create problem-solving strategies, and communicate the situation to involve others. The organization environment must welcome and encourage such messages. When executives treat people with ideas as "whistle blowers" rather than "truth tellers," the organization is doomed. Poor quality, poor performance, and cynical, uncommitted employees are the result.

Create an Ongoing Exchange and Sharing of Information

There is an old saying, "People are only as sick as their secrets." This is particularly true for organizations. Without knowledge and awareness, people cannot take action. Continuous process improvement demands an end to secrets. A reengineered operation must be imbued with these capabilities and values:

- There must be methods for anticipating problems.
- Data is nonjudgmental and should be viewed as an opportunity for improvement. Whether it spells good news or bad news is a matter of perspective.
- Transmitting problem solutions and improvement ideas is a critical worker and managerial function. There is no need for every work group to reinvent the wheel by replicating another group's painful experience or situation. Groups should learn from each other.
- Information sharing should be proactive—a part of the basic work function. People should not have to go looking for information—information sharing should occur on a daily, biweekly, or weekly basis as dictated by the job-improvement needs.
- Never "kill the messenger." People should be rewarded and encouraged to share information.

Quality process improvement really begins when people stop dictating solutions and start listening to others. People must have the behavioral and communications skills to:

- Unite people into a team with a common purpose
- Encourage people to focus on the real problems and issues they face, even if this makes them uncomfortable
- Mobilize people to encourage rather than discourage each other's ideas

In one company, for example, a project team started sharing simulation feedback data with another project team voluntarily and unilaterally. The teams began to meet regularly to coordinate plans and share problems and successes. Both project teams improved customer acceptance of their respective projects. Both were able to share new technology and avoid duplicative development efforts. And because of input from the original project team, the other project team changed its plans, which allowed a database they needed to be built earlier than anticipated. Costs were contained on both projects.

Quality Is Driven by Individuals, Not Organizations

Improvement happens because people care, because they are committed to the best performance and quality they can deliver. They believe they can always improve. It doesn't mean everyone becomes a perfection-ist. It *does* mean that people consider their work to be a reflection of themselves. They want to improve themselves, improve the process, and discover and learn from any source possible. Peter Senge calls it "Personal Mastery"—the need to see life as a curious adventure and discovery process. Personal Mastery is more than increasing one's personal skill and knowledge set. It's continually striving to increase one's contribution to the groups to which one belongs—at work, home, and play. Personal Mastery is possible only in an environment that encourages and rewards improvement at *all* levels.

CHAPTER 3

KNOW WHERE YOU ARE GOING

To survive a month-long safari you need a more detailed plan than you would for a trip to a neighboring city. But clear vision is essential to both kinds of trips and will help you survive many of the obstacles you encounter in strange territory. The same applies to business reengineering projects. Complex reengineering projects require a compelling vision of the new organization, including the values that will support that vision and a set of well-formulated goals that map out and measure progress toward attainment of the vision. For smaller-scale projects, the future may be described by answering the question, "What's the operation going to look like once we change?" In either case, the project vision must be inspiring enough to overcome the inertia, shifting priorities, prickly resistance, and fear of failure that accompany a business reengineering project team on its implementation journey.

Creating the Vision

Much has been said and written about the power of "visioning" in the past few years. Organizations routinely create vision statements, some inspired, some mundane. The more powerful these visions are, however, the likelier they are to come true. What makes a vision powerful, particularly for a reengineering project? Unlike organizational visions that are often lofty and idealistic, visions for reengineering projects are made powerful by their *specificity*. Like the architect's scale model, they bring concreteness to that which is only imagined. Powerful reengineering visions are *customer focused*, recognizing that the future of the business relies on a conscious recognition of the strategic role of its customers. Reengineering visions depict a future that truly *integrates process, people, and technology*. Reengineering visions signify a new way of doing business, proclaiming *bedrock changes* to the very systems that make the organization run. Visions for reengineering projects are *proactive*. They project what is possible, not what needs to be fixed. They answer the question, "If this business operation could work any way you want it to, how would it look?" Powerful reengineering visions create a new reality. When spoken or written in the present tense, they literally force the collective subconscious of the group to make it happen. They exemplify the reversed axiom, "believing is seeing." A vision should express the desired values of the new organization. It is at this level where people resonate with the vision. One organization incorporated these values into their vision:

> We are committed to serving our customers, fostering professionalism at all levels of our organization, and building an environment of innovation, effectiveness, efficiency, resourcefulness, and integrity. To this end we:
> - Develop partnerships with customers through open discussion and consensus building
> - Are receptive to new ideas and are responsive to customer needs
> - Take full responsibility for our performance
> - Deliver the maximum return on investment in terms of personnel and material resources
> - Make practical choices
> - Hold the welfare of the organization and its people above individual goals
> - Encourage initiative, risk-taking and teamwork
> - Respect and value each employee as a unique individual, recognizing contributions, achievements and excellence, and profiting from our diversity
> - Learn from our mistakes and celebrate our successes

When this vision was created, few people in the organization believed these values to be part of the culture. A core group representing customers, workers, managers, and executives struggled over the articulation of these values, and then many months were spent communicating them to the rest of the organization. No one disagreed with the values, but many were skeptical. This is not unusual, particularly when reengineering a complex, multifunction business operation. Vision and values must be translated into concrete, achievable goals that link the vision to the organization's strategic plans.

Establishing Goals

Over and over again, the momentum from the initial "visioning" effort dissipates from a loss of commitment. Just as with total quality management (TQM) efforts, business reengineering projects need concrete targets on which to set their sights. The solution in both cases is goals. Goals shift attention from what is possible to what needs to be done to make it possible. Goals provide top-down guidance and work priorities. Study after study proves that success can be tied directly to goal commitment, yet in most organizations goals receive lip service only. One of the problems we have discovered is that people do not know how to set goals.

> "Cheshire Puss, would you please tell me, please, which way I ought to go from here?" "That depends a good deal on where you want to get to," said the Cat. "I don't much care where," said Alice. "Then it doesn't matter which way you go," said the Cat. "So long as I get somewhere," Alice added as an explanation. "Oh, you're sure to do that," said the Cat, "If you only walk long enough."
>
> LEWIS CARROLL, *ALICE'S ADVENTURES IN WONDERLAND*

Those embarking on a reengineering project cannot afford to wander in Alice's Wonderland. Too much is at stake. Goals specify expectations around performance and give direction to the individuals and teams responsible for achieving the reengineering vision and to the executives who are sponsoring the reengineering and providing funding. Without goals, people get locked in an "activity trap," spinning their wheels but getting nowhere. Goals frame and focus the reengineering effort by:

• Specifying the expected business outcomes—the tangible products

and services to be produced by the reengineered operation; these outcomes must be *customer focused*, not process focused
- Including the *measures* that will be used to assess the quality of products and services—time to produce, time to deliver, percentage of resources used, involvement of how many personnel, percent accuracy, and so on
- Stretching the organization to change, proactively creating the future
- Exploding perceptions of the past and current beliefs that may or may not apply to future scenarios
- Assuming that whatever must be done to satisfy customer needs will be done

Goal setting should emphasize anticipating customer needs rather than process improvements. The success of the reengineering effort will ultimately be measured by the value created for the customer, *as determined by the customer*. Figuring out who the customers are is a challenging starting point for many organizations. They forget that customers exist both inside *and* outside of the organization.

For example, after developing its vision, one information technology department identified four goals to be achieved in a one-year time frame.

Goal: Implement a strategic planning and prioritization process based on customers' needs.

Measure: Customers will seek direction from the Information Technology department for business and technology planning.

Goal: Implement an application development process that involves customers up front and assures quality.

Measure: Meet 100 percent of customers' expectations for delivery dates and functionality. Most (95 percent) of our customers will rate our delivered products as excellent or very good in meeting their business requirements.

Goal: Implement a performance mastery process for all employees.

Measure: Within three months all employees will have a written

           assessment of their skills, knowledge, and developmental
           requirements for making the transition to the vision.
           Within six months all employees will have completed at
           least one developmental activity.

Goal: Implement a customer satisfaction and assessment
           process.

Measure: Feedback is timely, accurate, and complete.

Deriving goals from the reengineering vision takes time and effort. Goals should concentrate energy in those areas where the greatest return on investment will be realized. Goals also should lay the groundwork for continuous process improvement after implementation of the reengineered operation. Those involved in the goal setting process begin to think differently, essentially becoming both architects and builders of the new business operation, developing the skills to continue remodeling, and refining as the need presents itself in the future.

What makes goal setting so difficult? Most people in organizations believe, and rightly so, that no matter how much time they spend planning, some crisis will arise and take precedence. Establishing priorities seems to be a fruitless activity at best when any phone call can send the organization into upheaval. Unfortunately, business reengineering, particularly at the stages of visioning and goal setting, is often seen as just one more response to a crisis. Leaders and managers involved in the reengineering effort must stick to their guns and refuse to be sidetracked by every crisis that comes along after the development of the vision. Organizational activity should be defined by vision and goals rather than by crisis.

Goals establish the basis for prioritization of all activities within the reengineered operation and must be linked to the strategic direction of the organization as a whole. Often the business reengineering process painfully illuminates a lack of such strategic direction. In these cases, the project can provide a springboard into strategic planning. This, however, should not be the responsibility of the reengineering team. This is where project scoping and boundary setting are critical. It's easy to become swayed by the bigger issues and begin to dilute the efforts committed to reengineering. This is why goals are so important.

The Visioning and Goal Setting Process

Vision building and goal setting begin with stripping away the blinders created by old values and attitudes, the informal and formal rules that regulate and inhibit change, the rigidity built into the structure of hierarchy and roles, and the comfort of past experience. This creates an environment of inquiry and dialogue. Following are the steps for facilitating this process.

1. Provide training on the characteristics and components of a vision.
2. Develop the vision for the business reengineering project. Begin by conducting an idea-generating session, asking, "What do you see as the vision and values for this reengineering effort?" Then, using consensus-building techniques, draft the composite vision.
3. Using facilitated workshop sessions, focus groups, or written feedback, gather reactions, comments, and suggested changes, additions, and deletions to the vision from all those affected by the vision. Include executives, customers, and suppliers. Incorporate changes in the vision and communicate the revised vision to the organization. Gather additional feedback and comments and revise the vision until there is wholehearted agreement from everyone.
4. Provide training on goal setting and measurements.
5. In facilitated workshop sessions conducted with the reengineering project team:
   - Identify the *business* products and services of the reengineered operation. Use brainstorming, nominal group technique, and consensus building to generate ideas and commitment.
   - Develop measures for assessing the quality of products and services. Measures should be customer focused and quantifiable and include acceptable targets or standards.

Problems Encountered Along the Way

Vision Idolatry

When people create visions and goals they believe in, they naturally feel a strong sense of ownership. What begins as excited commitment can turn into rigid adherence to a new set of rules, with the intent or spirit of the vision lost. Instead of an ideal, the vision becomes an idol to be worshiped. To prevent this, visions and goals must be seen as transforming as well as transformational. A means for revising and revitalizing the vision is part of the business reengineering process. People should be encouraged to suggest improvements or amendments. These can be adopted as the organization sees fit. To avoid vision idolatry:

- Present vision building and goal setting as processes, not events.
- Involve as many people as appropriate in the drafting and revision process.
- Establish a means for gathering suggestions from the organization to improve or change the vision and goals.
- Periodically review and revise the vision and goals in light of the changing environment and suggested changes.

Tunnel Vision

Business reengineering goals can also suffer from a narrowness of perspective. "We have never done it that way around here." "No one will ever buy into this." These phrases are often heard at the beginning of a change effort. While business reengineering expands the peripheral vision of the organization, many people prefer the security of familiarity. There are many legitimate reasons for this response, but a common cause is tunnel vision. Many people believe that what they see is all there is— that the walls of their tunnels are permanent and impenetrable. The business reengineering process provides a relatively safe environment for people to begin to think "outside the box." During the visioning and goal setting stages, participants should be encouraged to:

- Use their imaginations
- Envision two and five years into the future, even more if possible
- Focus on what could be, not what is
- Be proactive, not reactive
- Consider all points of view
- Set aside biases and assumptions

To *vision* is to see beyond the tunnel, to answer the question "What if . . . ?" In this way, business reengineering allows us to create a new reality—one, perhaps, never imagined before. It is a powerful experience when people are given the freedom, through visioning and goal setting, to take control and responsibility for their work lives.

Habitual Thinking

Like tunnel vision, habitual thinking is a serious barrier to reengineering. History, culture, experience, and beliefs all come together to create thought patterns that seem to work. The critical word here is *seem.* Very few of us take the time to think objectively about thinking, and, when we do, we usually decide that our thinking is "right." Too many business reengineering projects stagger and fall because of a failure to break through habitual thinking. The visions and goals created by those stuck in the past tend to perpetuate the past rather than create the future. To overcome habitual thinking, business reengineers must be given opportunities to:

- Explore the effects of their biases and world views
- Practice "trying on" new ways of thinking (How would someone else, for example, Thomas Jefferson, Martin Luther King, my spouse, my boss, Isaac Stern, respond to this situation?)
- Build multiple scenarios of the future
- Reframe the business improvement opportunity in a variety of contexts
- Experience and relish ambiguity
- Shift and change their perspectives on time

These and other exercises will begin to break down the barriers of habitual thinking. Now people can begin the change process. They become less rule bound. They recognize and value paradox. They develop a sense of wonder as they begin to see the world as a child would. It is in this state that vision building and goal setting are possible. In his book, *The Dance of Life*, Edward Hall states:

> There is an underlying hidden level of culture that is highly patterned—a set of unspoken, implicit rules of behavior and thought that controls everything we do. This hidden cultural grammar defines the way in which people view the world. . . . Most of us are either totally unaware or else only peripherally aware of this.

Hall goes on to say that few people are willing to radically change the way they think in order to open their minds. In successful business reengineering projects, people do change the way they think. The process changes those "unspoken, implicit rules of behavior and thought." The work changes, and so does the worker.

Practical Thinking

Short-term practical thinking is one of the most cunning and seductive enemies of business reengineering. Although it can attack at any step in the process, it is deadliest during vision building and goal setting. Practical thinking, often disguised as "we need to get results quickly," "this is going to cost too much," and other such "realistic" objections can kill a project before it begins. Vision building and goal setting for business reengineering demand that people escape the confines of today's practicality. Too often practical thinking translates into near-term results, activity for activity's sake, or fear of failure. We are not saying that to be practical is necessarily bad; in fact, long-term practicality is invaluable. The vision and goals must fit within the future possibilities, not the highly improbable. But attention focused solely on the short-term practical results or tasks can seriously shortchange the reengineering process. Good ideas are precluded, judged as impractical. The now-orientation of practical thinking, clouded by the operating constraints of today, is the antithesis of visionary thinking. Practical thinking often focuses only on immediate cause and effect relationships, missing systemic faults. The "Beer Game" described in Peter Senge's book, *The Fifth Discipline*, is a perfect example of the problems created when practical thinking reigns. Typically, the players in the game make "practical" decisions assuming that what is happening right now will continue to happen. The systemic consequences of decisions are never anticipated. The result is chaos—predictable, but still chaos.

Because our culture values pragmatism highly, it can be difficult to manage in a business reengineering project. Most organizations reward people for what they can deliver this month or quarter rather than for their futuristic or systemic thinking. To shift people, even temporarily, away from the near-term reality, the business reengineering facilitator can use a number of tactics:

- Map the group's orientation toward practical thinking, and use this as a way to recognize biases during reengineering sessions.
- Use the "Beer Game" or a similar exercise to build awareness of the consequences of pragmatic thinking.

- List (on easel sheets) factors people use to judge ideas or suggestions. Note those that fall under the heading "practical." Create a new list of criteria by which to judge ideas, eliminating any that could be considered practical.

Sizing the Project

What should we include in the business reengineering project work? If a project team attempts to solve all organizational problems, the project will bog down and die of its own weight and complexity. On the other hand, if a project is defined too narrowly, real performance improvements may remain elusive. The project becomes incremental process improvement that can be accomplished without a special project team. Theoretically, any operation, no matter how large, can be reengineered. But the need for massive resources and a sustained commitment over long periods of time make success highly improbable. Reengineering means radical upheaval, which, if improperly scoped, could destroy a vulnerable organization. In the 1970s, the Bell System tried to establish a single automated accounting system for all 21 Bell companies. The project began with 50 people and a five-year schedule. Twelve years and hundreds of people later, the project was still unfinished. Determining the size of a reengineering project, then, is not just a practical matter, but one critical to its success. To properly size a project, we must address the issues of scope, boundaries, timing, and resources.

Scoping the Project

The core of any business reengineering project is the set of processes that will be redesigned to achieve the vision. This set of processes is identified during project scoping. This stage is so critical that, without it, the project will quickly lose its focus, expanding and contracting erratically. Executives and managers will find themselves warring over boundaries, leading the project team to endless frustration, delayed schedules, and unnecessary and costly distractions.

Street-smart business reengineers use six rules to define clearly where they are going (Figure 3.1).

Defining project scope begins with the identification of those business processes that must be reengineered to achieve the vision. Processes are

---

- Limit the project to no more than seven and no fewer than four interrelated processes.

- Scope should not exceed the control or influence of the highest-level person sponsoring the project.

- Processes included in scope must relate directly to the vision.

- Include only those processes that *are broken;* that is, *not working*.

- All processes included in scope must share inputs and outputs.

- Processes included in scope will share a common culture.

Figure 3.1 Rules for Scoping Business Reengineering Projects

what the business does, not *who* performs the work. Separating *what* from *who* is critical to scoping. A process must meet these criteria:

- Produces or manipulates data or physical materials
- Adds value to distinctive business outcomes (work products)
- Can be performed by one or more individuals or teams of people
- Is triggered (started) by one or more events
- Consumes resources

A process is *not* a task. It is *not* a business function. It is *not* a department. A business process typically contains four to seven subprocesses. If there are fewer, the process definitions probably are aggregated at too high a level. For example, to reengineer a corporate training center operation, the business processes potentially within the scope of the project might be:

- Define training requirements
- Develop training
- Certify instructors
- Process students
- Conduct classes
- Maintain training history
- Manage facilities

From a potential list such as this, we select the business processes for the project scope by applying the rules for scoping the project.

Limit the project to no more than seven and no fewer than four interrelated processes. Our list contains seven apparently related processes, so we pass this first test.

Scope should not exceed the control or influence of the sponsor of the project. When many different groups perform the process in many different ways, building commitment to a common set of business practices may not be feasible, either politically or physically. Too many variables and differences within the operation make commonality impossible, even though there may be significant problems. For example, if the business process, "define training requirements," was controlled by seven different line business units, the director of the training center (the reengineering project executive sponsor) may not have the political power to force a common-requirements analysis and planning process across the business line divisions. And, on closer scrutiny, each division may require a different process solution given the uniqueness of their business products, services, and operations. However, the training center director could set a standard for the requirements information delivered (input) to the center by those seven business divisions.

Processes included in scope must relate directly to the vision. The vision for this project focused on improving the development and delivery of training. Facilities management, although related to the other processes, did not directly relate to the vision.

Processes included in scope will share a common culture. The facilities management process is managed by an external contractor, and there is no intention to integrate that process into the culture of the training center.

Include only those processes that are broken, that is, not working. Even where it is politically and physically possible to reengineer a business process, there may be no need for a radical realignment. If it already performs well, continuous process improvement—the gradual tweaking to increase performance within the current configuration—may be perfectly acceptable. For example, the "certify instructors" process may function well even though it is an integral part of the training center's business operations. Information produced for output and required as input for those business processes within the project scope can be standardized to ensure smooth interaction and communication.

All processes included in scope must share inputs and outputs. Some processes do not directly relate or interact with the rest of the operation. They may operate in isolation or service different customers or constituencies. If an isolated process or set of processes requires radical change, establish a separate project to do if.

After applying the scoping rules, we include four of the seven processes in the project:

• Develop training
• Process students
• Conduct classes
• Maintain training history

There are risks to excluding business processes from the reengineering project. Sometimes the problem that indicates a need for business reengineering cannot be solved if the project scope includes only those business processes that exhibit symptoms. For example, one company had a significant rebate problem that was costing them millions of dollars. Commercial customers expected certain payments for discounts on products they purchased. When they did not receive the payments they expected, they would subtract the rebate amount from their invoices. Payment reconciliation groups spent many labor-intensive (and expensive) hours verifying that customers actually were entitled to the rebate amounts. Research revealed that the payment reconciliation and invoicing processes needed some automated improvements to provide better tracking. The real problem, however, was with the business processes preceding the payment reconciliation and invoicing processes. There were no payment standards or business practices for negotiating discounts with customers and communicating that information to the payment units within the business operations in a timely manner. To exclude those up-front processes would have prevented any significant improvement in rebate performance.

The next step in scoping a business reengineering project is to define the interfaces that connect the selected business processes to the rest of the operations. Identifying, controlling, and reengineering the interfaces can indirectly cause changes in parts of the organization over which the project executive sponsor has no control. For example, the requirements information produced by the business process "define training requirements" in the seven business divisions is an input interface into the processes within the project scope. Reengineering that interface will force each of those business divisions to define training requirements according to a new set of quality and information standards. This, in turn, could change the way they operate. We must inform those business managers of these potential changes during project scoping to ensure smooth implementation of the new business operation. Such attention to interfaces as well as processes builds credibility and acceptance in the early stages of the project (Figure 3.2).

Setting Project Boundaries

With the project scope defined, it becomes easy to identify the organization units responsible for performing the processes and supplying inputs or receiving outputs through the interfaces. We can document this using a matrix diagram that maps processes to organization units (Figure 3.3).

Within these identified organization units are the people who will be affected directly by the reengineering project and intimately involved in its implementation. They could be facing changes such as:

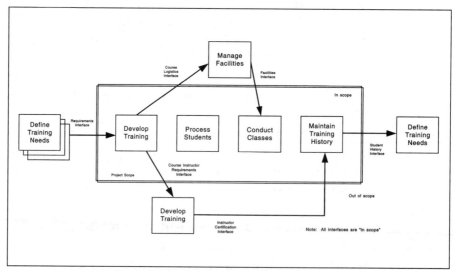

Figure 3.2 Business Process and Interface Scope

54

- New work methods or skill requirements (working directly with customers, using computer systems, eliminating reviews to make decisions directly)
- Redefined roles and responsibilities for work tasks, decisions, or supervisory accountabilities
- Lost job positions

With boundaries for the project identified, it is now easy to select:

- Executives to be members of an executive sponsor team for the reengineering project
- Managers and professionals to be members of the reengineering project team with decision-making approval authority and implementation responsibilities

Project scoping and bounding for business reengineering are, in the end, judgment calls based upon what is reasonable given the political power issues of the project executive sponsors and the perceived economic and customer relationship environments. For example, in one organization, the choice was between dramatically standardizing product offerings or redesigning the business processes to support product cus-

	Corporate Training Center	Division Employees	Vendors	Division Managers	Internal/ External Instructors
Develop Training	✔		✔		
Process Students	✔	✔			
Conduct Classes		✔			✔
Maintain Training History	✔	✔		✔	
Requirements Interface	✔			✔	
Course Logistics Interface	✔		✔		
Course Instructor Interface	✔				✔

Figure 3.3 Organization Boundaries

tomizations. At the start of the project, the team chose the latter option because it was perceived to be easier to sell process redesign than product-line simplification. However, after seeing the investment costs required to implement the new processing environment, the executives were more willing to explore product-line simplification even though it meant facing tough policy decisions that would affect both customers and very powerful general managers.

Time Available to Complete the Project

Executives and managers often have extremely unrealistic expectations about how long it actually takes to reengineer a business operation. They expect a situation that took years to create to be remedied in six months. The first part of any reengineering project, if approached in a structured and disciplined manner using accelerated design techniques, can be completed within four to six months. However, this work delivers only the reengineering design (the Blueprint) for the business operation and a plan for its implementation. The actual implementation may take many additional months or even years, depending upon the following factors:

- Number and complexity of business processes
- Severity of the changes
- Number and size of organizations directly involved and impacted
- Amount and type of new technology applied
- Resistance of the culture to change

For example, the effort to create common business practices, technology, and methods to support five common processes performed in seven separate operating companies affecting over 4,000 people took only six months to design and plan for implementation. However, because of the culture's aversion to risk, the number of organization units involved, and the financial investment required for new technology, the implementation will take at least three years. In fact, during the implementation's first year, only one common practice and a few interim solutions will be installed. Only after a proof-of-concept test is conducted (or a major financial or customer crisis reinforces the need for radical change) will additional implementation funding become available.

Even with approval for full implementation, the team often underestimates the amount of time the reengineering implementation will require. The basis of such shortsightedness may be any of the following false assumptions:

- Executives have only to "say the word" and it will happen.
- Process change is easy.
- Training in new technology or business practices is not required or can be informal and unstructured.
- The technology will work as promised.
- Technology can solve what is actually a business policy and practices problem.
- People do not take change personally.
- Everyone can see the big picture and work toward the greater good.
- Everything will go as planned.

Therefore, if the time for the project is limited—that is, less than one year—we recommend the following:

- Narrowly define the project scope and boundaries.
- Focus on changing business policies and practices and support changes with heavy doses of training and on-the-job hand-holding.
- Use accelerated decision making and high-involvement techniques, such as facilitated workshops, to design and plan for implementation within the first two months of the project.
- Limit expected improvements to smaller, less radical changes.
- Implement technology solutions using existing technology.

But, be careful—the result may not be radical enough to turn the business operation around. If the processes are truly broken, these narrow changes may bring only temporary relief. You have accomplished only process improvement on a broken process. Therefore, it is bound to break again soon.

Resources for the Project

There are three key resources for any business reengineering project: financial, facilities and equipment, and human. If resources are limited, the reengineering project should be downsized and controlled very carefully. The costs of developing a reengineering design (the Blueprint) and implementation plan are easily contained and moderate (approximately 10 to 15 percent of the total project cost). The least predictable reengineering costs occur in the implementation effort. Therefore, careful and specific task planning for implementation is critical to successful resource management. The more limited the resources for a project, the more implementation must be restricted, either by implementing only part of the reengineering design, by spreading the implementation over a longer time period, or by limiting the reengineering to a portion of the organization. Costs escalate when these types of implementation mistakes are made:

- Investments focus on the technology rather than on changes to business policies and practices and training. Studies have shown that most failed change efforts devote an estimated 85 percent of their costs to technology and only 15 percent to business changes. Successful projects reverse those numbers or at least keep them more balanced.

- Technology development proceeds without clear and definitive specifications of performance for transaction-processing and information needs. Studies have shown that failed technology projects have only 10 to 15 percent of the effort devoted to analysis and design activities. Successful ones have 30 to 40 percent of the time spent on this front-end work. As a result, the time required to test is 5 to 10 percent rather than 50 percent of the development effort.

- Human support for implementation is not made available. In failed projects, people are not given the time to learn and absorb the new changes into the line organizations and support staff. Accountability for training, coordination, and problem solving is not assigned. In some cases, no one is held accountable for the implementation.

- Measures to monitor progress are not an integral part of the implementation. In successful projects, specific implementation milestones and performance targets are tied to the performance goals for executives and managers of the affected organizations and tied to their compensation. Periodic and consistent forums for reporting progress and for problem solving must be available during the implementation so progress can be measured, accomplishments celebrated, and course correction made.

Project Sizing Critical Factors

A business reengineering project team should consider these factors in sizing the project, setting reengineering goals, and estimating time frames:

Number of business processes. The average business has 10 to 15 primary business processes. Each of these divide into three to five specific, identifiable key processes. If more than one primary process is included within the scope of the project, the project is considered large and may take many years to implement.

Diversity of business processes. The more unlike or disparate the business processes, the greater the differences in work methods, practices, and culture. This diversity increases project complexity because it will require more effort to bring a common set of business policies and practices to such a complex environment.

Number of organization units. The greater the number of organization units and people within each of those units affected by the project scope, the longer it will take to get buy-in from all the decision makers. If the organization units are also separated physically or do not interact in the current environment, it will take longer for the project team to create a common knowledge base about the project and obtain agreements and buy-in to the vision and reengineering design.

Organizational relationships to processes. The greater the number of organization units that perform the set of scoped business processes, the more complex the project will be. This overlap of accountabilities can produce redundancies and many over-the-wall handoffs of work. Organizational overlap requires simplification and much effort to resolve power and control issues during the process redesign activities.

Organizational politics. The more intense the organizational politics, the greater the potential for mistrust, hostilities, and territorial behaviors by executives and managers facing radical change. Additional time may be required to build trust, reduce hostilities, and create true commitment to the project.

Risk-aversion nature of the culture. If people have not been rewarded for making changes and thinking strategically and creatively, resistance will be profound. Executives and managers may exhibit this resistance by focusing from a short-term tactical perspective rather than a more strategic long-term perspective. More dramatically, these executives may initially commit to the project and then begin to backpedal once funding for implementation is requested. Obtaining funding for a costly implementation will take extra time when decision makers demand proof that the changes will deliver the promised performance improvements.

In chapter 5, "Prepare for the Journey," the first step of the reengineering work is called "Frame the Project." Within that step is an activity called "conduct a current situation analysis." The project is sized during this activity. We can apply many techniques in this analysis activity, including:

- The diagnostic tool described in appendix A to define a need for reengineering to solve current problems
- Market and customer analyses to identify future business needs and the potential contribution to that future of a business operations reengineering effort
- Observation and formal data collection to uncover specifics about the problems in operations
- Root cause analysis to identify project scope

A Special Note on Root Cause Analysis. The goal of root cause analysis is to look systematically beyond the symptoms of a problem to find its actual causes. Root cause analysis is fundamental to TQM methodology as well as business reengineering. Without a systematic approach, the search for problem causes is likely to become random and biased, which can lead the team down the wrong path. Most problems are rooted in product or process complexity. In other words, the way work is done causes the need for rework (error correction), inefficiency (too long a response time), breakdowns/delays, and variation in output quality or work procedure. As discussed earlier in this chapter, the symptoms may not appear in the process that causes the problem. In most cases, the causative processes feed the processes displaying the symptoms—that is, upstream business processes cause downstream symptoms (Figure 3.4).

There are a number of techniques used to determine which processes to include within the scope of a reengineering project. These techniques come from a variety of disciplines, including continuous process

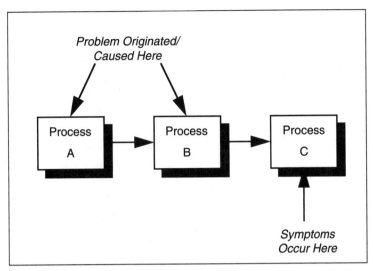

Figure 3.4 Problem Causes and Symptoms

improvement. In his book, *Continuous Process Improvement*, George D. Robson states that the analysis techniques should meet these criteria:

- Help the team use the knowledge it has about the problem.
- Logically address the possible causes.
- Work systematically from what the team knows to what it doesn't know.
- Utilize the expertise of people who know the problem firsthand.

The techniques most often recommended are simple and straightforward and do not require complex formulas and statistical calculations. (Some of these techniques may also be used in the process redesign work as explained in chapter 5, "Prepare for the Journey.") As discussed by Robson, Peter Schotes in the book, *The Team Handbook* and other experts, the techniques include but are not limited to:

Decomposition diagram (Figure 3.5). Sometimes called a top-down flowchart, this technique identifies and defines the hierarchy of business processes. Each level of decomposition should have no more than four to seven processes.

Process flow diagram (Figure 3.6). This technique examines the relationship of the processes in terms of inputs (the materials/information fed into the process) and outputs (the

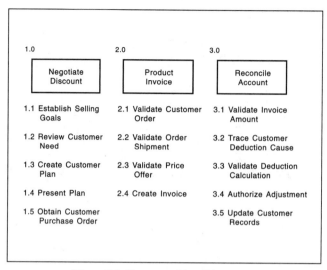

Figure 3.5 Decomposition Diagram

results of the process activity). For each process, it also identifies the controls (the environmental information used by the process to determine what can be done), the mechanisms (the resources that influence the process), the process customer (who receives the output), and the supplier (who provides the input).

Decision flowchart (Figure 3.7). Also called a detailed flowchart,

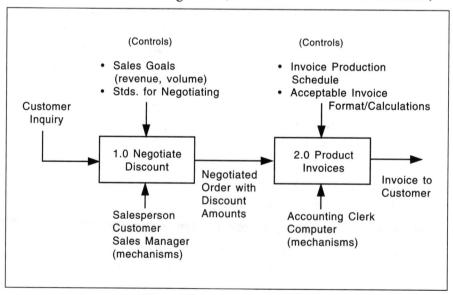

Figure 3.6 Process Flow Diagram

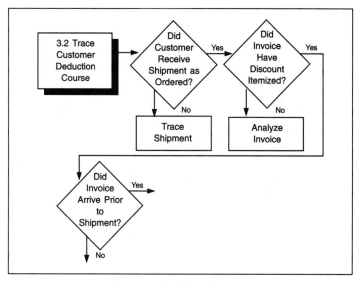

Figure 3.7 Decision Flowchart

this analysis technique identifies the key decisions and processing paths based upon the results of those decisions. This approach provides an information analysis rather than a task analysis of a business process.

Work-flow diagram (Figure 3.8). Charting the flow of transactions and physical movement of people within a business operation can sometimes be useful in analyzing problem causes.

Deployment chart (Figure 3.9). The deployment chart, a type of

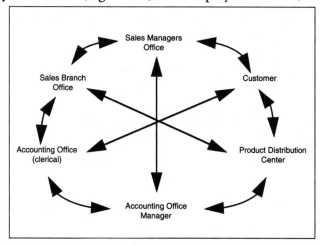

Figure 3.8 Work-Flow Diagram

63

Process	Sales-person	Acctg. Clerk	Sales Manager	Customer
3.1 Validate Invoice Amount		A		
3.2 Trace Customer Deduction Cause	C	A		C
3.3 Validate Deduction Calculation		A		
3.4 Authorize Adjust-ments		C	A	
3.5 Update Customer Records		A		C

A = Accountable   A = Approval Needed
C = Consulted/Involved

Figure 3.9 Deployment Chart

matrix diagram, depicts the relationship of "who does the work" to "what work is done." It can identify who is accountable for what processes, who is involved, and who has approval authority.

Pareto chart (Figure 3.10). This chart focuses on the frequency of problems as an indicator of problem impact. Usually types of

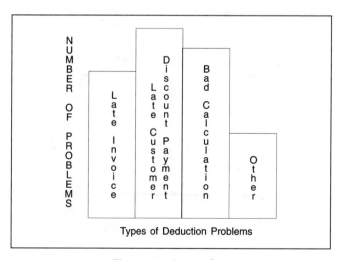

Figure 3.10 Pareto chart

64

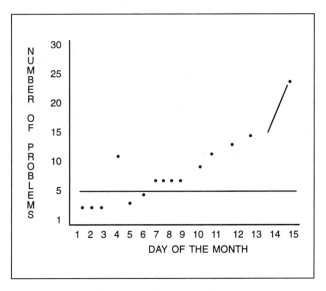

Figure 3.11 Frequency Chart

problems and their frequency are compared in a bar chart.

Frequency chart (Figure 3.11). Charting the frequency of problem occurrence against time helps to identify problem patterns. Adding upper and lower control limits to the display or other calculations, like averages, can assist in understanding problem variability.

Dot plot diagram (Figure 3.12). Data plotted over time can be converted to a dot plot diagram to check the distribution or spread of the data. Both abnormal and normal patterns can indicate

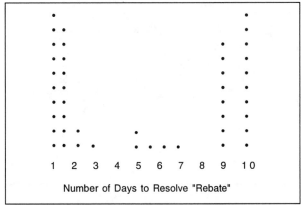

Figure 3.12 Dot Plot Diagram

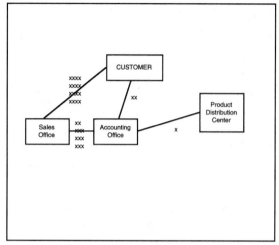

Communications Failure Occurrences

Figure 3.13 Defect Concentration Diagram

sources of problems. The version of this diagram that uses actual measurement data instead of dots is called the stem and leaf chart.

Defect concentration diagram (Figure 3.13). Another charting technique for problem identification is to visually mark where

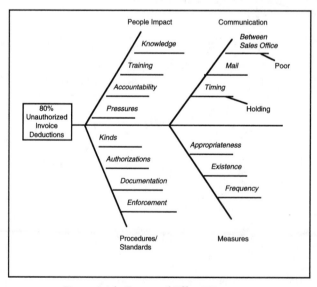

Figure 3.14 Cause and Effect Diagram

66

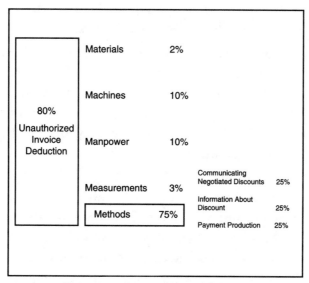

Figure 3.15 Structure Tree and 5 Ms

defects appear on a physical work product or on a diagram of the business process flow. The concentration of marks indicates a consistency and predictability of problem appearance.

Cause and effect diagram (Figure 3.14). Also called an Ishikawa diagram or fishbone diagram, this technique breaks down a given

80% Unauthorized Invoice Deduction	Is Occuring	Is Not Occuring	Therefore
WHERE			
WHEN			
WHAT KIND HOW MUCH			
WHO			

Figure 3.16 Satisfaction and Is/Is Not Matrix

problem into organized groups of possible causes, allowing people to see the possible relationship of the factors.

Structure tree and the 5 Ms diagram (Figure 3.15). This analysis technique forces an examination of any problem in terms of five probable causes—materials, machines, manpower, measurements, and methods (the 5 Ms). A percentage of the cause is assigned to each, and then the possible root causes of that percentage are identified. The goal is to focus on those causes that contribute most to the problem.

Stratification and is/is not matrix (Figure 3.16). This technique attempts to pinpoint where a problem does and does not occur by mapping the where, when, how much, and who of a problem against the patterns of occurrence and nonoccurrence.

Scatter diagram (Figure 3.17). This technique allows the examination of two process characteristics to determine if one characteristic influences the other. The pattern of points on the diagram will indicate the possible relationship. There may be no pattern, a trend pattern, or a clustering pattern.

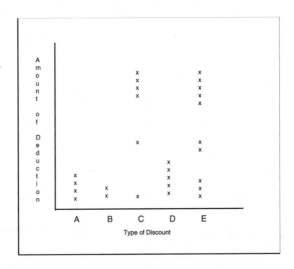

Figure 3.17 Scatter Diagram

Although most diagrams are self-instructional, you can find detailed instructions for their use in numerous texts, including those listed at the end of this book. The matrix in Figure 3.18 summarizes when to use the different analytical techniques.

Analysis Technique	Process Definition	Process Relationships Examination	Problem Cause Definition	Problem Data Examination
Decomposition Diagram	✔			
Process Flow Diagram	✔	✔		
Decision Flowchart	✔			
Work-Flow Diagram	✔	✔		
Deployment Chart	✔	✔		
Pareto Chart				✔
Frequency Chart				✔
Dot Plot Diagram				✔
Defect Concentration Diagram				✔
Cause & Effect Diagram			✔	
Structure Tree & 5 Ms Diagram			✔	
Stratification and Is/Is Not Matrix			✔	
Scatter Diagram		✔		✔

Figure 3.18 Diagram Application for Root Cause Analysis

CHAPTER 4

DON'T WALK ALONE

The seasoned, street-smart traveler knows that there is safety in numbers when wandering through unfamiliar territory. It's also more enjoyable, since burdens as well as pleasant sites and experiences can be shared with fellow travelers. Traveling with a group enables you to bring along everything you'll need for your journey and provides the necessary mix of skills to survive the adventure. That includes everybody from a good navigator to interpret the maps and road signs to a friendly fellow to ask the local people questions, seek out good sites, and overcome local suspicion and resistance. For street-smart business reengineers, the same concept applies. No one person can single-handedly bring radical business change and sophisticated technology to an organization, no matter how simple the situation may appear. The project director must assemble a team of people who can expand the group's awareness, involve people from all parts of the organization, and bring to bear the many skills needed to reengineer a business successfully. Without a team, the business reengineering project director is like a lost soul wandering down a dark alley in a strange neighborhood. Unusual sounds seem sinister, and strangers appear threatening. The team is the more powerful, capable way of warding off dangers and taking advantage of situations that are not available to the single traveler.

The Essential Nature of an Effective Business Reengineering Team

A reengineering team is more than a group of people who have been pulled together and told to redesign the organization. It is a group of people who have developed a successful way of communicating, solving problems, and working together. Leadership can come from the formally appointed project director or can be shared by the team members. In either case, the effective business reengineering team has the ability to learn within the context of the work itself. Team members utilize and maximize each others' skills. The team can expand and vary its membership without affecting its effective functioning. In other words, the business reengineering team is a model of what the organization can become. Team members model behaviors for the rest of the organization to emulate. The team must model the principles of business process redesign in the reengineering design (the Blueprint) they create. They must implement the project using the transformation principles. Furthermore, the team must model the principles of continuous process improvement through their continual assessment and improvement of how the team runs the project.

All effective business reengineering teams must possess three core competencies. These competencies must exist and mature as the project moves from the vision and design stages into the implementation phases. *Without these competencies, even the most appropriately reengineered business process will not survive implementation.*

Ability to Learn

The first critical competency is the ability to learn. This, of course, includes learning how to function as a team and execute a business reengineering methodology. But the ability to learn is critical to the nature of the business reengineering itself. Reengineering any operation, no matter how small, requires the redesign of business processes that cut across traditional and often rigid organizational and hierarchical boundaries. The team enters unchartered territory, encountering interdependencies, lack of accountabilities, and work complexities (which often caused the problems that triggered the project). More than likely, there is no clear solution. It is only through a systematic discovery and learning-based approach to the project that the appropriate solution, or set of solutions, emerges.

The project provides a natural setting for learning. Because of their different skills, knowledge, on-the-job expertise, and mental abilities, team members both learn from and teach one another. The team must be structured to nurture this learning relationship throughout the project. As the project matures through its life cycle, the team must be able to shift its focus and skill set, change team members, and continue learning. Underlying this learning competence are the following skills, knowledge, and abilities:

- Ability to listen carefully to others and to ask questions to uncover assumptions, biases, and perspectives. An "I already know the answer" attitude is a surefire formula for disaster. It leads to ignoring others' ideas and perspectives, making sweeping generalizations, dictating to others what to do, and creating political roadblocks to implementation.

- Ability to let go of old "proven" practices and ideas, which can prevent the reemergence of good ideas that were stifled in the past. When people let go of old ways of thinking and acting, they open themselves up to new perspectives and creative solutions.

- Ability to work in a systematic way. In addition to creative thinking, learning requires systematic follow-through—the ability to gather and carefully analyze data, to develop and test alternatives. Learning requires the ability to discriminate patterns and trends, anticipate problems, and translate experience— whether it be mistaken or successful—into principles and ideas for future behavior and situations.

Political Savvy

The second critical competency is political savvy. Business reengineering brings change. Centers of power and authority can be wiped out or moved, job positions can be eliminated or redefined, the work itself can change dramatically or disappear, and new technology can require completely new skills. Such changes don't come without pain. In some cases, executives and managers cannot fully imagine a successful reengineering outcome. Resistance may appear from all levels of the organization, even from supporters. The business reengineering team must have the political smarts to manage change from the project's inception through implementation. It must possess the skills and knowledge to:

- **Create trusting relationships and alliances throughout the organizational hierarchy.** The team must be able to create momentum and a positive climate for change. Line managers and executives with organizational credibility may need to speak for the team. The team certainly will need the support of these managers when it comes time to implement the changes and reinforce the required infrastructure and value behaviors in their own groups. Relationship building requires the ability to determine who needs to be brought into the fold, who needs to be approached one-on-one, and what sequence should be followed to talk with people so no one will feel offended or bypassed.

- **Keep from making unnecessary compromises in the reengineering design and implementation plans.** Sometimes it is the pressure to make the quick fixes or a reluctance to make the capital and training investment. It could be not comprehending the need for job training and support or the inability of executives to live with the ambiguity of long-term change. The reengineering team must operate from a position of strength and inclusion rather than of weakness and exclusion. Unnecessarily bargaining away of the design will reduce anticipated benefits of the reengineering effort.

- **Tell a story that captures the imagination.** There is an ongoing need to increase awareness and educate people about the project. The team will need to repeat the story to people over and over again. A truism in sales work is that it takes five calls to get the appointment. The same applies to the buy-in for business reengineering change. People need to hear the message repeatedly before they begin to commit to the benefits that can accrue to the organization and to themselves. The team must have the selling and presentation skills necessary to command attention, stimulate curiosity, and confidently answer questions and concerns that will arise.

Committed Persistence

The third critical competency is the ability to maintain a committed persistence throughout the life of the project. The team must have the tenacity of religious zealots. A business reengineering implementation will take from 12 to 24 months or longer. There will be "lows" when the team questions whether anything will really happen. Some team members will be reluctant to pay continual and absolute attention to implementation details, refusing to provide the "nursemaid" follow-up sometimes required to inspire people to action. There will be times when the team members are the only ones who believe that the project can succeed or who fully understand what must be done to make the project "happen." Executive sponsors will gloss over the details and assume that the job is complete when, in reality, the implementation has only begun. Managers will resist, erecting roadblocks and ignoring the need for their own and their workers' skill development. The computer staff will most likely have problems with the technology, overcommit and underdeliver, and complain about the lack of programming staff and vendor incompetencies. Reengineering always brings some ambiguity and chaos. The project team must be able to analyze obstacles and develop workable, practical solutions. Street-smart reengineers see this as a natural state of affairs. Project implementation is the most formidable and circuitous phase of a business reengineering project. The team must relish the "opportunities" that arise rather than be frustrated by them. It is the nature of reengineering work, nothing more and nothing less.

IS/IT Role in Business Reengineering

Information systems groups, also called information technology (IT) groups, have a unique opportunity to be catalysts for business reengineering projects. In their search for a productivity solution, business people often approach the IS organization with the need for a new system. In one organization, for example, the business decided salesperson productivity would be improved by laptop computers that could travel to the client location. In these situations, the IS/IT group is perfectly positioned to ask questions that lead business people to realize that productivity requires more than automation. However, "catalyst" is a different role from "driver." IS/IT can be the match that ignites the need for business reengineering, but the business must take over from there. Change must come from within the organization; it cannot be imposed from the outside. Project leadership and executive sponsorship for business reengineering projects must come from the business side of the organization.

IS/IT groups supply more than technology. In successful business reengineering, technology must be embedded into and aligned with the business. Single-source information sharing and access, along with sophisticated communication and networking technologies, are often required to bring business reengineering designs into reality. Business people need to understand all aspects of technological capabilities (and noncapabilities), which means that IS/IT must function as a partner and enabler in the reengineering. IS/IT people must perform these roles in business reengineering projects:

- **Awareness builder and educator.** The IS/IT community knows the direction and potential capabilities of existing and emerging technologies. More importantly, they understand the limitations, constraints, and implementation issues of various technologies. IS/IT groups can play a significant role in raising business people's awareness of potential applications within a particular business environment.

- **Project partner.** Joint project leadership is often an appropriate approach for accountability on business reengineering projects. As co-project operations manager, an IS/IT person can relieve his/her business co-project operations manager from the burden of directing and managing the technological side of the project. And, as co-project operations manager, the IS/IT person can ensure that technology and business needs are properly integrated and balanced. This is also a good position from which to manage technological expectations. Technology cannot deliver the reengineering solution, but, without it, the reengineering solution cannot be implemented.

- **Project team member.** The disciplined, structured approach, and analytical skills of a professional IS/IT engineer provides valuable skills to the business reengineering project team. Team members provide direct knowledge and skills about current and potential automation capabilities and the existing systems environment that must be converted to new technologies. Without IS/IT on the team, the project team will flounder in a sea of marketing literature and unfulfilled promises from vendors or, worse yet, ignore technology altogether.

Business Reengineering Team Structures

As you will soon read in the next chapter, a business reengineering project follows a life cycle that has eight distinct steps. The reengineering team will need a variety of different skills and knowledge for each step. Therefore, the team's structure must be flexible enough to accommodate required changes in membership and size throughout the life of the project. In the beginning, a small project team might conduct research to analyze the need for business reengineering and to create the business case. For the reengineering design and implementation planning, the team will expand to include representatives from all affected business units and to bring in other subject-matter experts. During the implementation, the team will change and expand again. From beginning to end, however, the team must include a core of politically savvy, committed, and persistent team members. Therefore, we recommend a structure (Figure 4.1) for the business reengineering project team that consists of these members:

- Business executive sponsors for vision creation, reengineering design, and implementation execution
- Project director
- Core project coordination and support group
- Business unit champions
- Advisory and subject-matter experts
- Implementation SWAT groups

The key advantage of this team structure is that it puts the ownership for the reengineering project in the hands of those who will live with the results. It involves as many people as possible to increase knowledge and buy-in and provides the driving energy and focus to keep the project from splintering during implementation.

Business Executives Sponsors

The project role of executive sponsorship belongs on the business side of the organization. At the beginning of the project life cycle, where the

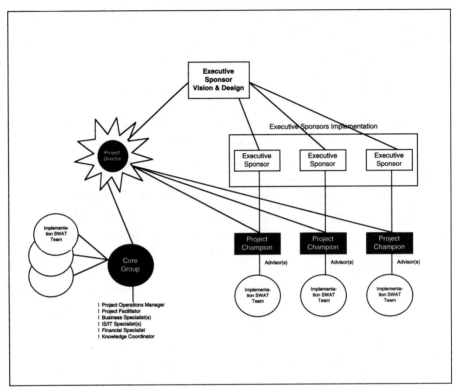

Figure 4.1 Business Reengineering Project Team Structure

focus is on creating the vision, developing the reengineering design, and planning the implementation, sponsorship can reside in a headquarters organization and/or directly in the line organization. During the implementation phase, executive sponsorship must come from the line organizations and be supported by the headquarters executive sponsor. The executive sponsors usually have the title of vice president or executive vice president. An individual may be the executive sponsor, or a small group of executives may form a sponsor team. If a sponsor team is formed, the only requirement is that they function as a team. The executive sponsor's organization will be affected by and benefit from the reengineering effort. Often it is the executive sponsor's budget that funds the reengineering project.

Throughout the project, the executive sponsor must demonstrate commitment to the project through a variety of actions:

- Speaking to reluctant peers and subordinates to encourage and direct their involvement in the project

- Attending and speaking at selected project team meetings and sessions
- "Walking the new vision" by participating in education and awareness-building sessions in person or on video
- Making the necessary policy decisions in a timely manner so the reengineered operations can be implemented
- Communicating upward to ensure organizationwide approval

The accountabilities of executive sponsors during the initial project phases include the following:

- Persuading line managers to commit champions to the project and realign job responsibilities and performance goals to ensure their participation on the team
- Clearing the calendars of other individuals selected to participate in design workshops, project team meetings, and planning sessions
- Making the decision to implement
- Modeling the communication and transformation behavior wanted for the rest of the organization

Once implementation is approved, project executive sponsorship becomes more action centered and includes the following accountabilities:

- Encouraging line managers and staff to accept the new operational vision and let go of the past
- Removing obstacles to change
- Resolving sensitive policy issues that can't be resolved at lower levels
- Incorporating implementation goals in each key executive's performance plans and holding these executives accountable for their achievement
- Modeling the communication and transformation behavior wanted for the rest of the organization
- Providing the funding and long-term support the project needs for successful implementation
- Updating the project team on external events and situations that may affect the project's implementation

Project Director

You may notice that the title is project *director* rather than project

79

manager. Business reengineering projects require a tremendous amount of leadership, which is not the same as management. The project director is accountable for the success of the project. Therefore, he or she must be an employee of the organization, not a consultant from the outside. Although the core group will report directly and the champions indirectly, the project director has little or no direct influence over most of the people involved in the project. He or she must inspire all of these people, including the executive sponsors, to action. The project director must maintain a delicate balance between the visionary future and the long-term practical realities. He or she must be politically astute. This means building relationships and commitment across organizational boundaries. It means communicating and negotiating among diverse sets of special interests. It means removing obstacles, selling policy changes, and helping project champions gain and maintain their power and credibility within their own organizations. At the same time, the project director must make sure that the project remains a high priority in the eyes of executives to ensure ongoing funding. The project director must be action-oriented, yet able to delegate detail work to core team members. In large and complex reengineering projects where multiple cultures must be integrated, there is a natural tendency for each group to try to go its own way. The project director must know when to push the various errant groups into alignment and when to let them be on their own. This is a special role requiring an experienced and skillful leader.

Core Coordination and Support Team Members

The core group normally contains three to seven people who run the project. They provide coordination and support to the champion decision makers. Initially, this may be the group that frames the project, builds the original business case, and obtains the funding for the reengineering design and implementation planning work. Members of the core group are normally assigned to the project full-time. The core group members must fulfill the following roles: project operations manager, business specialist, IS/IT specialist, project facilitator, financial specialist, and administrative specialist. One person may fill more than one role or two or more people may fill one role. There should be a formal job description for each core group position, and performance evaluations can be based on the individual's performance of that job as well as on the team's overall achievement. The executive sponsor selects the project director, and the project director fills all other core group job positions. If all personnel are not available internally, vendors may be used for some core group roles. Likely candidates for vendor support include project facilitator, IS/IT specialist, and administrative support. It is the job of the core group to:

- Provide the project strategy and process
- Research and provide alternatives for champion decision making
- Advise and counsel champions on their decisions
- Coordinate all internal and external communications
- Manage the issue research and resolution process
- Plan and conduct all decision-making and review meetings
- Produce all project documentation
- Coordinate the design, development, production, and communication of all common-usage implementation materials (systems, procedures manuals, training, and change management programs)
- Develop draft designs, plans, and other relevant materials for approval and change by project champions
- Communicate with and seek approvals from business sponsors
- Monitor and provide support to the champions' organizations during implementation
- Provide a central resource for information about the project
- Manage the quality and activities of implementation SWAT groups developing common solutions for use by all the business units

The core group is a fundamental part of the project team. Without the core group, there is no coordinating force for the project, no rallying point or support source for the project champions. However, the core group does not make decisions. That is the role of the project champions.

Project Champion Team Members

Project champions are the decision-making team members and may number anywhere from 3 to 20. Each team member represents a distinct business unit affected by the reengineering. The champion role is normally filled by middle managers who can communicate up and down their organization. They are formally appointed to the project team by the executive sponsor (and by their management), and their performance goals include measurable achievement of reengineering project success. Project champions understand the politics and managerial style of their organization. And, most importantly, they have influence and are recognized as people worth listening to. They understand the business processes that are within the project scope and the issues and problems that exist at the organization's operational levels. At the beginning of a project, these champions may have other duties besides project team membership, although they should commit at least 50 percent of their time to the project. As the project progresses, they may need to commit 100 percent, especially during implementation. The champions and core group team members are partners, sharing collective responsibility for the success of the project. The champions rely on the core group for support, focus, and direction but have the power to reject core group proposals. It is the role of the project champions to:

- Fully participate in all design, planning, and implementation activities
- Ensure that their own organizational issues and concerns are addressed while remaining focused on the total benefits of change
- Approve all project designs, plans, and products
- Customize, if necessary, common products developed for implementation in their own organizations
- Direct and manage the implementation of the reengineering design in their own organization
- Manage the quality and activities of the implementation SWAT groups working in their own organizations
- Apprise the core group of all actions, situations, and implementation progress in their own organization

Advisory Team Members

From time to time, the core group and the project champions will want to involve others, either from inside or outside the organization. These advisory team members are invited to participate in meetings and workshop sessions when their expertise is needed to validate ideas, provide additional perspectives, or offer additional input. These team members are ad hoc in that their participation is part-time and they are not accountable for the project unless they receive a specific task assignment.

This becomes more likely as the project nears implementation, and these participants become implementation SWAT group members with full-time implementation responsibilities. Until then, their managers are not likely to hold them accountable for project success in their personal performance plans. At any project team meeting or session, there may be none or up to 10 advisory team members.

Implementation SWAT Groups

When a business reengineering project moves from the design and planning steps of the life cycle into implementation, some tasks cannot be performed by the core group and project champion team alone. Specialized groups called implementation SWAT groups are established to produce common project products that can then be installed across the total organization. These groups, with their specific assignments, will report to the core group or to the appropriate project champion (directly or indirectly). Core group or champion team members also may be SWAT group members. SWAT group assignments may include such implementation tasks as:

- Design and/or develop business practices and related reference materials
- Design and/or develop new systems and technologies
- Install new systems and technologies
- Design and/or develop skills training
- Deliver training to field and headquarters organizations
- Provide consulting support to managers who must restructure their work units and jobs during the reengineering implementation
- Provide posttraining support as people start to execute the new processes
- Provide postinstallation support on systems and technologies
- Transfer new training and systems support into the work units' support systems after implementation
- Monitor performance and conduct critical reflection with work units to identify the process improvement needs of the implemented processes

The size of a SWAT group will vary depending on the scope and complexity of its work. Members must possess well-developed technical skills that fit the work requirements so they can act quickly and effectively. The implementation SWAT groups must establish strong and healthy working relationships with the core group and champions.

A Closer Look at Core Group Roles

Project Operations Manager

Day-to-day project management is the responsibility of the project operations manager. This person must have excellent management and follow-up skills to ensure deliverable quality and project effectiveness. The project operations manager normally coordinates all project tasks and promotes good relationships and communications at the working level among all team members. This includes managing the issue research and resolution process, removing obstacles, and planning and managing the work of the implementation SWAT groups.

Project Facilitator

The project facilitator should be an expert in leading groups to achieve their own objectives. The facilitator creates the process, structure, and climate for the various project meetings and sessions. The role requires skills in group process, team building, and relationship building; and techniques in conflict resolution, consensus creation, and barrier reduction. Through facilitated meetings and workshop sessions, the project time line can be accelerated and the team members focused for action. This person must facilitate meetings with the core group and executive sponsors, workshops with all project team members, formal meetings and presentations throughout the organization, and sessions with implementation SWAT groups and others for such purposes as "critical reflection" process improvement. In addition, the facilitator can provide one-on-one support, counseling, and coaching to individual team members, help others to confront issues, manage competing priorities, and balance the needs of all project participants.

Business reengineering projects are messy, particularly when they involve lots of people over long periods of time. Emotions will run high. People will be frustrated, angry, elated, combative, depressed, and withdrawn. The project facilitator plays a critical role in managing these emotional reactions. He or she must give team members the space to be themselves, but still keep the focus on the team's goals. Individuals do not lose their personalities when they become members of the team. They bring with them baggage from the past as well as expertise. A good facilitator is a coach, a teacher, a parent, a friend, an advocate, a therapist, and a judge.

The facilitator also should be an expert in business reengineering techniques and methodology. In essence, the facilitator is responsible for the work process followed by the project team. For this reason, the project facilitator is often an internal or external organization consultant who is specifically trained in facilitation and business reengineering. Business-specific subject matter expertise is not necessary and, in some cases, may be counterproductive.

Business Specialist

A core group should include at least one experienced business person with personal, in-depth knowledge of the processes and the people affected by the reengineering. If at all possible, one or more line or field persons should fill the business-specialist role. Although managerial rank is not necessary, organizational respect and overall credibility is. The business specialist is not a decision-making champion, but someone who can keep the core group in touch with "how things really work out there." Sometimes a project team can become detached from the operational world, becoming too theoretical and idealistic. Once the reengineering design is created, theory must give way to "nuts-and-bolts" activities during implementation. As core group team members, business specialists are most likely to work with champions and their organizations on business policies and practices, education and training, and communications with the field organizations. Their purpose is not to represent a field organization, but to ensure that business issues are raised and addressed throughout the project life cycle and across all the business units.

IS/IT Specialist

A knowledgeable expert on systems, technologies, and communication networks is crucial to a well-functioning core group. The IS/IT specialist must be able to speak fluently with external vendors and internal IS/IT groups about the technological options and issues. This person must understand complex technological options and risks, but, more importantly, he or she must be able to explain those issues in plain English that the business-oriented project team members can understand. In other words, the IS/IT specialist must be multilingual. His or her ideas and creativity can be critical to the design of the technology contemplated for the reengineered processes. He or she must be able to adapt and use appropriate systems life cycle methodologies in planning the technological implementation activities. And, because of the multitude of conversion and transitioning issues that must be addressed during implementation, the IS/IT specialist must be able to suggest interim alternatives for technology support. This person also should direct the implementation SWAT groups that have been assigned technology-related activities.

Financial Specialist

Finding the money to fund the various implementation activities is not easy in times of tight budgets and economic stagnation. A financial specialist can help the project director and the project champions analyze financial data, create business cases for funding, creatively present the data to funding decision makers as well as track actual costs against the budget. Not all reengineering projects require the full-time commitment of a financial specialist. The project's size and complexity will dictate its financial requirements. If the reengineering design calls for major changes in financial policies, practices, and controls, then this role can also take on design and implementation accountabilities.

Knowledge Coordinator

Although most core group members should be fluent with PCs and related software, a knowledge coordinator is usually required to ensure that the project runs smoothly and to maintain project information. All project outcomes must be created and maintained. The knowledge coordinator may use sophisticated technology to produce these, in addition to organizing, tracking, and maintaining project history files, presentations, distribution lists, meeting and session logistics, correspondence, workshops, and project equipment and materials.

Project Team Operational Techniques

The business reengineering project team is a well-trained working team that is fully responsible for the reengineering project. Sharing many characteristics with self-managing teams, the reengineering team has a wider range of cross-functional skills and is invested with greater authority and decision making powers than traditional teams. The reengineering team decides how to approach its work, sets its own priorities, organizes and coordinates its work with others, evaluates itself, and initiates its own corrective action. The team solves its own problems, schedules and assigns work tasks, and, in many cases, deals with its own personnel issues, such as absenteeism and member selection and evaluation. In most cases, the business reengineering project team has accountabilities that may change over time, and the team members are rewarded based upon team achievement as well as (or in lieu of) individual achievement. Not all business reengineering teams achieve complete autonomy and meet all the criteria of a self-managing team. For example, the project director job position may not rotate among team members, and the executive sponsor may request periodic updates on implementation progress. But, in most respects, by the sheer nature of the work, business reengineering project teams operate as self-managing teams and exist outside the traditional organizational reporting structure.

In order to succeed, then, the business reengineering project team must meet these critical success factors:

- **Commitment:** The project executive sponsors must empower the team to do its work and be ready and able to accept the results. They must trust the team to do the right thing, given sponsor guidance and strategic direction setting. The team members must be willing to take risks and share information among themselves as well as with outside groups. They must have access to skilled help when they need it and enough time and resources to accomplish their tasks.

- **Communication:** It is the project team members' responsibility to make their needs known and assert themselves with the executive sponsors when necessary. The team members must directly and honestly confront issues that put the project at risk. Their purpose is not to paint a rosy picture but to establish and maintain realistic expectations among all stakeholders. They must educate others about the project, its benefits, risks, and needs. They must assure all stakeholders about the future and acknowledge the ambiguity and anxiety that accompanies major changes. And, most importantly, the project team members must model the behavior they wish the rest of the organization to adopt.

- **Training:** The team members must be trained to conduct a business reengineering project independently. They must be prepared for the natural ups and downs of self-direction and the business reengineering process. This training, which should be supported by the project facilitator, should include some formal classroom education as well as on-the-job skills development.

- **Support:** The team must be supported by its management structure as it assumes authority traditionally held by supervising managers, as well as having access to coaches. The organizational infrastructure, including systems, policies, and procedures, must allow the project team to operate in a self-managing environment. In winter sailboat racing, "winter rules" allow boats to race safely by not following standard racing practices. Winter rules may also be necessary in a reengineering effort to establish team-based reward structures and objective-setting systems, develop technical training and consultation, institute direct links into all parts of the organization at all levels, and jointly develop outcome requirements and team boundaries.

- **Information:** The team must have access to both corporate and business unit information as they need it. The members must have the authority to access information without going up the hierarchy each time to get permission. They must be able to work peer to peer.

The project team members must develop healthy interpersonal relationships with each other and with those outside the team. This includes being willing to change long-held attitudes and beliefs, sharing one's knowledge and expertise, coordinating efforts with others to reduce duplication and overlaps, creating an environment that rewards collaboration and values relationships, and developing performance strategies that encourage teamwork.

Project Team Evolution to Maturity

Business reengineering teams go through a natural evolution (Figure 4.2). When the team first comes together, there is an initial period of ice-breaking and formation. Members are uncertain of roles, authority, and project goals, and mutual trust may be minimal. Some members may hold back, waiting to see who takes charge. An appointed, appropriately skilled leader or facilitator can minimize this initial stage by helping the team decide how to communicate, assign roles, conduct its work, and report its progress. When team members can relinquish the comfort of

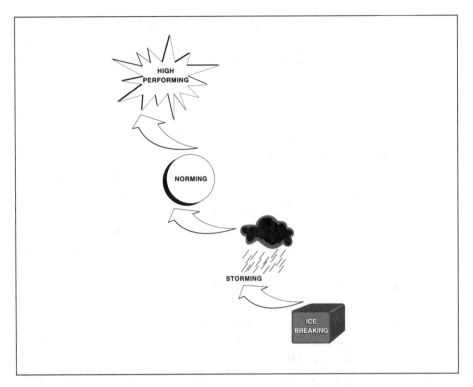

Figure 4.2 The Stages of Business Reengineering Team Evolution

nonthreatening topics and risk the possibility of conflict, they have matured to a second ("storming") stage of team development. Now members scrutinize and challenge almost everything about the team and its work. This includes the leader's policies and assumptions, individual roles in the power structure of the team, and their own ideas and biases about how the work should be done. During this stage, the project team may experience internal conflicts. Members need to learn to listen each other and jointly develop an operating structure that gives everyone a voice. When members complain and whine about how poorly the team functions, they must take their complaints to the team, not to someone outside the team.

If the team overcomes these storms, it moves to a problem-solving ("norming") stage and members learn to respect one another. They begin to share skills along with all types of information. The team can define team and member roles, and people are willing to take on the "right" assignments. Creativity is high; interactions are characterized by openness and sharing at both the task and the personal levels. There is, for the first time, real team spirit. The biggest drawback to this stage is the team's fear of being broken up or having their ideas rejected. In one project, when the training consultant transformed a team-developed product into a different form for training purposes, almost all team members initially rejected the design because the consultant had changed their creation. In another instance, the project team came to feel that executive politics would prevent their reengineering design from ever being implemented and that the organization's managers would water down the design during implementation. This "us vs. them" perspective will continue until the team sees its role not only as "designer" but also as "implementer" and "politics manager." The team can then adjust to the situation's requirements, having developed the selling skills to frame messages for a variety of audiences and to build alliances throughout the organization. The team has now matured and is committed to having the total organization achieve and succeed with the project ("high performing"). The focus moves outward, and the team begins to see itself as a catalyst to the learning process for the whole organization rather than as a savior. Where new team members once found it difficult to gain position, they now integrate easily into the team structure and are welcomed into the mature, high performing team. Finally, when the project is complete, the team must assure that their skills are embedded into the organization so continuous process improvements can be made. There must be recognition for member participation and achievement as the team formally disbands.

We strongly recommend additional reading and training on teamwork for every business reengineering team. We also recommend that the project facilitator play a key role in team development. Not every team is located in a single facility, which can make team building and communication even more difficult. Because the core group forms the hub of the project, it should be located together. The project champions are disbursed in their organization units. Like spokes on the hub of a wheel, champions bring stability to the rest of the organization. It is through the champions that the project will succeed or fail. Facilitation of the core group and project champion relationship and decision making can dramatically assist in creating a strong, healthy, committed project team.

CHAPTER 5

PREPARE FOR THE JOURNEY

The more the traveler knows about how to reach his destination, the more likely he is to arrive safely and on time. He won't get lost and, in fact, will probably enjoy the trip. By plotting his route on a map, using landmarks to measure progress, and knowing when to rest and reenergize, the street-smart traveler can navigate easily and successfully. Similarly, business reengineers use a methodology to guide their way. A well-structured methodology enables the business reengineering team to plan and track its activities, measure project achievements, define deliverables and outcomes, and accurately estimate project costs throughout the life of the project.

This chapter describes the methodology that is the basis for all successful reengineering projects—it serves as the street-smart business reengineer's road map. Like any map, it shows many routes to the same destination. The steps within the methodology represent essential landmarks encountered on the journey. How long each step takes, its difficulty, and even its importance to the final destination will vary. But without a methodology, you may never get there. A disciplined and structured methodology actually allows more room for flexibility and midcourse modifications to keep the project on course.

If you have a negative reaction to the words *disciplined and structured methodology* you need to check your biases. There are key decision points in every business reengineering effort. The methodology described in this chapter can make a significant difference in your life! What you are about to read defines those critical decision points, how to collect and organize the information required for that decision making, and the strategies and tactics required to make the most appropriate decisions.

There are eight decision points in any business reengineering project. They are:

1. Do we need to reengineer this business operation? Is there a simpler solution? If we do need to reengineer, what are the boundaries, scope, and interface points for the reengineering? How should we structure the project? Who should be on the team?

2. What is the end vision of the results of our reengineering? What are our priorities and goals? What values and principles are reflected in this vision?

3. What is the detailed design for our reengineered business operation? How do the processes function? What does the organization look like? What systems do we need? What infrastructure is needed to support it? What belief systems and culture must be in place?

4. Will our new design for the business operation work? Do we need to make changes in the design?

5. What is the plan for getting that design implemented? What is required to make it happen? How long will it take? What are the risks? What will it cost?

6. Should we fund the implementation of the business reengineering design?

7. Is the implementation going as planned? What corrections and changes should we make to ensure complete transition to the vision environment?

8. Is the reengineered business operation ready to take on responsibility for continuous improvement to the processes? If yes, let's give people the skills and knowledge to do it right. If not, let's keep working with them until they are ready.

These decisions are the framework for our methodology. The methodolo-

Step	Name	Outcome	Elapsed Time
1	Frame the Project	Framework Statement	2 weeks - 6 months
2	Create Vision, Values & Goals	Vision, Values & Goals Statement	1 day - 2 weeks
3	Redesign Business Operations	Blueprint	1 month - 2 months
4	Conduct Proof of Concept	Benefits Statement	2 weeks - 6 months
5	Plan the Implementation	Implementation Plan	2 weeks - 4 weeks
6	Get Implementation Approval	Funded Resource Request	1 week - 2 weeks
7	Implement the Redesign	Measurement Results	6 months - 3 years
8	Transition to a Continuous Improvement Environment	Higher Performance Standards	Ongoing

Figure 5.1 A Business Reengineering Project Methodology

gy's purpose is to get you answers to these questions as efficiently and effectively as possible. Figure 5.1 summarizes the information requirements and estimated times for each step in the methodology.

In step 1, a conscious, rational decision is made to start or stop the project. During steps 2 through 5, the reengineering design and the plan for implementation are created. In step 6, the resources for and commitment to implementation are obtained. (There are a lot of surprises here!) During steps 7 and 8 the environment is reengineered. Each step has a specific purpose, one or more decisions to be made, supporting outcomes against which to measure project achievement, and a set of activities for performing the work.

We developed the methodology using a TQM approach—that is, the first two steps ensure that the desired outcome is achieved the first time. The approach forces people to think before they act and to examine the biases and assumptions that shape their behavior. We recommend facilitated focus group and workshop techniques to execute many of the steps. Involving those directly affected by the reengineering outcomes is a critical success factor. Facilitation techniques help to ensure acceptance of the solution throughout the organization. In addition, these techniques can dramatically shorten the time required to reengineer an operation. Other techniques have been tried with unsatisfactory results, from simple rejection to flagrant sabotage. In one organization, a team of four "experts" from the research and development laboratory created a new way to deliver customer support services using the latest technology. It took them four months. They were very proud of it. However, the last time we checked, they were still trying to convince the four line organizations that replacing some of their people with technology was going to solve their problems. Because they didn't involve the line decision makers, managers, and influential professionals, a potentially great idea met with months and months of unnecessary resistance.

In our never-ending attempt to "keep it simple," we describe each step of the business reengineering methodology in the following terms:

- *Statement of purpose* to explain why the step is important
- *Outcome definition* to clarify the specific decision support outputs of the step activities and tasks
- *Key activities* to accomplish what needs to be done
- *Tips and techniques* to acquaint the reader with some do's and don'ts for success

---

Purpose: Decision to proceed/not proceed with project. Define and structure the project.

Outcome: Project Framework Statement

Key Activities:

1. Assemble analysis team.
2. Draft project frame.
3. Conduct a current situation analysis.
4. Produce the Framework Statement.
5. Recommend project go/no-go decision.
6. Contract with executive sponsors.

Figure 5.2 Step 1: Frame the Project

Step 1: Frame the Project

Statement of Purpose

Every business reengineering project needs to have established and validated objectives, measurability, and an established scope. Like building a home, the foundation for the project must be constructed. Without a solid foundation, costs will soar out of control or the project may collapse halfway through. To frame a business reengineering project (Figure 5.2), you must identify the following:

- Functional scope, organizational boundaries, and interface points
- Potential benefits
- Political, environmental, and cultural issues surrounding the project
- Root causes of the current situation
- Risks of action and nonaction on the project
- Factors critical to the project success
- Assumptions, limitations, and constraints to guide methodology application decisions

In addition, before moving forward with the project, assess and agree to:

- Organizational readiness
- Commitment to the project
- Establishment of the reengineering project team to conduct the situation analysis
- Project methodology and techniques to be applied in steps 2 through 6

The project should proceed to step 2 only if the following conditions are met:

1. The radical change of business reengineering is the right approach.
2. The project team can be expanded to include those directly affected by the project implementation.
3. Executive sponsorship for the project has been secured.
4. Resources have been committed for steps 2 through 5 of the methodology.

Without proper project framing, we can guarantee that at least one of the following situations will endanger the project's success:

- Ambiguous project scope, leading to ever expanding and unending work (In other words, scope creep absorbs all resources.)
- Lack of agreement on scope, creating territorial and organizational power conflicts
- Insufficient data to quantify the severity of current problems, preventing recognition of the need for reengineering
- Inadequate or no executive sponsorship resulting in a lack of funding

- The inability to relate the reengineering project to business strategies, leaving the reengineering project a low priority
- Undefined measures by which to assess achievements and benefits
- Failure to involve stakeholders, creating unnecessary resistance to change

Step 1 Outcome: Framework Statement

The Framework Statement provides the concrete evidence (or lack of it) of the need for the reengineering project and the data required to create a vision of the reengineered business operation. The Framework Statement concisely and clearly delineates:

- Business history and context for the reengineering
- Problems and their causes within the environment
- Business goals/objectives driving the reengineering
- Scope, boundaries, and interface points
- Enhancers and inhibitors to project success
- Limitations, constraints, and assumptions surrounding the project
- Recommendations for involvement and project team membership

The Framework Statement should be distributed widely to raise organizational awareness. You want to stimulate a great deal of discomfort, remember? It should present a compelling story that elicits and reinforces commitment and decision making by the executive sponsor. If business reengineering is the right answer, the Framework Statement provides a benchmark against which the ultimate success of the reengineering project will be measured.

Step 1 Key Activities

Work in step 1 may take from two weeks to six months, depending upon what is currently known about the organizational culture, the project scope and boundaries, how anxious people are to commit to change requirements, and the project team's skill in getting the work done. This work requires serious attention. Here are the basic activities:

1. *Assemble an analysis team.* These people typically become a part of the core group of the project team. Core group membership criteria are described in detail in chapter 4.
2. *Draft a project frame.* The analysis team begins by taking a first cut at the scope, boundaries, and interface points for the

reengineering effort. Scope and boundary affect all aspects of the project. The greater the effect on the organization as a whole, the more important it becomes to articulate clearly the costs, risks, and benefits of the project. Without this clarity, efforts to gain commitment are often futile.

3. *Conduct a current situation analysis.* Using the diagnostic and analysis tools described in appendix A and earlier chapters, the analysis team gathers data and analyzes the current situation. This means conducting focus group and individual interviews, observing work flows, and determining root causes of problems related to production volumes, timing cycles, errors, and the systems supporting the processes under investigation. The group must analyze the data within the context of customer relations, market conditions, and the organization's culture. The results should prove or disprove the need for radical change to the business operation. As stated earlier, controlling costs should not be the only reason for business reengineering. Depending upon the availability of data and the potential scope and boundaries of the reengineering effort under consideration, this work may take from a week to three months.

4. *Produce the Framework Statement.* The analysis of the current situation is documented in a Framework Statement.

5. *Recommend a project go/no-go decision.* Do not recommend going forward with a reengineering project if the problems uncovered in the analysis can be fixed through the "tweaking" of process improvement. If the operation is totally broken, then reengineer. If the decision is to reengineer, then you must recommend a project structure. The project structure includes a project process, team membership, schedules, and funding requirements for steps 2 through 5. If the situation analysis supports the necessity of a reengineering project, then the analysis team must recommend how to proceed. Specify desired outcomes and describe the techniques necessary to achieve them. Identify executive sponsor(s), a project director, core group, and champion team members by name and organization unit (see chapter 4 for details). Develop schedules and allocate funding. In effect, you are developing the game plan.

6. *Contract with executive sponsors.* Through the hard knocks of experience, we have learned that many executives suffer from selective hearing. That is, they hear only what they want to hear, which may be a great deal less than you want them to hear when you make your recommendations for the project. Therefore, be clear with your executives that you want a contract to create the reengineering design and develop an Implementation Plan. Make it clear that you are not asking for implementation funding—otherwise you may create unrealistic expectations and unnecessary pressures. Your team may find itself in trouble like this team did—because of unclear communications, the president of a large company sent a letter to all employees announcing that the business reengineering project that began in June would be completed by December. He thought he had funded the total project, not just the design and planning pieces.

Step 1 Tips and Techniques

If at all possible, a project facilitator trained in business reengineering techniques should help the analysis team conduct the meetings and interviews. Develop standardized worksheets (forms) to record observations and collect data to ensure completeness, consistency, and accuracy. To create the worksheets, the analysis team should identify the specific data to be collected and then define terms—for example, does a "day" equal eight hours? Everyone needs to be counting apples. Once the data is collected, you may use a variety of analysis techniques, including pareto diagrams, matrix diagrams, process flowcharts, and other graphical display options (see chapter 3). In projects that are potentially very large, and thus very costly to implement, the analysis team may decide to automate the data collection. If accurate data is not available (which is often the case), sampling and simulation of the current environment may be necessary. A lack of measurements—measurements being the consistent and timely collection of data and feedback to the business operation—can be both a symptom and a root cause of the organizational chaos leading to the need for reengineering.

Publishing the Framework Statement should create a tremendous amount of discomfort among the organization's managers. If this is the case in your organization, congratulate yourself. Discomfort, denial, and rebuttable of the data is a sign of success and should be treated as such. As discussed earlier, many people put off changing until the status quo feels worse than facing an uncertain future.

Purpose: Create a picture of what the operation wants to become.
Outcome: Vision, Values, and Goals Statement

Key Activities:
1. Prepare for project kickoff meeting and vision session.
2. Conduct the project kickoff meeting.
3. Conduct the vision session.
4. Create the Vision, Values & Goals Statement.
5. Validate the Vision, Values & Goals Statement.

Figure 5.3 Step 2: Create the Vision, Values, and Goals

Step 2: Create the Vision, Values, and Goals

Statement of Purpose

With the project established, it is now time to create a common perspective and future vision for the reengineered business operation (Figure 5.3). In the best of all possible worlds, the executives who asked the team to look into the situation in the first place should be able to communicate the overall vision and strategy for the business. It certainly makes creating the more specific vision of the environment after the reengineering easier. The project executive sponsors and the project team must agree to this environment vision and its supporting values and goals before beginning the business operation redesign. This vision serves as the inspiration for the redesigned business operation. Without a vision, there is nothing solid for which to aim or by which to measure. And, sadly, executive business vision and strategy can be either nonexistent or not communicated. This makes the project team's job in step 2 even more difficult. Team members must create the overall business vision as well as a specific vision of the reengineered environment. Getting the executives to participate directly in the visioning sessions can help overcome this problem.

Step 2 Outcome: Vision, Values, and Goals Statement

The Vision, Values, and Goals Statement is a succinct document that helps people envision how the business will operate when the reengineering is complete. Although idealism is certainly a factor in a successful reengineering project, the vision and values should appear reasonable and attainable. The goals are the performance outcomes and the excellence criteria by which the business operation can be measured. Without vision, the project will lose direction and fail.

Step 2 Key Activities

Developing the Vision, Values, and Goals Statement may take from several days to several weeks, depending upon the project's scope and boundaries and executive strategic guidance. These are some typical activities:

1. *Prepare for the project kickoff meeting and vision session.* Preparation for all reengineering sessions and workshops is critical, particularly in the initial stages of the project. These early stages create the project culture. The right message must be sent and received. These sessions should be more than just meetings—they are symbolic expressions of the "new world." It is important to invest significant time *before* beginning the project kickoff meeting and vision sessions. Address and document issues relating to the project's content, structure, and logistics in the form of detailed agenda and facilitation scripts.

2. *Conduct the project kickoff meeting.* To promote and formally announce the project, the reengineering project team and executive sponsors lead an awareness-building meeting for all interested parties who want to participate. The purpose of the meeting is to:

   • Promote the project within the context of the total organization

   • Demonstrate executive sponsor commitment to the project team and its success

   • Empower and energize the project team

   • Educate interested people about the project scope, objectives, and process

100

- Answer questions, overcome objections, and create an environment for decision making

This one- to two-hour meeting can be held up to a week or immediately before the vision session.

3. *Conduct the vision session.* The reengineering project team comes together to develop and agree on the vision, values, and goals for the project under the direction of the project facilitator. An example of an agenda and script for a vision session conducted in a facilitated workshop format is provided in the appendices. If the corporate strategic direction for the business operation's products, services, and role within the total context of the business are not clear to the team, it is important that the executive sponsors participate in these sessions. Otherwise the reengineering vision, values and goals may be completely "off the radar screen" in the executives' perspective. For example, if your company had decided that it was critical to reengineer the product development process, it would be important to know what importance executives give to that process. Is it to be the driving force for the business because corporate survival depends upon new product development? Is integration of different ways of working critical in their eyes or should diversity be supported at all costs? Is the priority processing efficiency? How should that be valued in relationship to enhancing the customer relationship? If the two values are in conflict, which should take priority?

4. *Create the Vision, Values, and Goals Statement.* The results of the vision session are synthesized and transformed into a succinct, eloquent, and intelligently written document. The importance of this document cannot be overstated. It not only sets the stage for the future; it becomes the primary means of communicating the purpose of the reengineering project throughout the organization. The document validates and celebrates the contributions of everyone involved. Everyone needs to be given credit!

5. *Validate the Vision, Values, and Goals Statement.* The reengineering project team revises or refines the statement before its publication. This process is often performed in a facilitated

meeting after the vision statement has been circulated throughout the organization. This gives those who have not been directly involved in the visioning sessions an opportunity to participate.

Step 2 Tips and Techniques

The most common technique for creating vision, values, and goals is the facilitated workshop or meeting. Chapter 6 explains how to prepare for, conduct, and document facilitated workshops and meetings. The project facilitator and, to a lesser extent, the project team core group are responsible for the workshop and meeting activities.

As the vision, values, and goals are being developed in the vision session, many questions and issues will arise. Recognizing questions and issues and assigning specific individuals to resolve them will overcome skepticism. The team members need to be reassured that their concerns are valid and will be addressed.

This first session to develop a vision is also a test of commitment to the reengineering project. If invited team members do not attend or the session participants cannot agree on the vision, values, and goals, there probably are serious cultural, power, and attitude problems within the organization. These problems must be addressed before the project can proceed. Corrective actions may include:

- Changing executive sponsors or reengineering project team members
- Proposing alternative schedules for sessions

Purpose: Design a new way of doing business that is in alignment with the vision, values, and goals.

Outcome: Reengineering Blueprint Consisting of Physical/Technical, Infrastructure, and Value Components

Key Activities:
1. Prepare for the Blueprint sessions.
2. Conduct the Blueprint sessions.
3. Document the Blueprint.
4. Validate the Blueprint.

Figure 5.4 Step 3: Redesign the Business Operation

102

- Encouraging executive sponsors to elicit more commitment from key managers
- Providing rewards for participation
- Holding a special meeting to address the organization's lack of readiness to proceed
- Meeting privately with resistors to discuss their needs, issues, and concerns
- Asking the executive sponsors to resolve any "killer" issues that arose during this first session

Step 3: Redesign the Business Operation

Statement of Purpose

This is the heart of reengineering, where current processes are "blown up" and redesigned to conform to the new vision (Figure 5.4). It goes beyond correcting current processes, instead forcing a complete rethinking of the organization's operations in light of its strategic business goals. Remember that reengineering does not change what *is*—it creates what is *not*. It is thinking the unthinkable. The business redesign is the blueprint for change. Use the seven principles for process redesign (see chapter 2, "Lighting the Way") as a guideline for evaluating the redesign quality.

Step 3 Outcome: Reengineering Blueprint

The Blueprint documents the three major components of the reengineered business: Physical/Technical, Infrastructure, and Value components (Figure 5.5). These components ensure that, if implemented, the reengineering will be successful. Without all three components, the implementation of the redesigned processes will fail. The Blueprint provides the foundation for a realistic and feasible implementation, enabling the team to estimate implementation costs and forecast implementation benefits (Figure 5.6).

Your first reaction to what follows may be, *"Is all this detail really necessary? Can't we put together a high-level overview of what we're thinking?"* Our question to you is, "How do you cost out a high-level overview? How can you tell people how things are going to change with only a high-level overview?" A contractor cannot build you a house with only a high-level overview or a general description such as, "I want a ranch house with

Physical/Technical Component
    Process Model
    Information Model
    Organization Model
    Technology Model
Infrastructure Component
    Management Strategy
    Measurement System
    Reward Programs
Value Component
    Culture Precedent
    Power Utilization
    Belief Systems

Figure 5.5 Business Operations Redesign Blueprint Deliverable Outline

a big yard." He needs to know all sorts of details so that he can execute your vision of a ranch house to your expectations. The same applies to business reengineering. You need to create a complete picture of how things will work in the reengineered environment. Then, and only then, can your team estimate with some accuracy what it will cost to implement, develop a sound strategy for implementation, and test the new design if needed.

Physical/Technical Component

The Physical/Technical component answers these questions for people:
- What work will be required to produce our products and services? What business policies, practices, and controls are needed to ensure effective performance?
- What information do we need to operate effectively at all levels in that environment?
- Who will do what work and how must the organization be structured to support peak performance of the operation?
- What computer systems, communications networks, and other technologies must be used to enable the work to be done effectively?

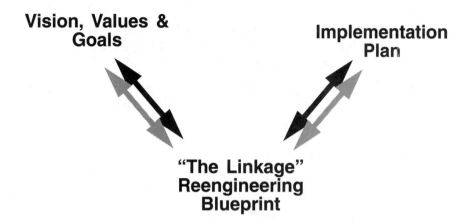

Vision, Values & Goals

Implementation Plan

"The Linkage" Reengineering Blueprint

Figure 5.6 Linking Vision to Implementation

To answer these questions, the Physical/Technical component of the Blueprint is structured into four distinct models, which together describe the reengineered operational environment. The models represent processes, information, organization, and technology. Each is described below.

Process Model. The core of the Blueprint is the Process Model. The Process Model depicts work processes in the reengineered environment, independent of who will perform the work. The number of processes included in the model can vary dramatically depending upon the level of detail in the design and the scope of the reengineering effort. A Process Model normally consists of:

- Key business outcomes (e.g., products, services) and criteria for judging their quality
- Business processes required to produce and support the business outcomes
- Description of how those processes relate to each other, including work flows, information flows, and timing dependencies

So what is a process? Technically, to be considered a valid process, it must create or transform physical items or data. In other words, a process must add value to an outcome.

What do we need to define about each process? Our recommendation

105

is that the process definitions in the completed model should contain the following information:

- Unique process name and reference number (Hint: The name starts with a verb and has a noun; for example, Create Inventory, Plan Sales Calls, and Establish Training Needs.)
- Business outcome or part of a business outcome (processes should be grouped to organize the work around business outcomes) produced by the process
- Standards (excellence criteria) by which the quality of the outcome will be measured
- Triggering event(s) for process execution
- Inputs (physical and informational) required to execute the process
- Business practices and controls to be followed in executing the process, including authority and empowerment to make decisions
- Steps required to perform the process from beginning to end
- Skills and knowledge required to perform the process
- Performance frequencies and volumes for both normal and peak production periods

The process business practices and steps will be documented as methods and procedures for those who perform the work once the processes are implemented. Expansion and refinement will be required for this to happen. Application of business practices will be the subject of much education and skills training and automation.

Information Model. The Information Model describes all data required to perform and make decisions within the reengineered business. For business people, this model provides the new language and common terminology for the reengineered workplace. For technology (IS) people, this model (along with the process model) provides the basis for evaluating software packages and designing or enhancing systems to support the business. The Information Model normally contains:

- Definition of the information groups (e.g., customers, orders, and products) that perform the business processes and make business decisions
- Dependencies among information groups (e.g., an order can't exist without a customer; a customer may have more than one order at any time)
- Characteristics of each information group (e.g., how many can the

business have; how much history do we need; how many times and at what volume do we add the information group, change data about it, access it or remove it from our business)

- Definition of the data we need for each information group (e.g., for a customer we need to know the name, mailing address, billing address)
- Characteristics of each data item (e.g., how it is created, permitted values, default value, the kind of data it is, other names it is called by, whether it is required for a record of the information group to exist)

At times the Blueprint work should begin with the Information Model, particularly when dealing with processes and/or departments that use different languages. For example, in one company we found that the word *customer* had at least 10 different meanings depending upon which division and department you were talking to. In another, everyone used the words *part number* to identify a manufactured object, but each division had its own part-numbering system. These kinds of problems have to be resolved (or at least clearly identified and understood) if a team of people from those divisions and departments are going to succeed in redesigning processes in which they are all involved.

The Information Model should be mapped into the Process Model to define how data is created or transformed by the redesigned processes and whether data is used to make decisions and/or to produce products. Both models should be mapped against the existing automated systems and databases to assess requirements for new or integrated systems to support the redesigned processes.

Organization Model. To the uninitiated, business reengineering often, mistakenly, means restructuring the organization. So, it is important to help people understand that organization structure, embodied in the ever changing organization chart, is only one of nine dimensions of business reengineering. And that structure is only one piece of a complete organization model.

The Organization Model defines the new or existing organization structure, job positions, and job configurations (such as team structures) required to perform and support the redesigned processes. To develop an effective Organization Model, we recommend these guidelines for both individual job positions and teams:

- Jobs should involve meaningful work that provides people with a sense of accomplishment and a sense of their contribution to the organization's mission. As stated earlier, jobs should be organized around a process or group of processes that produce definitive outcomes.
- Jobs should incorporate accountability and accurate performance measurements. Organizing work around subprocess tasks clouds accountability.
- Jobs should incorporate feedback systems that provide direct results so that people can improve their operations and the quality of outcomes immediately and effectively.
- Jobs should facilitate direct and easy communication with internal and/or external customers. Hierarchical barriers to communication must be eliminated.
- Jobs should provide access to resources. The organizational structure must not inhibit information flows and resource sharing. Individuals and teams must have the resources they need (such as budget and purchasing authority, equipment and information access) to perform work without delays or hindrances.
- Jobs should provide opportunities for learning so that people are being continually challenged and expanding their skills and knowledge. This protects the organization from depending on a single individual and builds redundancy of skills and knowledge without redundancy of people.

There are many options for organizational structures. Creating and discarding job titles and positions are often necessary to structure the reengineered business operation effectively. Organizations can have many or few hierarchical levels. Work can be organized around cross-functional teams or by function. Some organizations centralize both physical location and reporting relationships. Others disperse jobs to different physical locations and establish reporting relationships that are centralized, dispersed, or matrixed. Some organizations outsource (contract with firms outside their corporate organization) work; others do not. There are benefits and risks to each organizational structure.

Theoretically, current employee skills/knowledge and personalities should not be considered in creating the Organization Model—matching individuals to specific positions is an implementation issue. However, personalities often get in the way. Recently, in one government organization, it was clear that the chief-of-staff position should be accountable for operational management of the department unit. But, because the department head wanted a long-time associate who was very loyal to him in that position, a special position to handle "operations" was created to manage the department's operation, leaving the chief of staff to focus on policy issues.

Document the Organization Model with this information:

- An organization chart (this may not look like the pyramids of the past)
- Narrative descriptions to support the organizational chart that identifies locations and reporting relationships for all job positions and teams
- List of advantages and benefits of the structure
- List of risks inherent in the structure that need to be managed
- Number of teams and number of job positions on each team
- Number of each job position
- Team and individual job position descriptions that document:
  —All business processes (from the business model) for which performance responsibility and accountability is assigned
  —Skills/knowledge required to perform all assigned business processes
  —Reporting structure required to support the job positions and teams, given the extent of authority assigned directly to working-level job positions

Technology Model. As we said earlier in the book, much of what distinguishes today's business reengineering from earlier attempts to improve an organization's effectiveness is the potential of today's technologies for distributing and managing work, providing expertise, supporting decision making, communicating with people directly at any time, and accessing common information by employees, customers, and suppliers. Whole books focus on this aspect of business reengineering. For example, in their book, *Paradigm Shift*, Don Tapscott and Art Caston detail the potential applications of existing and emerging technologies. But do not be fooled into putting all your design emphasis on technology. It is only through the simultaneous design of the business processes and the application of technology to those processes that you are going to get something that can really work effectively. Technology alone spells failure. For example, one company gave its sales people state-of-the-art notebook computers housing a variety of software applications for customer information storage, work planning, cost estimating, and order taking. After they were distributed and the sales people were trained in their operation, everyone was very pleased to receive the computers, but only 10 percent of the sales force actually used them in their work on a regular basis after the first six months. Why? Only a few sales people took the time to figure out how to use the computer in their jobs. Additionally, there was no incentive to use it. The project team that selected the hardware and software did not define how to integrate the automation into the daily sales processes. Only after a special team of sales people, managers, and systems specialists was brought together did they discover how to make the technology really perform as intended. Only after dramatic changes were made to existing sales processes and to the software systems and all the sales people were retrained did utilization increase to 85 percent after another six months. Don't let yourself get caught in this kind of backward business reengineering.

Technology can provide access to accurate and timely data to support decision making; provide direct feedback for self-correction and process improvement; allow people to conduct work simultaneously rather than sequentially; allow people who enter data to process it; enable decisions to be made as close to the customer as possible; and enable physically disbursed people to work together.

The Technology Model documents the databases, applications, communications, and networking required to support the redesigned business processes. This requires an analysis of technological capabilities and availability, the business process and information models, and the existing systems and databases. In addition, the Technology Model should include requirements for:

- Security for information protection and confidentiality
- Quality assurance and control for auditing, disaster recovery, backup, and error correction
- Speed, volume, and user interface performance requirements
- System administration
- Hardware and software platform standards
- Communication network protocols and standards

It is easy to see from this description of the Technology Model that there must be strong technology-specialists on the reengineering project team. Their role is to show the business team members how technology can make a significant difference in the operation. The techology-specialist team members can be catalysts to truly innovative thinking if they take the time to communicate clearly.

Infrastructure Component

The Infrastructure component answers these questions:

- What kind of supervision and managerial support does the redesigned business operation require? What roles should these people fulfill? What strategies and techniques should they use to motivate and support people within the operation?
- What data is needed to measure operational performance accurately and effectively? Where does that data come from, how often, and in what form?
- How can we incite people to perform to higher standards and in new ways?

The Infrastructure component of the reengineering Blueprint defines how to reinforce the behavior and actions required to operate the Physical/Technical component effectively. This component consists of the management strategy, measurement systems, and reward programs.

Management Strategy. The managerial style and performance management process required to support the organization model makes or breaks the implementation of the Physical/Technical component. An analysis of the Organization Model and Process Model relationships provides critical input for defining a Management Strategy. For example, the more empowered people and teams are at the working level, the less directive the management style of supervisors should be. As discussed extensively in chapter 7, "The Road Is Not Smooth, Look for Danger," supervisors and managers may be displaced completely from their traditional roles of information screener, work controller, and decision maker. New managerial positions may be created or existing ones permanently eliminated. A militaristic, hierarchical management style may need to give way to a participative, coaching, facilitative management style. In the reengineered environment, manager accountability may focus on planning, research, and employee development rather than on direct supervision of work tasks. The Management Strategy must define the following:

- Supervisor and managerial job descriptions that identify role
  definitions, accountabilities, authorities, and criteria by which job
  performance will be measured and rewarded
- Skills and knowledge required to execute each managerial job
- Business practices for setting all worker and supervisory
  performance objectives
- Business practices for evaluating and rewarding worker
  performance
- Business practices for creating and executing employee
  development plans

Measurement System. The Measurement System defines the data, process, and supporting business practices for collecting, evaluating, and displaying performance results for each accountable job position and/or team. The scope of the system should selectively target the data that will provide feedback on goal achievement and process performance. In the reengineered environment, people will be held accountable for meeting quality standards for all outcomes. To achieve continuing improvement, it is crucial to have accurate and timely information about the outcomes and the processes used to produce and support the outcomes. People can act only on what they know. Requirements for the Measurement System include the detailing of:

- Who is accountable for data collection
- What data must be collected (as defined in the project goals and
  process performance targets)
- When, to what level of accuracy and detail, and how often data
  will be collected
- How data will be displayed for appropriate analysis and decision
  making (such as 13-month rolling trend, percentage from
  standard)
- Who is accountable for analyzing and taking action on the
  measurement data
- How the data will be used (for example, for continuing process
  improvement, reward allocation, or both)

Reward Programs. As discussed earlier, Reward Programs should motivate people to produce, achieve, and excel. Ideally, the work itself provides intrinsic motivation to excel. At a minimum, however, reward programs should not discourage appropriate behavior in people. For example, if people should work as a team rather than as individuals, then team performance, not individual performance, should be rewarded. If people need to reduce costs and errors, then rewards for doing so should be given. The Reward Program should include both financial and nonfinancial elements. These may include (for each job or team):

- A description of the required performance, as defined by the reengineering goals and process performance objectives
- Measurement of the performance as defined by the Measurement System
- Type and amount of reward for each level of performance achievement
- Business practices (timing requirements, controls, documentation) for evaluating performance and conferring rewards

Value Component

The Value component defines the culture, power, and individual belief systems that must be aligned with the reengineering vision and values. In essence, the Value component describes the underlying philosophy and characteristics of the business culture that must be in place in order for people to embrace, nurture, and reinforce the reengineered business operation. For example, if a value of the reengineered organization is involving subordinates in decision making, the failure of managers to do so sabotages new ways of working. Such misalignments send clear messages to employees that the reengineering is not for real, that business can go on as usual.

With proper planning, the culture can and will change. It is important to define what is "out" and what is "in" in terms of behavior, the use of power, and individual belief systems in the reengineered business operation. During implementation, it is the responsibility of the organization's leaders to propagate this new culture through what they say and do. Everyone will look to them. If they are acting out the new values and beliefs, then others will adopt those behaviors. For example, in one company, a value incorporated in the reengineering vision was that the customer relationship was the most important aspect of the new culture. However, throughout the early stages of the project and into the anguish of obtaining funding and the first year of implementation activities, the organization's vice presidents displayed only frustration and anger when told they should invest in systems to meet needs. One vice president was heard to say, "It's our job to tell the customer what he will get from us and how we will do it. It's the salesperson's job to make customers understand and accept what we are doing." Implementation of the vision value at the working level is very difficult in such an environment. The lesson learned? If the project team does not hear the right words from their executives, they certainly aren't going to see new behavior in the organization.

Organizational Culture. Organization Culture defines the rituals, symbols, and behaviors that are observable in the reengineered environment. Organizational Culture defines matters such as whether people arrive on time to meetings and whether they work in team workrooms or individual cubicles. During implementation, the elimination or changing of symbols sometimes sends a stronger message to people than adding new behavioral requirements. For example, eliminating reserved parking spaces, private executive dining rooms, and central executive offices makes a more direct, visual statement to workers about hierarchy than actually reducing the number of executive levels. Talking to people without notes or overheads when historically everyone came in loaded with overheads sends a signal that dialogue is more important than "buttoned-up" solutions.

Power Utilization. Power is the ability to get things done. One kind of power is based on a person's job within the organizational hierarchy. This job power includes the ability to give or take away rewards in the form of praise, money, or promotions. From the negative perspective, job power includes coercive power—the ability to influence through actions, threats, pay cuts, termination, and layoffs—and includes the ability to decide matters such as work assignments, territories, performance standards, policies, and procedures. As long as there are job positions and formal accountabilities, an organization must assign job power. However, there is another type of power that has nothing to do with position power: personal power. People have personal power because of who they are rather than because of the job they perform. People at all levels of the organization have the potential for personal power. You can have four types of personal power:

- Referent power, when people like or respect you
- Expert power, because of your knowledge and skills
- Information power, because you have relevant and accurate information

114

• Connection power, because you can influence important people
(the position power holders) inside or outside of the organization

Power Utilization defines how people should use their job and personal power to accomplish work and motivate people. In most reengineered environments, coercive power should give way to increased reward power. Expert, connection, and information power become more important than job power in organizations where managers are coaches and obstacles removers rather than supervisors.

Belief Systems. Thinking structure—our capacities to value people, function, and system; the ability to clearly and accurately assimilate information to make decisions; and attentiveness to our total environment—forms the basis and drive for much of our behavior. Our thinking structure can enhance or inhibit performance. It becomes apparent when we talk about how things "really are" at work, what management and the "company" think about people, and whether we believe we can make a significant difference. In the successfully reengineered business operation, individual belief systems become aligned with the stated beliefs of the organization. For example, the capacity to value people as unique individuals regardless of their function or performance is a belief that the organization can reflect through fair and equitable support and assistance during a downsizing mandated by the reengineering.

Step 3 Key Activities

Redesign of the business operation and the creation of the Blueprint should take no more than four to eight weeks. The key is to work fast and effectively so the project does not get bogged down. You develop the Blueprint through these activities:

1. *Prepare for the Blueprint session(s).* To prepare for the Blueprint session, do the following:
   • Design session structure and process
   • Identify content, learning, and team-building requirements
   • Prepare the session script
   • Prepare documentation worksheets and forms
   • Select and reserve meeting room(s)
2. *Conduct the Blueprint session(s).* Under the project facilitator's guidance, the reengineering project team develops and reaches consensus on the business operation redesign.

3. *Document the Blueprint.* Production of the Blueprint requires synthesizing the session results and writing a succinct and understandable document.

4. *Validate the Blueprint.* Those who developed the original Blueprint should have the opportunity to refine or correct it before publication.

Step 3 Tips and Techniques

The Blueprint for the redesigned business operation should be specific to the organization's culture and needs. Don't be afraid to adapt a standard approach for your organization that is different from what you read in a book. Remember, documenting an approach is just someone else's way of speaking—many reengineering practitioners follow their own approaches.

To develop a jointly owned Blueprint of the future, involve people directly affected by the reengineering along with futurists and other subject-matter experts. This smooths the way for implementation.

It is sometimes difficult for people to escape their current reality and belief systems, which bias their thinking and perpetuate their limited views of what is possible. Even experts suffer from this. It requires thoughtful planning and mind-expanding approaches to teach people to think in new ways. Here are some of the "letting go" problems we encounter in business reengineering projects:

- **Separating what needs to be done (process) from who does it (organization).** Years of thinking of process and organization as one has encouraged this form of fuzzy thinking. For example, many departments are named by their function (accounting, order processing, customer service, sales). People must be taught to make the distinction. Once they let go of who does the work today, it is easier to change, delete, or create a new process.

- **Identifying customers and understanding that they may be internal or external to the organization.** Large bureaucracies and other noncustomer-driven businesses often find it difficult to define their work in terms of products and services produced for customers. For example, a workers' compensation group may see itself as administrators who process paper rather than as providers of services and products to their customers within the

116

corporation. People tend to focus on the tasks they perform rather than on what they produce and who they service. Their performance traditionally is measured in the same way. When they let go of the task orientation, they can think in terms of customers and products and services.

- **Not considering different perspectives in the redesign.** This includes finance, management, audit, control, production, and legal. If representatives from these organizational areas are not included in the initial redesign activities, the project may come to a halt right there.

- **Expecting a technological solution to solve a business operation problem.** The right technology is essential. But business policies and practices, organizational infrastructure, and belief systems play a much larger role in causing and reinforcing poor operational performance. Competent business redesign must focus on both technological and business solutions—balance is critical. To teach people to let go of their technology bias, explore their biases and assumptions about potential solutions before and during the redesign work. This ensures a good balance of technology and business policies, practices, and people.

- **Worrying about implementation issues when people should be concentrating on the business redesign.** People can't let go of "how to do it." They may dismiss creative and innovative ideas because they cannot easily visualize how to implement them. People need to be reminded about the difference between *what* and *how*. The Blueprint defines *what* they want, not *how* to get there. The Implementation Plan defines *how*. Writing implementation questions and issues on an easel sheet as soon they are raised helps people return to the "what" redesign activities.

The Workshop Approach

The most common technique for creating a Blueprint is the facilitated workshop (see chapter 6 for details on how to prepare for, conduct, and document facilitated workshops). Most redesigns will require two or more workshops, each of which will take from two to four days and include from 10 to 30 participants representing the various constituencies and stakeholders. The reengineering project team may want help from subject matter experts and other advisors with various components of the Blueprint. These may include industry specialists, organizational design experts, training and methods experts, and systems experts.

This facilitated workshop series is not always easy to arrange due to scheduling conflicts and work assignments. However, if executive sponsors are willing to ensure participant availability, the rewards are extensive. The facilitated workshop allows people to build strong relationships, commitment, and understanding across and at multiple levels within the organization. The workshop approach generates momentum and provides the cornerstone for implementation commitment. To the contrary, using only a small group of four or six outside experts to develop the Blueprint requires that the business design be sold to an uninformed organization. Resistance to changes developed by outsiders who "know nothing about the real world" have derailed many reengineering efforts. Therefore, we strongly recommend the broader-based workshop approach.

How productive is the workshop environment? Several years ago we conducted several studies to measure workshop productivity. In one study, a one-day workshop in a comptroller's organization defined the vision and goals for the organization. At the end of that day, all decisions and information gathered were posted and written up. An outside expert in interviewing techniques was called in to assess what had been accomplished and compare it to his approach. He looked around the room in disbelief. "Did everyone agree to what is here?" he asked. "Yes," we responded. "Well," he said, "you did in one day what would take three weeks of work using my process."

Modeling and Diagramming Techniques for Business Process Redesign

What follows is a review of some of the current modeling approaches and diagramming techniques in use. If you are not directly involved in business process redesign work, you may wish to turn to step 4 of the methodology, "Conduct Proof of Concept."

The modeling approaches your team can use include, but certainly are not limited to, business-oriented Integrated Definition Method (IDEF), Business Event Analysis, and the more systems-oriented Information Engineering and Object-Oriented Analysis. Each has its own unique (though similar) terminology and graphical display diagram techniques. In all cases, what the business does (the processes) are separated from who does them (the organization units), how the processes are performed (the technology, controls, equipment, and facilities required), and the information used to perform the processes. The goal is to create a detailed graphical depiction of the redesigned business operation. All approaches enable you to look at the business piece by piece (who, what, how, and data) and as a whole. The approach may ask you to define the processes in a certain manner, examine the pieces in a certain sequence, derive one piece from another, or define the relationship between two or more pieces. Figure 5.7 summarizes some of these distinguishing differences among business process redesign approaches. No one approach is best for all situations, and, in fact, it is sometimes more effective to draw on individual aspects of each to meet your specific project needs.

The eight diagramming options described in the rest of this section can be associated with one or more of the approaches listed in Figure 5.7. The techniques for creating diagrams vary depending upon the approach rules, the application of the diagram, and the experience of the group creating the diagram. The act of creating the diagram is as important as the documented end result in that it raises many issues that must be addressed in a structured and disciplined fashion to complete the business operation redesign. Training in the various techniques is available through many sources. The diagram information is introduced in Figure 5.8. We also provide a generic example of each diagram. The diagrams included are matrix, decomposition, dependency, data flow, state transi-

Approach	Focus	Analysis Approach	Diagrams	Philosophy	Origin
IDEF	Process & Data	Linear	Yes	Process First, then Data	Business Analysis
Business Event Analysis	Triggering Events	Linear	Yes	Process Derived from Events	Business Analysis
Information Engineering	Process & Data	Linear	Yes	Data & Process Independence & Integration	Systems Analysis
Object-Oriented Analysis	Data	Object	Yes	Data First, then Process	Systems Development

Figure 5.7 Approaches to Business Process Redesign

119

	Process Model	Information Model	Organization Model	Technology Model
Matrix Diagram	✔	✔	✔	✔
Decomposition Diagram	✔		✔	
Dependency Diagram	✔			
Data Flow Diagram	✔	✔		
State Transition Diagram	✔	✔		
Entity Relationship Diagram		✔		
Entity Table		✔		
Decision Table	✔			

Figure 5.8 Diagram Option Chart

tion, entity relationship, entity table, and decision table. You can obtain detailed instructions for using these diagramming techniques through the numerous vendor-training and education programs offered publicly and privately. Many organizations have this diagramming expertise in-house today through their own IS organizations.

Matrix Diagram. The matrix diagram describes the relationship between two unlike sets of information. Matrix diagrams are often used to look at business processes or events in relation to data used in those processes, the job positions involved in the events, the organization units accountable for the processes, existing automation systems used to support the processes, and/or the problems that affect the processes. This diagram is very useful in summarizing relationships, checking project scope, setting project boundaries, clustering processes or events based upon the relationships, and analyzing the extent of business problems and opportunities for change. The examples provided display the relationship between business processes and the organization units (Figure 5.9) and the relationship between business events and the job positions (Figure 5.10).

Decomposition Diagram. The decomposition diagram identifies the components of an information set using increasing levels of detail. Its purpose is to build a hierarchy of information sets where any level of decomposi-

Processes	Employee	Supervisor	Training Center Staff	Instructors	Vendors	Executive Directors
1.0 Develop Training	S	S	P	S	P	S
2.0 Process Students	S	S	P			
3.0 Conduct Classes	U		SU	P		
4.0 Maintain Training History	U	U	P			U
S = Source of Information P = Perform Process (Accountable) U = Use Generated Information Outcomes						

Figure 5.9 Matrix Diagram—Business Processes and Organization Units

Business Event	Training Registrar	Training Director	Instructor	Facilities Manager
Student requests course catalog	1,3			
Student registers for course	1			
Student cancels course sign-up	1			
Supervisor approves attendance	2			
Student completes course	2			
Manager requests course development		2		
Instructor begins class			1	
	1 = take action 3 = refer information 2 = collect data 4 = don't know			

Figure 5.10 Matrix Diagram—Business Event and Job Positions

tion is defined by the next level of detail. Decomposition forces consistent detail at any level. The diagram is often constructed when it is important to force definition and ensure a common understanding of what is being analyzed before more complex diagrams are created. It ensures that people are comparing apples to apples. The information sets most often decomposed in reengineering projects include business processes, decisions or events, organization units, problems and opportunities, and implementation plans. Figure 5.11 decomposes a business operation into two levels of process detail.

Dependency Diagram. The dependency diagram defines the relationship of items from any selected level of decomposition and typically examines business process dependencies. These process relationships may be based

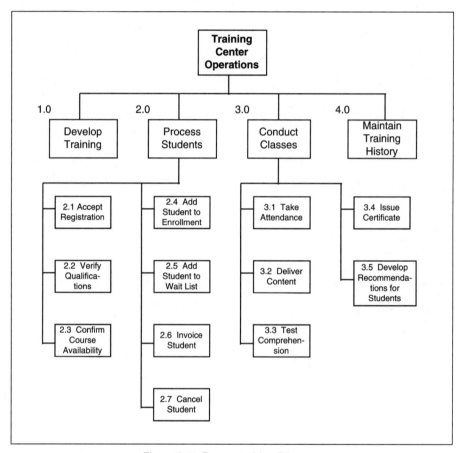

Figure 5.11 Decomposition Diagram

upon the information required as input from one process and/or output to another process, time, or work-sequencing dependencies. This diagram helps to establish normal and exception work flows, to confirm that all processes have been identified and properly defined, and to begin organizing processes into logical groupings for job position or team assignments. Some business processes or events may not depend on other processes or events and should not be analyzed using this diagram. Figure 5.12 displays a process flow based upon information dependencies.

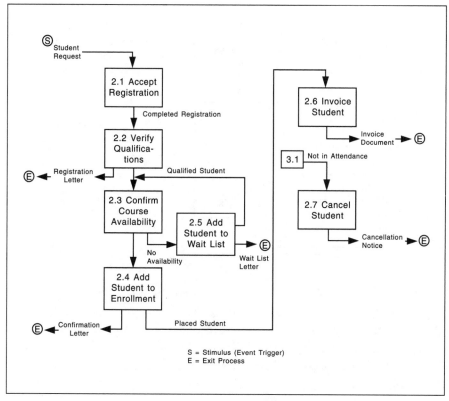

Figure 5.12 Dependency Diagram—2.0 Process Students

Data Flow Diagram (DFD). The data flow diagram expands the dependency diagram. In business reengineering projects, we use it to define information transformed (created, updated, or deleted) by business processes. In some approaches, such as IDEF, additional information such as controls, job positions, and mechanisms required to perform the process are added to the diagram. The DFD is normally constructed after the dependency diagram, the entity relationship diagram (ERD), and the entity tables are complete. The DFD also helps validate the completeness and accuracy of the ERD and entity tables. Data that appears in the ERD and entity tables but does not appear in the DFD is either unnecessary or used only for decision support. The DFD also validates the processes as true processes. If a process does not transform data, then it is not a true process and should be removed from the dependency flow. Figure 5.13 shows the data input into the processes on the left and the data transformed by the processes on the right.

123

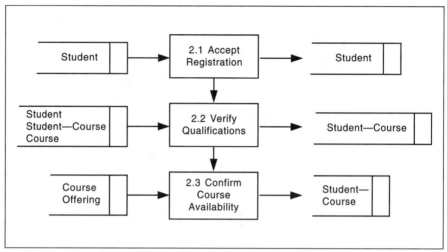

Figure 5.13 Data Flow Diagram (DFD)

State Transition Diagram. The state transition diagram identifies the processes required to transform a business object (for example, people, places, things, or events) from one status or state to another during its life cycle. In business reengineering, the objects that are analyzed through state transaction analysis are the essential business outcomes/products. In the training center, for example, the business outcomes/products could be students, training courses, instructors, catalogs, and certifications. This approach forces people to focus on value-adding processes rather than on traditional administrative processes. You can use the diagram to create new business processes as well as to validate business processes and data defined through other diagramming techniques. Figure 5.14 traces the life cycle of an object called a "student" in a training center operation.

Entity Relationship Diagram. The ERD identifies what the business needs to know about the objects that are essential to its operation. The information can be strategic, tactical, or operational. As discussed in the state transition diagram, these objects may be people (employee, student, manager), places (plant, building, facility), things (order, product, policy), events (holiday, conference), and intellectual concepts (calendar, contract, transaction, account). The characteristics that identify these objects are called attributes. For example, the attributes for a student employee might include name, student number, current job title, department code, building location, and current supervisor's name. The diagram defines

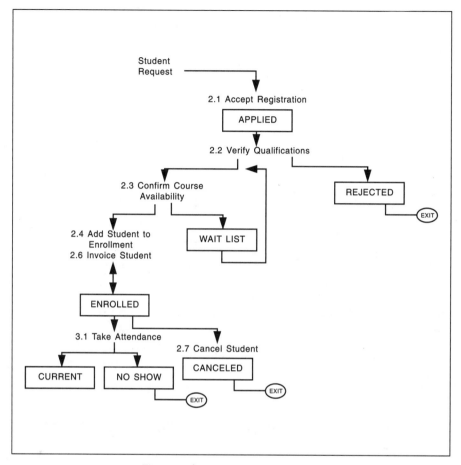

Figure 5.14 State Transition Diagram

the relationship of objects to each other in a nonredundant and clear manner. A completed ERD is guaranteed to define all the rules for data use in the business operation. The creation of the diagram forces people to define and document systematically the information they use in their business. A common language across business processes and organization units is developed and documented as a result of the ERD work. Figure 5.15 shows the relationship of objects used in a training center operation.

Entity Table. The entity table documents the attributes (the information we need to know about a business object) used in the business operation. The table is a simple way to display the attributes along with all the necessary examples of occurrences of the entity. Entity tables are created as a

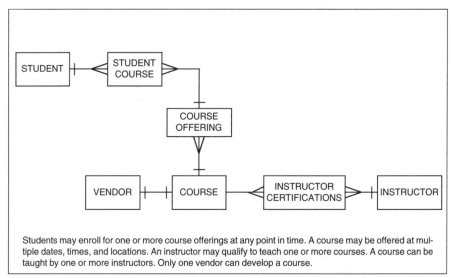

Students may enroll for one or more course offerings at any point in time. A course may be offered at multiple dates, times, and locations. An instructor may qualify to teach one or more courses. A course can be taught by one or more instructors. Only one vendor can develop a course.

Figure 5.15 Entity Relationship Diagram

result of the entity relationship diagramming work. Figure 5.16 displays information about a student.

Decision Table. The decision table identifies the rules for complex deci-

Entity: Student

Name	Loc. ID	Org. Unit	Current Title	Highest Degree	Career Goal
Jones, Tom C.	273-871	HRD	Manager	BA	Executive
Smith, Mary	044-982	ENGRG	Asst. Engr.	MS	Scientist
Ireland, Eric T.	101-880	MKTG	Planner	MBA	Economist
Mano, Chuck	044-960	HRD	Manager	BA	Executive

Figure 5.16 Entity Table

sion making in the business. This includes the conditions, their states, and responses to the different condition states and combinations of condition states. You can use the decision table to capture complex decision

CONDITIONS	1	2	3
Student meets preprequisite	No	Yes	Yes
Supervisor approves	N/A	Yes	Yes
Seat available	N/A	Yes	No
ACTIONS	RESPONSES		
Add student to enrollment		✔	
Send enrollment letter		✔	
Send wait list letter			✔
Send rejection letter	✔		
Update student record	✔	✔	✔

Figure 5.17 Decision Table

logic necessary for automation of decision making and rule use. These tables are normally built through extensive individual and group interviews with business experts. Figure 5.17 attempts to capture the decision making around enrolling a student in a course.

Step 4: Conduct Proof of Concept

Statement of Purpose

With the business operation redesign articulated in the Blueprint, it may be important to refine the expected benefits originally articulated in the Framework Statement of step 1 (Figure 5.18). The refinement is possible because the Blueprint includes information that was not available for the original business case. For narrowly scoped and simple reengineering projects, this step may not be necessary. But when hundreds of jobs may change, where multiple organization units must adopt a common set of business practices, where new technologies and information systems must be developed and installed, and where many customers and products/services are affected and the cost of implementation is substantial,

Purpose: To refine the estimate of the project's expected benefits and to see if the business operation redesign performs as expected.

Outcome: Benefits Statement

Key Activities:

    1. Determine need for proof of concept.

    2. Select a proof of concept approach.

    3. Develop proof of concept requirements and plan.

Figure 5.18 Step 4: Conduct Proof of Concept

you may require some sort of testing before full implementation to accurately assess expected benefits.

Step 4 provides an opportunity to demonstrate the expected return on investment through a proof of concept that simulates the redesigned business operation or through a pilot test of all or a critical part of the operation. The goal, in both cases, is to provide feasibility and benefits information without committing to a total implementation across the business. In the end, executive sponsors are more likely to fund a multi-million dollar implementation if some part of the organization has already experienced success with the redesign or there are specific numbers from a simulation to prove benefits. Figure 5.19 shows the alternative project flows for step 4.

As we mentioned, proofs of concept can be conducted through simulations and pilot tests. A simulation is the artificial execution of the Blueprint using manual techniques like a walk-through or computerized automation. For example, one automotive parts company wanted to reengineer its design and manufacturing process. After creating a Blueprint for the operation, they conducted a series of meetings where line managers, using matrixes and paper displays, walked through all 14 part-type situations to ensure that each part type could be handled in the new design. As a result of these meetings, several changes were made to the design. Another company used a computerized simulation to identify transaction capacities, potential bottlenecks, and error reductions.

A pilot test, on the other hand, is an actual live demonstration of the

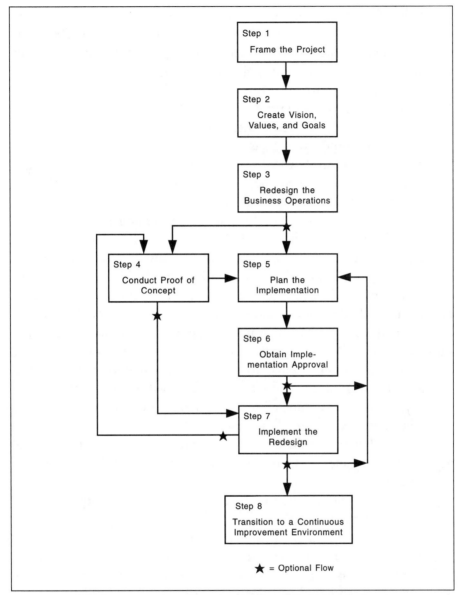

Figure 5.19 Business Reengineering Steps Work Flow Options

Blueprint. For example, the telecommunications industry has used the pilot technique called the "model office" to test how an operator service or customer service support might function using new technology.

Simulations can be conducted in a matter of weeks, running before or in parallel with implementation planning. A pilot, because it may take six months to provide solid results, should be conducted after implementation planning to avoid significant delays in the project. Which to choose? Or should you perform both? A simulation can be used to calculate the financial and physical processing aspects of the reengineered business operation. It will answer questions such as:

- Does the reengineered business operation have the capacity to meet our production goals?
- Are there hidden bottlenecks or other problems that must be fixed?
- Does the reengineered operation cost less? How much less? Does it generate more revenue?
- Does it handle all types of transactions, including exception and error processing, effectively?

Computerized real-time simulators are available today. You can run the operation over time and vary inputs such as job and organization structures, transaction volumes and types, and technology configurations. Simulators do require extensive and detailed data about the current environment. Preparation of simulator inputs may extend the planned simulator time in the overall project plan. A less accurate but simpler and more economical approach is to conduct a manual simulation using transaction and situation walk-throughs. This will force the reengineering project team to examine all process relationships and make financial and volume estimates for each process.

A side benefit of simulation is that its supporting data often exposes organizational issues and problems that were previously overlooked. Issues and problems that may arise include:

- Business policies and procedures that are routinely ignored or applied inconsistently
- Missing or inaccurate measurement processes
- Mistaken assumptions about how the business actually operates

The pilot test, as defined previously, creates the reengineered business operation in a controlled, small-scale environment. It should run for a limited amount of time (such as a single business cycle) and involve a limited number of people with easily controlled interfaces. One company tested three of the five redesigned business processes, using only two business units working out of one office serving four customers. A successful pilot test requires accurate "before" and "after" benchmark data from the test environment and a measurement process for collecting data. Unless the results provide concrete, measured benefits information, a pilot test wastes everyone's time and unnecessarily disrupts the work environment.

The pilot test provides several benefits not attained through simulation. These include:

- Actual, as opposed to estimated, proof of benefits
- Experiences that teach people how to ensure orderly change and avoid mistakes during implementation
- Training, materials, job structuring, and business practices testing
- Refinement to processes, business policies and practices based upon actual use
- Cultural change experience, so expectations and resistance to change can be addressed during full-scale implementation
- Organization awareness building
- Assessment and definition of detail not fully documented in the Blueprint

When the pilot test is over, the test environment should be able to continue the reengineered operation (assuming the test proves successful). People will not want to return to the old ways of working, decision making, and interacting while the large-scale solution is developed and rolled out. Therefore, if technological support is "rigged" for the pilot test, working alternatives must be available to install posttest. Policies and practices applied in the test should be continued even if they are not followed in the rest of the organization.

Step 4 Outcome: Benefits Statement

This document concisely presents the qualitative and quantitative benefits of implementing the business operation redesign based on the results of the simulation or pilot test. It presents the measures, the measurement data, an analysis and interpretation of the data, as well as recommendations for continuing the project. The recommendations may follow one of these directions:

- Implement immediately—results meet or exceed expectations.
- Enhance the design in specific ways to achieve expected results and then proceed to full-scale implementation.
- Refine the design of the business operation because it currently

does not yield sufficient results to warrant implementation across the organization.

- Stop the project. It is not feasible to continue the work.

Step 4 Key Activities

As stated above, a simulation can be completed before, during, or after planning the implementation. A pilot test should take place after implementation planning, since it demands more resources, and during the first six months of the implementation when foundation-building changes are being introduced across the organization. The activities for a proof-of-concept test include:

1. *Determine need for proof of concept.* Conduct a proof-of-concept test when the following kinds of conditions exist:
   - Executives are reluctant to allocate funds without "hard" data to guarantee expected benefits.
   - Competing priorities in the business require that benefits be proven to ensure commitment to implementation.
   - The reengineering Blueprint is sufficiently radical to require feasibility testing to define the types, intensity, and extent of communication programs, education and training, and change management support required for implementation.
   - Initial cost estimates for implementation require a second look at the Blueprint to ensure benefits will justify up-front retooling and conversion costs.
   - There is a history of project failures due to unrealistic expectations of what can work and be accepted within the organization.
2. *Select a proof-of-concept approach.* If a proof-of-concept test is required, determine whether to perform a simulation, a pilot test, or both. Simulation is appropriate where time is limited, a simulator can be rented or purchased, and accurate data is available from the current environment. A pilot test is appropriate if there is sufficient time, people mistrust simulation data, or organizational response to the reengineering implementation necessitates measurement and analysis.
3. *Develop proof-of-concept requirements and plan.* For the simulation test, define the following requirements:

- Data required to run the simulation. This usually includes current processes, triggers, flows, and dependencies; organization locations, job assignments, and labor rates; transaction types, volumes, and frequencies; transaction timing in each process and routes taken through the processes for each transaction type.

  In organizations with multiple business units performing the same processes differently, agree to a typical or average process environment for the simulation. Otherwise, the simulation can become more complex than the reengineering effort itself.
- Standard data collection worksheets/tools and support materials to consistently and accurately capture current processing environment data.
- Resources, tasks, and assignments for using the simulator.

For the pilot test requirements, define the following:
- Scope of the pilot test. This includes selecting the business processes and practices to be tested; identifying the products, services, and related transactions, customers, organization units, job positions, and geographic location(s) to include; and defining the technology to use during the test.
- Preparation of the test site. This includes obtaining the commitment of line business people, preparing materials, conducting training, collecting benchmark data, and installing technology.
- Time frames of the test.
- Measurements to use during the pilot test. This includes defining the measures, the collection process, the frequency, and the start date for data collection.
- Resources, preparation tasks and assignments, how to implement and monitor the test.

4. *Conduct the proof-of-concept test.* Those assigned to execute and monitor the test begin their work. This includes collecting data and analyzing results of the pilot test or simulation as they become available, changing the test environment as necessary to improve the redesign, and reporting preliminary results to key managers and the project team.

5. *Produce the Benefits Statement.* At the end of the simulation or

133

pilot test, analyze results and document them in the Benefits Statement.

Step 4 Tips and Techniques

Do not view the proof of concept as a win/lose event. If achieving the benefits in the Vision, Values, and Goals Statement does not seem feasible, then the right decision is not to proceed. However, a no-go decision is not typical. Instead, proof-of-concept testing typically reveals what must be tweaked to achieve the desired results. The proof of concept is not a science experiment that must be conducted in a hands-off manner. Rather, it is an exploration of possibilities that should reduce the risk of implementation problems. Its purpose is to prevent people from making theoretically correct but impractical decisions.

Purpose: Develop a realistic action plan for implementing the reengineering Blueprint.

Outcome: Implementation Plan

Key Activities:

     1. Prepare for the implementation planning sessions.

     2. Conduct the implementation planning sessions.

     3. Document the Implementation Plan.

     4. Validate the Implementation Plan.

Figure 5.20 Step 5: Plan the Implementation

Step 5: Plan the Implementation

Statement of Purpose

Developing the reengineering Blueprint is easy compared to implementing it. Without a carefully thought-out strategy, the redesigned business operation will never become a reality (Figure 5.20). No one voluntarily disrupts their business, gives up power, or forces abrupt change on already overburdened people unless they believe their company's very survival depends on it.

Although the Blueprint for radical change can be created quickly, the change itself takes much more time—always more time than anticipated.

You must obtain funding and sustain it throughout the period of change. You must get approvals for new structures and job positions. Business policies and practices must be documented and integrated into existing reference manuals and computer systems. People must be taught how to change and given new skills and knowledge. After existing automation technology is assessed, systems must be enhanced, purchased or developed, tested, and installed. Many questions must be answered; expectations and egos must be managed.

Therefore, the purpose of step 5 is to:

- Develop an implementation strategy that addresses the politics of change and creates the least disruption to the organization
- Provide a realistic plan that can be funded as benefits become visible
- Detail an activity plan that clearly identifies tasks, deliverables, roles, accountabilities, timetables, and costs

In our experience, no executive will allow change to disrupt his or her organization without knowing why and when it should be done, what it will entail, how much it will cost, and who is accountable. We have also found that the most successful implementations involve as many people as possible from the affected organizations. The team members who are champions coordinate and drive the implementation work within their own units. The core group team members provide support to the champions and the implementation SWAT groups as described previously in chapter 4, "Don't Walk Alone."

Any implementation is multidimensional. Like a spider web with threads reaching out in all directions, the implementation extends across many areas of the business (Figure 5.21). The questions that must be answered include:

- How should the different organization units be transitioned to the reengineered environment? One at a time? In groups?
- If an organization is geographically dispersed, does it make sense to phase in certain geographies before others? By region? By state? By country?
- Should the organization invest in completely new technology, or are there interim solutions that can minimize technology investment without undermining the project? How will legacy systems be phased out?

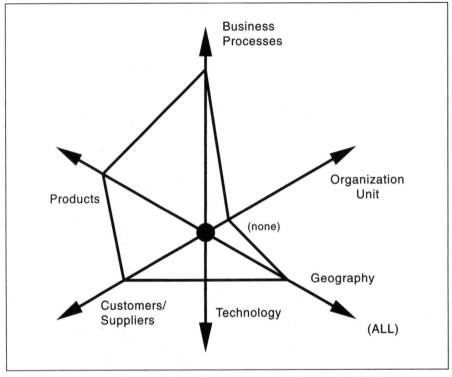

Figure 5.21 The Complexity of Reengineering Implementation Phasing

- Should customers and/or suppliers be brought into the reengineered environment one at a time? In groups or all at once? By type? By how much must they change to interact with the reengineered environment?
- Should all products be processed through the reengineered environment at the same time? Should they be phased in by type? By volume sold? By transportation need? By sales tactic?
- Should the redesigned business processes be implemented at one time? Should the front-end ones go first? Should we start with the middle ones?

The reengineering project team must determine what is logical, cost effective, and politically feasible. The everything-at-once, "flash-cut" approach to change generally won't work for large projects. Therefore, implementation phasing is almost imperative. What should be done in the first phase? Obviously there is no one formula, but many business reengineering projects start with two or three items—foundation building, quick fixes, and possibly pilot testing. To build a foundation means to install across all of the affected organization a common language and a supporting set of business practices that position the organization for future change. For example, one company had all training groups across the company begin to use a new language for training information on all communication and data sharing in the first phase of their reengineering implementation. They also introduced a standard catalog and description format for publicizing training courses and standard formats for processing training requests in all units. Later phases changed the training support processes, installed a new training database that everyone was to use, and consolidated some of the training units.

Quick fixes or interim solutions are changes you make to disarm a crisis. It is like emergency room treatment. You stop the bleeding any way you can; then, when the life threatening crisis is over, you fix the wound in the proper way. For example, as a quick fix to automating invoice payments, one company had everyone use two existing software packages that did not share data and met only 50 percent of the data requirements. In later phases of the project, the company installed an integrated automation solution with all the necessary functionality. The quick fix was then abandoned. However, unless quick fixes and interim solutions are carefully managed, employees can mistakenly view them as the end instead of part of the first phase of reengineering. When are quick fixes and interim solutions necessary? Here are some typical situations that call for them:

- Foundation-building work (for example, initial policy and practices changes) required as a first step in implementation may not deliver quantifiable performance benefits. For example, all organization units using a new language for their work conveys the soft benefit of increased clarity but not the hard benefit of being able to process significantly increased transaction volumes.

- The best technological solution may require an extensive and time-consuming investment in new databases, hardware, and systems. For example, in an organization with fragmented systems, the interim quick fix was to develop an extraction database from multiple existing legacy systems. The best technological solution

BUSINESS REENGINEERING: THE SURVIVAL GUIDE

was the development of a single-source database and the conversion of the existing databases to that single source—a change that would require 18 months to implement.

- A pilot test is required. Such a test may take six months. However, it is not politically feasible to do nothing until then. Therefore, a quick fix adopting some new business policies and practices would signify progress without requiring full-scale implementation. For example, as an interim solution, one company eliminated several approval signatures for certain types of work but did not change the work process.

Step 5 Outcome: Implementation Plan

Each phase of an implementation for a major reengineering project normally takes from 6 to 12 months. If a total plan can be assembled and costs estimated, so much the better, although it may be difficult to estimate costs accurately beyond the first year of implementation. Therefore, we recommend that the first year (one to two phases) expressly be detailed and costed. Other phases must be scoped and have resources estimated, but do not have a detailed activity schedule. Each phase should include activities that assess achievement, measure benefits, improve the implementation process, conduct next phase detailed planning, and acquire funding. Each implementation phase can be introduced in the following manner:

- Organization and implementation team structure and roles
- Phase strategy and scope—the dimensions of impact (Figure 5.21)

Example Possible Activity	Possible Action									
	Acquire	Analyze	Design	Develop	Document	Test	Deliver	Install	Monitor	Ongoing Support
Project Team Maintenance: Team Member & Exec. Sponsor	✔				✔					✔
Team Management, etc.				✔					✔	✔
Decision-Making & Issue Resolution Processes			✔			✔		✔		✔
External Project to Project Coordination		✔			✔				✔	✔
Implementation Monitoring			✔	✔					✔	✔

Figure 5.22 Implementation Planning Matrix

138

- Phase objectives and measurable expected accomplishments
- Risk factors to be mitigated during implementation
- Total resource requirements and costs
- Expected return on investment
- Schedule and timeline for all activities

Within each phase, group implementation activities into categories such as Project Team Maintenance, Communications Program, Training and Education Program, Cultural Change Program, Technology Development Program, and, optionally, the Pilot Test. Each category should identify the specific actions of these activities such as acquire, analyze, design, develop, document, test, deliver, install, monitor, and provide ongoing support. Figure 5.22 provides a sample implementation activity planning matrix.

For each category of planning activities, activities to be included might be:

- Project Team Maintenance
  —Team membership and executive sponsorship
  —Team management, accountabilities, operations, and communications
  —Decision-making and issue-resolution processes
  —External project to project coordination
  —Implementation monitoring and accomplishment reporting
- Communication Program
  —Objectives—inform, sell, reinforce
  —Target audiences—customers, employees, managers, executives
  —Content
  —Media and vehicle options
  —Materials, kits, and so on
  —Briefings, meetings, and so on
- Cultural Change Management Program
  —Expectations management
  —Business policies, practices, and work methods decisions
  —Organization structure
  —Job positions and staffing requirements
  —Performance objectives
  —Measurement systems
  —Reward and incentive programs

139

—Management and employee transition support
- Education and Training Program
  —Business policies, practices, and methods reference materials
  —Skills and/or knowledge requirements
  —Target audiences—customers, employees, managers, executives
  —Format and media options (for example, self-instructional, instructor led, on the job)
  —Posttraining reinforcement
- Technology Development Program
  —Hardware, software, and communications requirements
  —Current environment capabilities
  —Marketplace offerings
  —Standards, protocols, and platforms
  —Logical designs
  —Code generation or package purchase
- Proof-of-Concept Test
  —Some or all of the subject areas listed in categories above

For each activity defined in an Implementation Plan phase, the following information is required:
- Activity name and purpose
- Assignments to identify who is accountable for the work, any approval requirements, who to involve and consult in the work, and who to inform of progress or results
- Start and end dates for the work
- Outcomes/deliverables of the work that can be measured for achievement of excellence
- Criteria for outcome excellence
- Work techniques to use in executing the activity
- Downstream (or upstream) activity dependencies
- Estimated direct costs for consultants, equipment, facilities, travel, and so on
- Estimated number and identity of people accountable and/or involved in the activity and their expected hours of work

Step 5 Key Activities

For small-scale reengineering projects, step 5 work should require two to three weeks. Even for larger efforts, it should require no more than four weeks. It is an intensive effort to assemble a carefully thought-out and detailed plan.

1. *Prepare for the implementation planning session(s).* Preparing for the session includes defining content, session structure, and logistical arrangements. A format and strategy for the planning should be prepared.

2. *Conduct the implementation planning session(s).* The reengineering project team and advisory expert come together to develop and reach consensus on the Implementation Plan under the project facilitator's guidance. We recommend a small group of not more than 8–10 people.

3. *Document the Implementation Plan.* The production of the Implementation Plan requires synthesizing the results of the developmental session(s) into a succinct and intelligible document.

4. *Validate the Implementation Plan.* Those who developed the original Blueprint should be able to make any necessary refinements to the Implementation Plan before its publication and presentation to the executive sponsors to obtain funding approval.

Step 5 Tips and Techniques

There is always the question of presenting the reengineering Blueprint to the project's executive sponsors before developing an Implementation Plan. The primary advantage of this "one-two-punch" approach is that separating what should be done from how to do it allows the team to get agreement and feedback on the design without confusing the executives with implementation issues. The disadvantage is that they may not be able to comment on the radical change until they know more about the feasibility and timing for implementing the change. As one executive we know put it, "It's easy to like to a new idea, but I won't be able to support it until I know the impact on my organization." Therefore, whether you create the Implementation Plan before or after the Blueprint is presented is a strategic selling decision of what works best in your environment with your executives.

If you have ever developed a detailed implementation plan, you know that effective and convincing implementation plans are not created in a single draft. Most project reengineering teams will need to make additional changes as each new draft reveals new overlaps or inconsistencies. They may require interim reviews with executive sponsors to obtain direction and corrective feedback.

Some planning efforts require multiple scenarios. The project director should discuss the types and number of scenario plans and get agreement to them with the project's executive sponsors before the planning effort begins. Don't do work that you don't need to do. Otherwise, the reengineering project team is liable to suffer extreme frustration when management repeatedly asks "What would it cost if we . . . ?" and "What would the effects be if we . . . ?" Document each requested scenario with clearly identified benefits and risks, the activity's details, and timelines. Selecting scenarios for planning depends on many factors, some of which may seem arbitrary and elusive to regular working folks. One scenario might depict "tight-money" situations by reducing the number of activities and resources and increasing the timeline for each activity. Another scenario might portray an "ideal" implementation; another might depict a "realistic" version with specific constraints. Another scenario may define a quick-fix phase to set the stage for a second-year phase of full change in a limited number of business units, and then a final third-year phase to cut over the rest of the organization after the partial implementation has proven effective. The second- and third-year plans may depend on the results from a pilot-test phase with activities conducted to parallel a quick-fix phase in the first year.

The most common technique for creating the Implementation Plan is the facilitated workshop. Most implementation plans require one to three workshop sessions of two days each, with 8–10 people representing the various constituencies and stakeholders. A larger group (up to 30) may be best for reviewing and finalizing the Implementation Plan. Between workshops, core group meetings may be necessary to clarify details, calculate costs, and resolve implementation issues that come up as the plan develops. In reengineering projects that affect multiple business units or organizations, each unit may need to develop its own Implementation Plan in addition to the overall plan. You can then integrate these unit level plans into an overall project plan or use them to supplement an overall plan.

Be warned that implementation planning can generate new resistance to change. Why? This is where the team and its executive sponsors come face-to-face with the reality of changing the organization. Instead of "fantasy" time, it becomes "let's really make this happen" time. For the first time, people will begin to see how their own power and comfort with the status quo will be affected. People can start to get very stubborn and back off previous commitments. We'll talk more about this in chapter 7.

Purpose: To get the funding and resources to begin Blueprint Implementation.

Outcome: Funded Resource Request

Key Activities:
    1. Develop the approval strategy.
    2. Ask for approval.

Figure 5.23 Step 6: Obtain Implementation Approval

Step 6: Obtain Implementation Approval

Statement of Purpose

Were you ever involved in a project that was scheduled to start implementation the week after the design was completed, but you had to wait two months for approval for funding which put the whole project behind schedule and raised everyone's frustration levels about 80 percent? The purpose of step 6 is to put some reality into that scenario (Figure 5.23). Funding approvals take time. They are not automatic. If the first five steps of this methodology are performed correctly and the politics are properly managed, this step should be relatively straightforward. Informal briefings all along the way should have prepared executive sponsors for what they will hear in the formal presentations. Life isn't perfect, however, and external events or a change in management can create a nightmare of last-minute presentations, massaging of the Implementation Plan, or even a reselling of the reengineering need. Whatever the case, it takes time to obtain the final approval and funding for moving to implementation. Plan for it! Getting approvals is as much a part of the project work as creating diagrams to document the redesigned processes or developing new systems.

Step 6 Outcome: Funded Resource Request

The outcome of this step is a decision to proceed as demonstrated by the approval and allocation of the resources required to execute the first phase of the Implementation Plan. These resources should include at a minimum the necessary:

- Human resources for the implementation activities
- Facilities and equipment
- Direct budget for external consulting, training, and so on

Step 6 Key Activities

Step 6 should require from one to two weeks, but may take several months. The activities required include:

1. *Develop the approval-process strategy.* The reengineering project team and the executive sponsor(s) must ensure that all stakeholder executives have the opportunity to become involved in the decision making for the implementation. This may require presentations to one or more executive operating committees and their line managers, which should be scheduled in advance. The presentations may be made at regularly scheduled or special meetings of key decision-making groups. Each presentation should be meaningful to its audience, and the presenter must be credible. A presentation may be public with many attendees, or it could be a private, one-on-one meeting with an individual executive. Whether the path to approval is straightforward or circuitous, know what it is and follow it! Don't let the reengineering project fail because of political mistakes.

2. *Ask for approval.* The outcome of the formal presentations should be approval to proceed with the project implementation as defined in the Implementation Plan. However, executives have been known to act unpredictably, so be prepared to respond to these types of directions in order to get approval:
   - Go ahead, but at a slower or faster pace.
   - Go ahead, but at a later date.
   - Go ahead, but change the scope of the implementation.

• Go ahead, but do it more cheaply on the same schedule.

Step 6 Tips and Techniques

Making the required formal and informal presentations requires a certain amount of stage presence as well as a good command of the facts. The outcomes from the previous steps are available as source materials for creating the presentations. These include:

- Background Statement
- Vision, Values, and Goals Statement
- Blueprint
- Benefits Statement (optional)
- Implementation Plan

Don't overdo the details, but don't gloss over important points. Be sure to include hard facts and figures, but don't forget that they must "own" the vision of what is possible before they will commit. Talk about the risks of not proceeding, but don't encourage unrealistic expectations. The presenter should find a way of engaging his or her audience while answering these questions:

- Why did we get involved in this project in the first place?
- What are we trying to accomplish? Why is radical change needed?
- How do we get there?
- Why won't quick fixes do the job?
- What are the risks?
- What's in it for you (personally and for the executives)?
- What will happen if we don't do anything?
- When will we see the first benefits and what will they be?
- What specifically do we want you to approve?

Step 7: Implement the Redesign

Statement of Purpose

If you have gotten this far in your reengineering project, the team should have had a big party to celebrate its success at creating and selling a radical design for change. Now the hard work begins as the team turns the Blueprint for business operation redesign into reality (Figure 5.24). The Implementation Plan provides the road map. The core support

Purpose: To transition the business operation from the current environment
to the reengineered environment.

Outcome: Measurement Results

Key Activities:

    1. Consistent periodic meetings.

    2. Celebrate success.

    3. Conduct critical reflections.

Figure 5.24 Step 7: Implement the Redesign

group and champions not only do much of the work, but also coordinate and support the work of the implementation SWAT groups. The implementation SWAT groups are assigned accountability for specific implementation activities. Materials get developed, people are trained, policies and practices get changed, systems are developed, and organizations get restructured.

Step 7 Outcome: Measurement Results

Improvements in the business operation should be visible and measurable as the implementation proceeds. Measurement results should show movement toward the reengineering goals as stated in the Vision, Values, and Goals Statement. These may include such qualitative and quantitative measures as:

- Frequency and volumes of transactions
- Number of customer inquiries, complaints, and responses
- Number of errors, discrepancies, changes and corrections
- Elapsed or dedicated time required for process cycle
- Number of people required to produce the process outcomes
- Customer satisfaction with services performance and products delivered

Step 7 Key Activities

Step 7 lasts as long as it takes to conduct all phases of the Implementation Plan activities. Every 6 to 12 months, as an implementation phase comes to an end, formally evaluate the progress that has been made to determine if adjustments are necessary. In addition, pursue detailed planning for the next phase along with funding acquisition. The key activities during implementation should include:

1. *Consistent periodic meetings.* The reengineering project team must meet regularly to share learning, monitor implementation progress, and resolve issues as they arise.
2. *Celebrate success.* As improvements become visible, the people who made them happen should be rewarded for their work. Formal celebrations are called for here! Rewarding the positive behaviors, modeling those behaviors for the rest of the organization, and having fun at work is important. When you climb great heights, looking back at how far you've come is inspiring. Celebrations also help keep priorities focused and executive commitment strong. Everyone wants to be associated with a winner.
3. *Conduct critical reflections.* The project team should work proactively with the line organizations to anticipate problems with the implementation work. Use a critical reflection process, as described in chapter 8, "Form the Neighborhood Watch," with work groups on a regular basis to uncover implementation needs and make adjustments in the implementation activities. The project team may need to change its support based upon the learning from such sessions. This critical reflection process is the continuous process improvement aspect of project management.

Step 7 Tips and Techniques

Good follow-up is the most important characteristic of successful project teams during an implementation. Getting people to take the right actions requires persistence and the ability to anticipate and remove obstacles. During implementation, follow-up is demonstrated by talking with people to:

- Uncover what they need to get the job done
- Ensure they attend the meetings and events to which they are invited
- Check to see that actions are taken as promised
- Uncover issues and problems
- Remove obstacles that inhibit progress
- Provide needed resources or support to get the job done
- Ensure that quality is delivered

Purpose: To bring closure to project team activities and have line organizations continue to improve the reengineered environment.

Outcome: Continually Improved Performance

Key Activities:

Ongoing measurement and critical reflection by operations units.

Figure 5.25 Step 8: Transition to a Continuous Improvement State

Step 8: Transition to a Continuous Improvement State

Statement of Purpose

As a business unit transforms itself into the reengineering vision, it becomes self-sufficient, no longer requiring the special support of the reengineering project team. That is when reengineering ends and continuous improvement begins. The "big bang" is complete. It is now time to begin tweaking operations to achieve continuous improvements in process performance over time. To do that, people must embed measurement and self-correction techniques into the daily and weekly work processes of the business operation. Step 8 ensures that the organization acquires and internalizes the skills and knowledge needed to conduct its own continuous improvement process.

Step 8 Outcome: Continually Improved Performance

When work is intrinsically rewarding to those who perform it, continuously increasing levels of performance are guaranteed. Whether it is finding a way to reduce the production cycle or adding a customer-requested feature without increasing production costs, people can become improvement-focused if they are rewarded for it and, much more importantly, if they are given the support and power to do it. When this happens, the culture is truly transformed into a learning organization.

Step 8 Key Activities

Once the continuous improvement skills, knowledge, and processes are embedded in the organization, step 8 is ongoing. The key activities for continuous process improvement (detailed in chapter 8) include:

- Measuring outcome production directly and continuously
- Analyzing the feedback from the measurements
- Creating corrective or improvement actions and testing them
- Rewarding success with improvements
- Transferring the learning to the rest of the organization

Step 8 Tips and Techniques

The boundary between reengineering implementation and continuous process improvement is often fuzzy and unpredictable. Some organizations can move quickly from installing radical change to improving upon the change as they work. Others seem to struggle for years.

If the reengineering project was executed correctly and step 8 is installed and supported, reengineering should not be needed again unless there is a major shift in the marketplace or in the corporation itself (a merger, for example). Why? Because with the proper foundation and a solid structural design, a business operation can prosper a very long time. Renovations may be needed occasionally, due to external forces; but, if proper organizational preventive maintenance is applied, the operation will "wear like iron."

The Life of a Business Reengineering Project

Here are some fictional excerpts from the diary of a project director. They are based upon the actual experiences of a project team that was given the opportunity to reengineer a major process in their multidivisional manufacturing company.

November 1991

After researching the executive vice president's idea that we need a common form for processing customer product-customization requests across our divisions, the team (which is only Sue, Tom, and me) has reached the conclusion that the problem is much deeper than he suspected. The data shows we're going to be in big trouble on error rates, and correcting them may cost millions 12 to 18 months from now. Hope we can sell him on the idea of reengineering the whole process. It would be good also to change the fundamental policies concerning customizations, but the marketplace and our internal political environment probably won't buy that. Everybody says their customers and products have unique needs.

January 1992
EVP is interested in our approach. Have to present to vice presidents and create funding letter for president to sign.

June 1992
Have finally gotten executive sponsorship, champions, core team and consultant on board to begin the visioning work (step 2). The red tape around here can really slow us down. One of the VPs resisted participating. That took two weeks to clear up. The kickoff meeting should have about 50 people attending. Have promised a Blueprint and Implementation Plan by the end of October.

September 1992
Why does everyone want to have their own way? Sometimes I don't think we're working for the same company. Have completed the Blueprint. Ended up with two versions—one that is radical and one that is not so radical. Champions agree that the less radical version is the one to sell after meeting individually with the VPs of each unit.

December 1992
The initial plan of three years and $5 million to save $20 million in two did not sell. Appears that next year's profits will be down and that change is scary to those guys. Will rework plan to show what we can do in 12 months and $0.5 million. They also want a set of interim fixes to stem the error rates. They keep wanting us to fix the back-end processes and not the front-end processes where the problems are occurring.

March 1993
Funding was finally approved for 1993 in January. It has taken two months to get the champions to commit to the business practices changes and standardization they agreed to last year. Each has established a SWAT implementation group to develop business cases for the training the core team is developing. The champions and I are trying to get some policy changes through to make the implementation easier and position us better for next year.

July 1993

First part of the training has been completed in all the divisions. What a relief. We found we needed to add a lot of detail and make some refinements as the training and reference materials were developed. Second phase has to be completed by September 30. We will have trained over 500 people in six months. But, other news comes from the front!! Error figures just released show our 1991 predictions for problems are coming true. VPs are demanding a new set of quick fixes. When will they see that Band-Aids® won't work? The core team and some of the champions wanted to go yell "we told you so" to the VPs. I suggested calm and that this is all part of the educational process. I hope I'm right.

September 1993

As the divisions start to use the new product-customization language, practices, and standard format for creating product customizations, they are finding that they can simplify a lot of it. We're getting a lot of positive feedback on the training. It also appears that many field people were expecting more changes than we are actually introducing. So much for managing expectations. The headquarters wants less change and the field wants more change.

October 1993

The results have stimulated the vice presidents to summon us to a meeting to discuss the possibility of extending the simplification work and putting more emphasis on reengineering how we plan for products and product customizations. Finally!!! It's time dust off that radical Blueprint of ours.

November 1993

As I leave this project and turn it over to my replacement, I leave knowing that we have brought the organization to a new level of understanding. Funding for 1994 will allow us to bring a common set of business processing to all the divisions and a standard set of customization options. This will achieve at least 40 percent of our expected benefits. And we have been funded to build a new database and system to support access to real-time data for both headquarters, manufacturing, and field sales people. Our organization is now ready, and the team can march ahead with solid support from all levels of the organization.

CHAPTER 6

MOVE WITH PURPOSE

Traveling in the neighborhood, the wise traveler uses the mode of transportation best-suited to his circumstances. For a short distance he may walk; at night, however, the same trip might require a taxi or a bus. If he's going to a distant neighborhood, he may take a plane or a train. Just like street-smart travelers, savvy business reengineers can choose from a variety of options for achieving their goals. And they have the necessary skills and knowledge to execute their options, including knowing when to hire consultant expertise from outside or inside the organization. Capable business reengineers don't trust their future to dumb luck. They move with purpose and know how to get things done.

For those who are responsible for managing a business reengineering project or participating as a team member, this chapter and the supporting appendices provide a detailed approach for managing a project and using the methodology outlined in chapter 5. The techniques and guidelines presented here and in appendices B, C, and D create an environment in which you will get the "right" Blueprint the first time; they also position the project so that implementation can take place successfully. This is one of the most effective ways to manage a business reengineering project. You will be introduced to three basic techniques—the focus group interview, the facilitated meeting, and the facilitated workshop.

Why These Techniques?

For over 10 years, the computer industry has successfully used structured and disciplined facilitated techniques to design and implement business information systems. Using these techniques has dramatically improved the quality of systems products (up to 400 percent) and reduced the time required to deliver those products (50 to 100 percent). See the book, *FUSION: Integrating IE, CASE and JAD: A Handbook for Reengineering the Systems Organization,* by Dorine Andrews and Naomi Leventhal for more details. Applying these techniques to business reengineering achieves the same positive results. In our experience, every day spent in a facilitated workshop saves the reengineering project team three to six weeks. In a power utility, facilitated workshops enabled the human resources organization to redesign its business operation and plan for implementation in three weeks rather than six months. The actual time spent in workshops was five days. This highly structured, facilitated approach derives its power from six distinguishing characteristics:

- **Unbiased facilitation.** Facilitation by an unbiased outsider enables project stakeholders to reach consensus rapidly. The facilitator brings the process, objectivity, and techniques required to create a cohesive team and teach them reengineering methodology and techniques. The facilitator is the project's truth teller. Having no political stakes in the project, he or she can confront the team in ways that would be too risky for other team members. The facilitator does not need specialized knowledge of the business operation, but must have a solid background in organizational theory, management practices, and information technology. The facilitator also must be specifically trained to recognize and manage biases.
- **Deliverable accountability.** Reengineering efforts often fail when accountability is unclear or absent altogether. Joint application development techniques build accountability into the process. Deliverables are defined and created within the context of facilitated workshops. Everyone is involved and everyone has ownership.
- **Definitive participant roles and responsibilities.** As discussed in chapter 4, "Don't Walk Alone," the reengineering project team should involve more than three or four experts working together

in a closed room. There should be core group support staff members, champions, executive sponsors, the project director, subject matter experts, advisors, the facilitator, and others involved in the reengineering effort. Each has clearly defined roles and accountabilities within the project and within the various facilitated sessions.

- **Process structure.** For reengineering projects, the process structure outlined in chapter 5, "Know Where You Are Going," defines a rigorous and disciplined methodology for conducting a reengineering project. The facilitated techniques within this chapter support that methodological structure. These techniques reduce the time required to complete each step and guarantee a higher-quality, more acceptable reengineering solution.
- **Forum structure.** There are three distinct facilitated forums or sessions: the focus group interview, the workshop, and the facilitated meeting. Each session has its own objectives, preparation requirements, operating rules, facilitation style, and participant responsibilities.
- **Exercise structure.** It is the project facilitator's job to design and conduct sessions that support all aspects of change: technical, cultural, and behavioral.

The project facilitator's job is to stimulate and direct the creativity of those brought together for the business reengineering work. We believe that this is best done by helping people to think and talk about the right things at the right time. By providing a structure and discipline to work through the methodology, we can keep people from dwelling on how to implement something before they know what it is that they want to implement; and we can help conceptual thinkers translate their "big" ideas into the step-by-step application to reality. There are many different approaches to stimulating people's creativity, and we encourage project facilitators to use as many of them as possible.

Facilitated techniques model the principles of business process redesign, continuous improvement, and transformation that are so important to a successful business reengineering project. For example, to support transformation principles, the facilitated techniques:

- **Force people to confront their biases and assumptions.**
  Reengineering facilitators help the project team members uncover and manage the beliefs and assumptions that shape their behavior.

155

- **Build credibility through behavior modeling.** By using facilitated techniques, the project team members say to the organization, *"Do what we do, not just what we say you should do."* The reengineering project team exemplifies leadership and change by modeling desired behaviors.
- **Think about the problem before deciding its resolution.** Unlike other approaches, facilitated techniques encourage the team to identify the problem and explore all possibilities before deciding on a single solution.
- **Accelerate the change process.** Facilitated techniques eliminate iterative, linear reviews and force joint discussions and decision making among all key decision makers. A winning Blueprint and Implementation Plan can be delivered in weeks instead of months.
- **Create acceptance through involvement.** In facilitated sessions, project decisions are made by those affected by the outcomes rather than by advisors or subject matter experts who walk away when the project is over. The participative nature of the process ensures buy-in to all aspects of the reengineering outcomes.

To support process redesign principles, facilitated techniques:
- **Organize all sessions around outcomes.** When people identify what they expect from a meeting, workshop, or interview, the reengineering project facilitator designs a structure and creates an environment to deliver it. Deliverable accountability forces the focus on methodology outcomes.
- **Empower the participants.** At facilitated workshops, participants come to the table with decision-making power, rather than taking information back to decision makers.
- **Build in open feedback channels.** Involving key stakeholders provides ongoing communication and interaction with the organizations affected by the reengineering. These people take open issues to the right players within their own organizations to speed resolution, enhance education, and increase the involvement of executive sponsors. Having multiple organizational levels and a variety of business disciplines at the same facilitated session ensures direct information sharing, increased understanding, and immediate feedback.

- **Enable direct access to customers.** External and internal customers are invited to participate in facilitated sessions. There is no need to second-guess what the customer thinks and wants.
- **Enable simultaneous work.** The facilitated workshops and meetings can include 25 to 30 people actively working as a team. Sometimes all of them work together, but more often they divide into subteams to simultaneously design, analyze, and make recommendations. This is extremely productive. As stated before, every day in a facilitated workshop equals three to six weeks in a conventional environment.

To support continuous improvement principles, facilitated techniques:

- **Pay attention to the lowest level of detail.** Facilitated sessions can create all types of outcomes: detailed performance data, high-level priorities, a Blueprint, or an Implementation Plan priced to the penny. Whatever your goal, facilitated sessions are the way to go. The key is knowing what information is required, when it is required, and including the right people.
- **Enforce improvement as everyone's responsibility.** A reengineering project facilitator involves the team in assessing session results so that the reengineering process and sessions can be improved as the work progresses.
- **Make improvement always possible.** Facilitated techniques are constantly improving and becoming more effective. Two years ago, biases were not considered. Today facilitated workshops and meetings provide numerous exercises and activities to reveal, explore, and manage our biases and belief systems.

Participation in facilitated reengineering sessions is an exciting team-building and learning experience. It is an opportunity to model all of these principles for the larger organization, and it builds the competence and confidence needed to survive radical change.

The Job of the Reengineering Project Facilitator

To facilitate means to make group decision making easier by eliminating barriers to agreement. Facilitation should create consensus, allowing everyone to participate in decisions and outcomes. Not everyone gets his or her way, but everyone who participates can live with the decisions. This is not design by committee, where each participant is there to protect his or her territory and power. Using facilitation, the participants jointly construct the solution that is most appropriate for meeting the reengineering objectives. It is the job of the facilitator to unite the group, focus their discussion, and mobilize them to resolution and action.

However, the reengineering project facilitator is more than a group discussion manager and process consultant. The facilitator models the behaviors that the team will need to lead the organization. The facilitator transfers to the team his or her reengineering methodology expertise and ability to merge traditional organizational development (OD) group process techniques into the highly structured and disciplined environment. During implementation, the reengineering project facilitator may be assigned to other projects as the core support team members take on the facilitator role.

The reengineering project facilitator has a tough job. From a technical perspective, it is the facilitator's job to help the project team scope, size, and structure the project and all required deliverables. The project facilitator must plan, prepare, and ensure proper documentation of all facilitated sessions. The facilitator must also have the technical skills and knowledge to select, design, and conduct facilitated sessions to produce all possible content, diagrams, charts, and models required of the reengineering deliverables.

From the political and behavioral perspective, the reengineering project facilitator must manage personal biases as well as those of the participants. The facilitator must help the project team elicit and sustain commitment from the executive sponsor and the entire organization. That means having the skills to sell ideas and inspire others to action. On a day-to-day basis, the facilitator must help the team identify and manage individual problems and disruptive behavior. Principles, not personalities, should drive the reengineering work. And he must have the skills to transform 6–30 individuals into a fully functional team. The facilitator must help the team confront organizational, political, and power issues that arise in every reengineering project. The facilitator must be the catalyst to action, the team coach and consultant, the proactive detective, the confrontational questioner, and nonjudgmental listener, observer, and provider of feedback. Effectively filling these roles creates a learning-driven project team focused on key outcomes.

The facilitator must change roles as the needs of the project change.

Figure 6.1 summarizes opportunities for facilitation support throughout a reengineering project.

What Does It Take to Be a Reengineering Project Facilitator?

What makes a project facilitator successful? Quite frankly, skills training is not enough. Anyone can learn to drive; very few successfully race cars. It is sensitivity, guts, and a can-do attitude that separate the amateurs from the professionals. There is often intense resistance to large and complex reengineering projects. The cynics want you to call it off because they "know it won't work. Nothing will change." The wimps want you to back down because they "don't want to make any waves or rock the boat." Project know-it-alls want you to restrict project participation because they "know what is best for everyone." The lazy ones want everything to stay at a conceptual level, because "laying out detailed plans and designs requires too much effort and thought." The facilitator must know when to ignore, when to confront, and when to be patient and supportive. Highly successful reengineering project facilitators must be willing to:

- Proactively work with the project team to structure a process that will produce the creativity needed for a radical solution.
- Accept that organizational politics are as much a part of the project as technology and process modeling.
- Challenge the status quo, even when people resist.
- See obstacles as opportunities for inspiring others to action.
- Face setbacks optimistically. Learning to walk requires a lot of falling down.
- Observe behavior and provide explicit feedback to people.
- Confront people with problems you see, even when you know they would rather not hear it.
- Remain focused on the vision. Repeat the words, "It's not what *is*, but what you *want it to be* that's important."
- Be flexible and patient, allowing people to discover solutions themselves.
- Get what you want by asking questions rather than by telling people what to do.
- Be persistent and tenacious where critical success factors are

159

Reengineering Process Step	Facilitated Meeting	Focus Group	Facilitated Workshop	Facilitator Role(s) for Emphasis
1. Frame the Project				
· Assemble Analysis Team	✔	--	--	team coach; team builder
· Draft Project Frame	✔	--	--	meeting leader
· Conduct Situation Analysis	--	✔	--	interviewer
· Produce Framework Statement	--	--	--	analyst; editor to team
· Recommendations	✔	--	(✔)	team coach; process expert
· Contract with Executive Sponsors	--	--	--	team coach; politics advisor
2. Create Vision, Values, and Goals				
· Prepare for meetings	✔	--	--	team coach; process expert
· Conduct kickoff meeting	✔	--	--	meeting leader
· Conduct Vision, Values & Goals session	--	--	✔	team builder; meeting leader
· Create Vision, Values & Goals Statement	--	--	--	analyst; editor to team
· Validate Vision, Values & Goals Statement	✔	--	--	meeting leader
3. Redesign the Business Operations				
· Prepare for Blueprint sessions	✔	--	--	team coach; process expert
· Conduct Blueprint sessions	--	--	✔	meeting leader; team builder
· Document the Blueprint	--	--	--	analyst; editor to team
· Validate the Blueprint	✔	--	--	meeting leader; team builder
4. Conduct Proof of Concept				
· Determine need for proof of concept	✔	--	--	meeting leader; questioner
· Select proof of concept approach	✔	--	--	meeting leader; process expert
· Develop proof of concept requirements and detail plan	✔	--	(✔)	meeting leader; team builder
· Conduct proof of concept	✔	--	--	meeting leader; questioner
· Produce Benefits Statement	--	--	--	analyst; editor
5. Plan the Implementation				
· Prepare for implementation planning sessions	✔	--	--	team coach; process expert meeting leader; team builder
· Conduct implementation planning sessions	--	--	✔	
· Document the Implementation Plan	--	--	--	analyst; editor
· Validate the Implementation Plan	✔	--	--	meeting leader; team builder
6. Obtain Implementation Approval				
· Develop approval process strategy	✔	--	--	team coach; process expert; politics advisor
· Ask for approval	--	--	--	team coach
7. Implement the Redesign				
· Consistent, periodic meetings	✔	--	--	team coach; process expert; politics manager
· Celebrate success	✔	--	--	team builder
· Conduct critical reflections	✔	--	--	meeting leader; process expert; team coach
8. Transition to a Continuous Improvement State (At this point, facilitation skills and process expertise should be fully embedded in the project team and in the line organizations through skill training, education, and experience.)				

Figure 6.1 Opportunities for Facilitated Technique Application

- Be persistent and tenacious where critical success factors are concerned.
- Encourage others to make decisions.

Focus Group Interviews and Other Data Collection Mechanisms

The focus group interview is a research technique. Originally developed by market research organizations to study consumer preferences, the focus group interview is now widely used in many disciplines. For reengineering projects, we use the focus group interview to collect data.

As the name implies, the interview involves a group of people (usually from four to eight) with similar characteristics. A discussion leader (normally the project facilitator) facilitates the interview, asking each group a series of 8 to 12 prepared questions. The interaction and sharing of information among participants provides a rich repository of information, which is documented by the discussion leader or a documentation specialist. In one or two hours, a focus group yields more information than the team could collect during an entire day of individual interviews or weeks of written surveys. The focus group interview is an excellent technique for performing step 1 (frame the project) of the reengineering methodology.

Let's look in on a focus group to see how it works. Imagine yourself behind a one-way glass observing the scene. Mary, the project facilitator, and her documentation specialist, Jake, enter a room where six people are sitting. They are all customer support people from the customer service units of the western division. Their job is to field inquiries and problem calls from customers. After introducing herself and Jake and having each individual introduce themselves, Mary begins.

Mary: We are part of a team of people who have been asked to find new ways to work with our customers to improve our relationship with them and streamline our internal operations at the same time. I'm talking with many groups of employees and customers about their ideas, perceptions, and issues in these areas. I'm going to ask you a series of questions—the same questions I am asking everyone.

After answering a few questions about the project, Mary launches into her questions:

Mary: What are the things that prevent you from working with customers and solving their problems?

There is a pause. People seem a little timid. Mary smiles and waits. In about 30 seconds, Jim speaks up. *We never seem to have the right information about the customers and their products. Sometimes the information is missing and sometimes it's just plain wrong. Since about half of our product support data is not computerized, we have to reference the manuals. And, we have to share those.*

With that statement, there is a flood of people wanting to speak. Mary smiles and points to Sarah.

Mary: Let's go to Sarah next. Then I'll work my way around the room so we can hear from everyone.

Mary is careful not to contradict what someone has said. She also keeps people from judging each other.

Mary: We don't have to agree here. All thoughts are welcome. Back to Sarah.

Sarah: I think the customers have to put up with a lot from us. I mean, in the last week I had to make three customers wait over two hours while I researched their problems and got approval from my supervisor to go ahead with my solutions.

Mary continues to collect responses to her question from the group. She asks several more questions relating to the work and how it is processed.

Mary: If you had the ability to redesign how you did your work, what would you recommend?

Tom: I'd create service teams who would always work with the same customers, just like auto service departments. They have the red team, blue team, and green team.

Jane: I'd let us make the decisions as long as it didn't cost over $1,000. Then we could bring our manager in on the decision.

Paul: I'd make us into product experts.

Sue: I'd make our supervisors talk with customers at least once a week.

And so the interview continued. Mary continued to listen and her documentation support person continued to take notes. During interviews that followed this one, she would look for repeating patterns of issues, problems, and ideas. After all the interviews, she and the team have a picture of the current operation with multiple perspectives and some patterns in thinking about possible solutions that the team should explore during its process redesign activies.

You may need to supplement focus group interviews with a few individual interviews in the following circumstances:

- You are meeting with a project executive sponsor.
- Someone asks to meet with you alone.
- There are many personal and confidential issues to discuss that would be inappropriate in a group.

In one company, for example, each director requested a private interview to describe personal concerns about the past and current organization leadership.

Another supplemental technique that may be required in addition to the focus group interview is the business operation walk-through. Often used in current situation analysis, a business operation is visually reviewed by literally "walking through" the current process and documenting transactions, bottlenecks, information gaps, problems, and breakdowns. Walk-throughs tend to focus on gathering accurate numerical data (e.g., numbers and types of transactions, errors, and complaints), while interviews tend to focus on perceptions, critical success factors, issues, priorities, hidden agendas, enhancers and inhibitors to project success, and conflicts among others. These three techniques—focus group interviews, individual interviews, and business operation walk-throughs—form an extremely effective data collection mechanism for business reengineering projects.

We do not recommend using paper or electronic surveys to collect data because they seem to yield inaccurate and incomplete results. In one company, the following problems arose:

- Each group that received the survey defined the terms used in the survey differently. The results counted "apples, oranges, and cantaloupes" together.
- The survey design did not provide proper space for the reporting needs of all surveyed groups. Respondees skipped sections or added information where it did not belong.
- Only half the surveys were returned, despite follow-up calls. Responding to surveys is not a priority for most people.

As a result, the analysis team had to make additional on-site visits to collect the data and clarify responses. The survey effort wasted four valuable weeks before it was abandoned.

For detailed instructions and procedures for conducting focus group interviews, see appendix B.

Facilitated Meetings and Workshops

In business today, meetings have a bad reputation. Too many meetings have no focus or clear purpose, and they waste everyone's time. The classic example is the "status meeting" where everyone reports what has happened over the past weeks. We asked people why they don't attend (or wish they didn't have to attend) meetings. Here are some responses:
- Nothing ever happens at the meeting.
- Meetings are not well planned and don't stay on track.
- Others don't show up, so why should I?
- Nobody took the time to ask me personally to come.
- I don't know why I should attend.
- Too many meetings are meaningless exercises in political fighting.
- Somebody always dominates and ends up getting his or her way, so why should I bother?

Unlike conventional meetings (the kind our interviewees would rather avoid), a facilitated reengineering meeting is designed to achieve specific results. People leave a facilitated meeting on time, having accomplished what they expected. They understand why they were there, everyone is still speaking to each other, and they feel they had ample opportunity to bring their own issues and ideas to the table. In essence, a facilitated meeting is a meeting that has been engineered for success.

Facilitated meetings and facilitated workshops differ in terms of time and objectives. A facilitated meeting lasts no more than one or two days; a workshop runs from three to five consecutive days. The objectives of a facilitated meeting can be one or more of the following:
- Rapid data collection from multiple sources
- Planning and preparing for workshops by project teams
- Problem solving on specific issues
- Disseminating information and educating participants
- Validating and finalizing outcomes from workshops

The objectives for a reengineering facilitated workshop always include the following:
- Building a team
- Building consensus and common perspectives among participants
- Creating reengineering process deliverables/outcomes (for example, Vision, Values, and Goals Statement; Blueprint; and Implementation Plan)

Our reengineering methodology presents many opportunities for facilitated meetings and workshops. Sometimes there is a choice between a meeting and a workshop. The nature and tenor of the individual reengineering project will determine which is more appropriate. Appendix C details how to construct effective facilitated meetings. The instructions also apply to workshops. However, workshops have additional needs that are addressed in appendix D. The recommended facilitated meetings and workshops for a reengineering project are listed in Figure 6.2.

The Jefferson Company Design Department

Although it is difficult to recreate the reality of an actual workshop within the context of a book, the following case tells the story of the Jefferson Company Design Department and their experience with a Vision, Values, and Goals workshop.

Joe Landover, the vice president of the Jefferson Company Design Department, knew his department needed to get closer to its customers—the other departments within the company. Over the past two years, the company had experienced rapid growth, and his department, in an effort to service its customers more effectively, undertook a massive effort to upgrade drafting and design technologies within the department. But Joe still had problems. His customers consistently complained that the work his people delivered was not always what was expected and that it was often late. Some customers were even starting to go to outside sources for design and drafting work. He knew his people cared and were trying hard, but whatever they were doing was not quite enough. Joe and his executive team, the three directors who report directly to him, decided to "reinvent" their organization. They contracted the services of a reengineering consulting group. Using the reengineering methodology described in this book, the consultants conducted a background analysis to confirm that reengineering was really needed. With that need con-

Reengineering Process Step	Event Title/Objective	Expected Outcomes	Participants
1. Frame the Project (1) Draft Project Frame	Project Framing (Definition) Meeting	• Decision to proceed • Impacted organizations • Drafted Framework Statement	• Analysis team and key business managers
(4) Produce Framework Statement (5) Recommend project process	Project Planning Meeting	• Validated Framework Statement • Project plan	• Analysis team and key business managers
(6) Contract with Executive Sponsors	Project Contract Meeting	• Agreement to proceed	• Executive sponsor • Project director
2. Create Vision, Values, & Goals (1) Prepare for kickoff meeting and Vision, Values, & Goals session	Step 2 Planning Meeting	• Kickoff meeting script • Deliverable detail • Technical agenda • Workshop script	• Project team (core)
(2) Conduct kickoff meeting	Kickoff Meeting	• Prepared workshop participants	• Full project team • Executive sponsor • Interested others
(3) Conduct the Vision session	Workshop(s)	• Data for Framework Statement	• Full project team
(5) Validate Vision, Values, & Goals Statement	Vision Validation Meeting	• Final Vision, Values, & Goals Statement	• Those who created the vision, etc.
3. Redesign the Business Operations (1) Prepare for the Blueprint sessions	Step 3 Planning Meeting	• Deliverable detail • Technical agenda • Workshop script	• Project team (core)
(2) Conduct the Blueprint sessions	Workshop(s)	• Data for Blueprint	• Subset of project team
(4) Validate the Blueprint	Blueprint Validation Meeting(s)	• Finalize Blueprint • Next step plans	• Full project team
4. Conduct Proof of Concept (1) Determine need for proof of concept (2) Select proof of concept approach (3) Develop proof of concept requirement and plan	Concept Test Planning Meeting	• Decision on need for and type of proof of concept • Implementation Plan	• Full project team
(5) Produce Benefit Statement	Concept Test Evaluation Meeting(s)	• Drafted Benefits Statement • Recommendations for proceeding	• Full project team • Test participants
5. Plan the Implementation (1) Prepare for the implementation planning session(s)	Step 5 Planning Meeting	• Deliverable detail • Technical agenda • Workshop scripts	• Project team (core)
(2) Conduct implementation planning sessions	Workshop(s)	• Data for Implementation Plan	• Full project team
(4) Validate the Implementation Plan	Implementation Plan Validation Meeting	• Final Implementation Plan	• Full project team
6. Obtain Implementation Approval (1) Develop approval process strategy	Approval Strategy Meeting	• Detailed Approval Strategy	• Project team (core)
7. Implement the Redesign (1) Consistent periodic meetings (2) Celebrate success	Implementation Monitoring & Action Planning Meetings	• Progress reports • Plan refinements • Problem solving • Action plans • Parties	• Full project team • Interested others
(3) Conduct critical reflections	Process Improvement Meetings	• Blueprint Refinements • Bus. ops. changes	• Full project team • Business groups/teams
8. Transition to a Continuous Improvement State	Process Improvement Meeting	• Bus. ops. changes	• Business groups/teams

Figure 6.2 Facilitated Meetings and Workshops for Business Reengineering

firmed, they planned a Vision, Values, and Goals workshop, a two-day event. Participants included Joe, his staff, their staff, a cross section of the department professionals, and four customers. The outside consultant facilitated the group, a total of 24 people, and designed the workshop to meet this group's specific needs. By the end of the two days, the group had developed and agreed to:

- A Vision, Values, and Goals Statement for the organization
- The behaviors each of them would display in living the vision and values
- A set of seven measurable goals to be achieved within the next 12 months in the implementation of the vision and values

They also agreed to dates for the next workshop to review the Vision, Values, and Goals Statement, to detail an implementation plan for goal achievement, and to appoint a project director. This was the organization's first exposure to facilitated workshops. When group members were asked what they thought of the experience, one participant summed it up for the group when he said, *"I have never seen us work together so well and accomplish so much in so little time. When we tried to do this two years ago, the project went nowhere—our customers weren't involved and none of us really understood what it would take. We just weren't committed. Now we are committed at all levels of the organization with a vision we all agree to. It could not have happened any other way."*

To ensure workshop success, the facilitator had created a script for this workshop. It provided a structure that allowed the group members to think creatively and have a rich and powerful dialogue with their customers and each other. The script designed for that workshop appears in appendix E.

Issue Resolution

Every reengineering project involves a myriad of business and technical issues. Everything comes into question—current policies, business practices, current technology capabilities, timing with other changes, and so on. Without a sound process for addressing issues as they arise, the project can bog down. The project team members must establish an issue resolution process that allows them to tackle the right issues, at the right time, with the right people. Such a process includes the following steps:

Step 1: Document issues on a standard worksheet as they arise, and assign a team member to fully define, classify, and possibly resolve the issue by an agreed-upon date that meets project timelines. The project team tracks issues weekly or as needed.

Step 2: If no resolution is obtained, the person assigned to the issue (and/or the project team) develops and documents alternative resolutions. Project risk for nonresolution is assessed.

Step 3: The issue, along with proposed resolutions and risk assessment, is presented to the executive sponsor. A date for resolution is negotiated with the sponsors and the project team.

Step 4: If the issue is not resolved as promised by the executive sponsor, the project team meets with the executive sponsor to negotiate a delay in the project or to call a project halt, if appropriate.

Step 5: If the issue is resolved, the project team and executive sponsor communicate the resolution to all affected parties.

Critical Reflection Technique—Continuous Process Improvement

Throughout the project, the reengineering project facilitator and the project team should assess the project approach. They should make this assessment periodically (weekly or monthly, for example) and after key events such as workshops. Nonteam members may be invited to attend. The recommended technique is called *Critical Reflection,* and it involves asking the questions outlined below. Critical Reflection can be applied in an hour or two. The answers to the questions constitute an effective assessment on which to base improvements to the reengineering methodology and approach.

- What has happened? Describe events/processes using nonjudgmental observation of actions and behavior.
- What happened that was good? These are the actions the project team wants to reinforce and continue.
- What happened that was not good? These are the actions the project team wants to change or eliminate.

- What beliefs, attitudes, or hidden agendas did the team bring to the situation that negatively affected the outcomes?
- What could the project team have done before, during, or after the situation that would have produced more positive outcomes?
- What beliefs and attitudes could the project team have brought to the situation that would have made the outcomes more positive?
- What should the project team do the next time?
- Who is accountable for testing out these recommendations and communicating them through the project and to other projects?

From our experience with many project teams, problems center around these areas:

- Lack of preparation and follow-up. For example, teams forget to telephone invitees to ensure their attendance at a session. Or the facilitator becomes lazy, departs from the script, and loses control of a meeting.
- Assumptions made about others. Many teams are quick to assume that others understand or "see the light," only to encounter unexpected resistance. In other cases, the team assumes its solution is the best, only to find that others feel hostile and alienated.
- Not involving the right people in sessions. Without the right people, decisions are not made, information is missing, accountability is elusive, and commitment to the project falters.

The Secrets to Successful Reengineering

We have learned, sometimes through trial and error, how to successfully reengineer a business. Using the following guidelines will help your project succeed.

Starting a Team

Take the time and provide sufficient opportunities for people to learn how to work as a team. Demonstate the principles of role clarity, leadership from within, information sharing, asking questions, planning, and experimentation through short (30 minutes or less) but intense experiential exercises. Team members often see each other only at facilitated meetings and workshops. Too many teams make the mistake of beginning task work before team building is complete. In big projects, the principles of teamwork must be reinforced periodically. In one project, for example, the 28-member team, which participated in twice-monthly facilitated workshops or meetings, began every other session with a team-building exercise. If they skipped the exercise, team members were disappointed and complained to the project facilitator. In addition to reinforcing the principles of teamwork, the exercise helped them shift gears from the outside world. The facilitator must find or create, conduct, and lead discussions after these exercises so that team members can apply what they learn to the work.

Facilitating like Attila the Hun

Reengineering projects force people to make decisions they would prefer not to make. If the reengineering project facilitator is not skilled in bringing people to consensus or enforcing critical success factors, then he or she puts the project at risk. Winning the respect of and gaining credibility with session participants is crucial. Enforcing the rules of operation in an uncompromising but pleasant manner keeps people on the reengineering track even when things get tough. Expressing determination is a matter of facilitator style. It can be done quietly or loudly, but it must be done. One 25-member project team was so attuned to its facilitator's voice that, when she said "Excuse me!" to a waiter at lunch, everyone at the table stopped talking and turned to her for direction.

Making It Real by Writing It Down

Even exceptional sessions become failures if the outcomes are not documented and communicated. Consensus becomes nonconsensus if no one can reference the actual decision. Everyone always interprets a session differently. Our senses are tuned to what we want and expect to see and hear. The project team must accurately document meeting outcomes. One team member must be responsible for documentation production and distribution, and distribution dates must be established. Information that has not been captured on worksheets or easel sheets or by automation ceases to exist—don't let that happen.

Focus, Focus, Focus

Like all projects, reengineering efforts can suffer from "scope creep." If people are not focused, they will wander from topic to topic, idea to idea, implication to implication. If scope creep occurs, the project may collapse under its own weight. The reengineering project facilitator must keep the project team working within the approved project scope, keep discussions on the topic, and ensure that team members remain committed to their accountabilities.

Putting Process Above Personalities

Working as a team doesn't mean working without conflict. All of us have personality traits that can irritate others. The reengineering project facilitator must help people value each others' strengths and work effectively as a team. Effective teams have members who can work together, exchange positive and constructive feedback, and directly express their needs and concerns. There is no blaming or excuse making. Effective teams understand that members have different priorities, perspectives, and needs. The project facilitator must help team members view differences as contributing to creativity rather than as the basis for conflicts.

The Committed Fanatic

One key to reengineering project success is in middle management commitment. Executive commitment to change is much easier because most changes don't personally affect executives (at least not in the first steps). Working-level commitment is relatively easy too. Just ask most people if they want less complicated work, more control, and less paperwork. One is likely to encounter the most resistance in the middle of the organization where roles are not clearly defined. There is potential or perceived loss of power, prestige, or control; and the job itself could be eliminated. It takes a fanatically committed project director and team to tackle these "middle" issues successfully, to push for necessary changes to infrastructure, and to demand change management and training support for middle managers and staff. Eliciting their buy-in of the reengineering can be the toughest job of all.

Practicing What You're Preaching

The reengineering project must mirror the values and behaviors required in the reengineered environment. You can't force empowerment on people. You must demonstrate how empowerment works; how to make decisions you previously were not allowed to make; how to work in

171

open teams rather than in small, isolated groups. If you want people to feel that they're part of the solution, they must become involved in its design. If it's important to value workers' opinions and ideas, then start by including them in the reengineering project.

Managing Team Bias

The more people work on a project, the more committed they become. Intense involvement often creates its own biases, which can get in the way of progress. Biases shoot down ideas and stop people from listening. The reengineering project facilitator must help people recognize and control their biases.

CHAPTER 7

THE ROAD IS NOT SMOOTH—WATCH FOR DANGER

No matter how well you plan your journey or how carefully you observe your surroundings, you can expect the unexpected. A fierce storm can blow down a tree that blocks your path. A road crew can set up a detour creating backups that clog the neighborhood arteries. A nice afternoon may bring many people outside, filling the neighborhood streets with double-parked cars and jammed sidewalks, making passage slow and frustrating. The journey is not smooth for business reengineering projects either. Unforeseen obstacles can derail even the most well-organized reengineering project team. Smart business reengineers are always on the alert for danger. They actively seek out and remedy potential problems, thus avoiding full-blown crises. This chapter describes typical dangers a team might encounter and provides defense strategies and tactics to improve the chances for project success. We can divide the typical problems into these categories:
- Leadership imperfections
- Terrorists and saboteurs
- The plight of middle management
- Anguish of cultural struggle
- Project paralysis

Leadership Imperfections

As was stated earlier, executive sponsorship and commitment are critical to project success. And we expect our organization's leaders not only to do what they say, but to sustain their commitment to the project. But expectations seldom live up to reality. In our experience, most organization leaders tend to be like everyone else—they need nurturing, feedback, encouragement, and guidance. We should treat each executive as an individual who requires special attention and support. But this support can't come from above; it must come from below—from the project team positioned in the middle of the organization. If the project team assumes that the executive will remain committed after the initial excitement about the project fades, the project can get into trouble. The loss of executive sponsorship can translate into loss of funding, project delays, and weakened efforts that cannot achieve the promised benefits.

Executives are not stupid or naive. They reflect their overall culture, especially if they have grown and succeeded within the organization they now oversee. The longer the executive has been part of the culture, the more likely he is to exhibit both its good and bad characteristics. Although a new executive might bring more objectivity to his vision, he may lack an internal network and the organizational savvy to win others over to his cause. For example, one government agency was headed by a woman with a Ph.D. who was brought in from outside the organization. As an outsider without field experience who had not worked her way up the organization, it took her five years to gain credibility among her peers. In another organization, the vice president of marketing and sales had worked his way up through the organization's marketing unit, so he received enthusiastic support from marketing, but was viewed suspiciously by sales. And because he had developed and implemented the processes that were being reengineered, he was more than a little reluctant to start with a clean slate.

The imperfection of leadership occurs most frequently in four situations:
- The executive lacks the skills needed to demonstrate leadership.
- The executive suffers from "control madness."
- The executive has "runaway" expectations.
- The executive lacks the skills needed to manage change and model new behavior.

Most executives receive little or no training in leadership skills, change management, and behavior modeling. They don't know how to sponsor a business reengineering project effectively. Instead of focusing on problems, change processes, and the ambiguity of creating a new environment, they focus on solutions and immediate results. Executives with this skill deficiency tend to restrict the project's scope, negating opportunities for daring improvements. For example, a vice president in one company told the project leader, "The problem here is that we need to fix the 'Must Do' priority list for which we hold the district sales offices accountable." This means that the "Must Do" list becomes a sacred cow that can be tweaked through process improvement but cannot be reengineered to dramatically improve organizational productivity.

Many executives find it difficult to see themselves as others see them. They have trouble listening, asking questions, and seeking clarification—they feel more comfortable dictating and seeking confirmation. As one department head said, "Everybody laughs at my jokes. They were never funny before I got this last promotion." Furthermore, very few business cultures encourage people to challenge their executives. Managers tend to report what executives want to hear, which means they support executive perceptions and screen out bad news. As Rosebeth Moss Kanter often says, "You know you have succeeded in climbing the corporate ladder when nobody disagrees with what you say anymore." In one organization, the executive director complained that her direct reports "don't make decisions on their own, but continually bring problems to me for resolution." She was oblivious to her own behavior, which in fact was the root cause of her subordinates' behavior. She would often seek data or hear out a complaint concerning her direct reports and take direct action based upon what she learned. Her subordinates felt their authority was undermined, and, instead of confronting her, their response was to cease making decisions. They felt that she was likely to counter their decisions or actions without consulting them and that she was not interested in their perceptions.

Some executives simply don't know how to sponsor a reengineering project. What is executive support? What actions and behaviors are required? What messages should they relay throughout the organization? Some executives are introverts, uncomfortable with the "people" side of executive sponsorship. They are insecure about speaking to groups of either subordinates or peers. These executives tend to "blurt out" their thoughts or stumble when interacting with people. The extroverted executive, on the other hand, is comfortable talking with people, but, if not properly briefed, he or she can communicate some damaging messages. For example, two months after the start of one reengineering project, an enthusiastic executive sponsor sent out a letter stating that "now that we have tackled the reengineering of the sales process, we can move onto . . . " When the project team members read their copy of the letter, they gasped. The project was not finished. It had just begun, but now the wrong message had been sent.

A fairly common misperception among executives is reflected in their tendency to focus on reorganization—a solution that can be implemented in one action. It is easy to do—everyone can understand changing structure, slicing positions, and changing titles. One company had six reorganizations in one year, and yet the problems persisted.

Sometimes education is the problem. Executives don't understand exactly what business reengineering is and therefore may apply the term to any kind of process change. Executives often confuse business reengineering with the more gradual and incremental approach of process improvement. In one systems organization, the director insisted on creating a new organizational reporting structure in the middle of the business reengineering implementation. This did nothing to change the process and only led to more confusion and chaos.

Control-focused executives demand detailed knowledge of project plans and insist on being involved in all design decisions. Rather than sponsoring the project, they become operational project directors. This occurs when the executive sponsor distrusts those in charge of the business reengineering project. There may be logical reasons for the mistrust. In one organization, an executive vice president had to become involved with a department operation because of the skill deficiencies of the department head. After the department head was replaced, the executive vice president became angry when he was not invited to participate in reengineering meetings sponsored by the new department head. In actuality, the VP was experiencing a sense of loss because his involvement was no longer needed. He felt left out.

Control madness can also be rooted in risk aversion. By becoming involved in design and planning meetings with the project team, the executive can measure and control the risk to which he is exposed. Risk aversion can also be a significant factor in executive reluctance and delays in implementations that require large infusions of capital, downsizing, and extensive training. Risk-averse executives should sponsor process improvement projects rather than business reengineering projects.

Few business executives are pessimists. They tend to be enthusiastic optimists who believe that almost anything is possible. This natural and desirable predisposition can, however, lead to runaway expectations for the business reengineering project. In large organizations, moving to new ways of working is like moving an elephant. Persistent encouragement and prodding are what gets the elephant moving and what builds momentum once the elephant takes its first slow steps. Even though most executives know this intellectually, they still want things to happen quickly. Some executives deny the complexity of the effort. Some forget that fundamental change takes time and requires continual training and support. Change is much more than a series of simple decrees and staged events. In this same vein, some executives are truly conceptual visionaries but are not detail oriented. Sometimes, they confuse their vision with the reality of making the vision happen. Such executives must be reminded that seeing it in their minds doesn't make it real, and that much work must be done to make it so.

Executives who are rewarded for short-term performance will always push for short-term results. This creates a very short attention span that demands quick fixes. A business reengineering project typically takes 12 to 18 months to deliver its first benefits. And the pain of change becomes more intense as people try to let go of old habits and assimilate new ideas and knowledge. The ambiguity and dysfunction of this transition is not easy for an executive looking for a quick fix.

Lastly, we must recognize that executives are subject to a barrage of outside pressures that can affect a business reengineering project. Customer demands, competitive changes in the marketplace, government legislation, and other projects all demand their attention. The more reactive the culture, the more likely these pressures will disrupt the reengineering project.

Defense Strategies for Leadership Imperfections

As in football, the best defense is a good offense. Since most project teams can't choose their executive sponsor, nurturing the one you have should be addressed specifically by incorporating the following activities in the reengineering project plan.

- Have periodic meetings with the executive sponsor to discuss roles and responsibilities, expectations for the project, and other needs and concerns.
- Hold briefing sessions with the executive sponsor and other key executives to educate them on business reengineering and alternative change strategies.
- Develop and get executive acceptance of a tactical action plan that provides the executive with specific recommendations for how to act, what to say, and how to sponsor the project. The executive sponsor should fully understand that he or she must model the new behaviors expected of the rest of the organization. These behaviors and how they will be demonstrated throughout the project should be developed jointly with the project team.
- Agree on the extent and types of involvement (meetings, written/electronic communications) required to make the executive sponsor comfortable with the project team's work. As trust builds, the executive sponsor can rely more on the team to initiate interactions on an as-needed basis. However, regularly scheduled meetings and other forms of communication are best at the start. Base all communications on facts and data. Clarity and reliability in reporting progress, issues, and plans are essential to building executive trust.
- Provide for periodic updates from the executive sponsor to the project team on pressures and influences that may affect project implementation or that must be managed or integrated into the implementation plan.

Nurturing an executive sponsor requires a sophisticated understanding of the executive's specific needs and personality. It is very important that the project team does not make the executive sponsor the target of its frustrations and anxieties. Such blaming behaviors will not help the project succeed. If the executive sponsor does not perform skillfully, the team should take responsibility and ask itself, "How can we help our executive sponsor perform as he should?" The project team is responsible for providing feedback, guidance, and direction to the executive sponsor. It is the team's responsibility to manage "up the organization" actively rather than wait for direction.

Terrorists and Saboteurs

In a reengineering project, acts of terrorism and sabotage do not take the form of fire bombs and sniper fire. Political attacks, passive aggressive behavior, and unpredictable acts more accurately describe reengineering terrorism and sabotage. The difference between terrorists and saboteurs and those who react normally to the prospect of radical change is one of purpose. Terrorists and saboteurs are driven by ambition, the need to control others, and other self-centered personal agendas. When the project does not take a direction that suits them, terrorists and saboteurs attack, either overtly, covertly, or both. Terrorists and saboteurs can be very intelligent people or blundering incompetents. They are not afraid of change—in fact, many relish it, surviving and thriving on chaos. For the vast majority of people, education, communication, training, and hand-holding will reduce fear and skepticism. This is not the case with terrorists and saboteurs.

Terrorism and sabotage may not surface during the early stages of a business reengineering project. Terrorists and saboteurs take a wait-and-see attitude and may even appear enthusiastic. The problems begin when the reengineering project takes on its own momentum and gains organizational credibility and changes begin to happen. The project team must be prepared for acts of terrorism and sabotage from everywhere in the organization, even the project team, and particularly from influential and well-positioned individuals who have the ear of executives and key managers. It would be difficult to describe all the acts of sabotage that can occur, so we have chosen to describe five types of behavior that we have encountered:

- The Lone Ranger
- The Game Player
- The Opportunist
- The Technocrat
- The Pretender

The Lone Ranger

Jim was both persistent and smart. When he first heard about business reengineering, he was one of the first to promote the idea to his executive director. He arranged for the director to meet with outside consultants who could help them reengineer their operations "the right way." Jim moved the paperwork through the contracting office so a purchase order could be cut in record time. The consultants saw Jim as being eager for change, enthusiastic, and committed to the project. They recommended that he be named project manager. During the background research interviews, however, interviewees asked to talk with the consultants alone—without Jim. The message seemed to be that Jim didn't work well with people. "How can this be so?" the consultants thought. Jim appeared to be a innovator who cared about people and the organization. The project progressed and the team developed a vision for the organization using the approaches outlined in this book. A second contract was quickly approved, again due to Jim's unique ability to push things through. The consultants relied on him for information about the organization's politics—he was their ear to the inside. He called them almost daily with new information. When the project team for implementation was established, Jim was its highest-ranking member. It was his role to address political issues and work with the executive sponsor, with whom he appeared to have a very good relationship. As the team members learned to work together, share responsibilities, and start work on implementation, Jim began to withdraw his support. He missed team meetings, and he discussed the team members and the project in "private" conversations with the executive sponsor and others. He began to look for a new solution to the organization's problems. Jim clearly saw his own power waning as others gained new skills and knowledge during the implementation phase of the project. The training sessions conducted by the consultants and the work performed by the implementation team were raising organizational awareness of work group effectiveness issues and how to resolve them. Within six months, Jim had switched from promoting business reengineering to promoting another outside consultant and an organization solution that was "better than business reengineering."

Lone-Ranger Defense Strategies

Direct confrontation regarding sabotage and terrorist behavior can be very effective. Look at how the consultants handled Jim, whose need for control and recognition drove him to separate from the reengineering project. Jim is highly skilled, and the project certainly could use his knowledge and political savvy. But if he isn't the center of attention, the lone hero, he refuses to contribute. The team needed to stop the sabotage and neutralize Jim so they could proceed with their work. They did so through quiet and direct confrontation—both with Jim and with his executive director. The consultants confronted Jim privately, saying, "What are we doing to cause your negative messages to the organization and the executive director? Your actions are being interpreted by us and the team as sabotage activity. Do you want to stop this project? We need to set up a meeting with the executive director to resolve these issues." Jim denied sabotaging the project, but the confrontation warned him that others would not tolerate subversive behavior. In a review meeting with key managers and the executive director, Jim presented a "private" survey he had conducted that concluded "nothing was changed." The lead consultant asked the entire group, looking straight at them, "Given these results, then, is the conclusion that we should leave and stop the project?" The lead consultant left Jim to defend his position with the executive director and key managers, who strongly disagreed with Jim. The conclusion of the meeting was that the project should go forward. Jim was relieved of all project responsibilities and moved into another area.

The Game Player

Laura was a respected internal consultant for the product development department. She reported directly to the vice president, Joe, and had been managing the development of the department's strategic plan for almost a year. When a business reengineering project was initiated to address overall business strategy, Laura joined the project team.

The business reengineering project had been commissioned by the executive vice president to whom both the product development and market research departments reported. Due to what appeared to be scheduling problems, Joe was not available for project research interviews. The project manager assumed that he did not want to be involved in the project due to other pressing priorities. The Framework Statement, which was based on the interviews, presented several controversial findings. The project team thought the vice president should have a chance to review the results before the Framework Statement's publication. Laura volunteered to take the document to Joe, her boss. She returned it to the project team saying that no changes were necessary. When the document was published, however, Joe marched into the project manager's office and yelled, "Why wasn't this document given to me for review before it went out?! The stuff in here is absolutely outrageous! This better never happen again!" Surprised, to say the least, the project manager said with great enthusiasm, "Well, Joe, I'm so glad that you're interested in the project. I guarantee that this will never happen again. Let's talk about how you need to be involved in the project so you can give it proper guidance." Not wanting to start a blaming session, the project manager did not mention what Laura did. The next week the project team convened the first business operation redesign workshop.

Game-Player Defense Strategies

Inclusion is often an effective strategy for neutralizing a saboteur. Laura had set up the project team for a confrontation with her boss. She had been in control of the planning process and the key counselor to her boss, and she perceived that the business reengineering project threatened her position. The project team decided that the best way to manage Laura was to keep her in the project. The project manager confronted Laura privately and said, "Laura, when you didn't review the Framework Statement with Joe, it resulted in some misunderstandings. What do I need to do to ensure that this situation doesn't happen again?" The project manager put her on notice that he would not tolerate this behavior. He also learned not to trust Laura and began to follow up carefully on each of her commitments. The project manager also began meeting directly with the vice president, thus avoiding the communication gap created by Laura. Laura was always invited and included in the meetings.

The Opportunist

Jeff had been champion for the parts division on the reengineering project. Because of his stellar performance, he was promoted just before the start-up of the implementation phase. His replacement, Mike, was new to the champion role. He had field experience, and the entire team was excited and pleased to see him commit to his new assignment and enthusiastically participate in the team meetings. After several meetings, however, Mike developed a pattern of trying to shorten team meetings.

He always seemed to be in a hurry. He was very busy and let others know it, sending electronic mail messages at 11:00 at night. Then, in one meeting, Mike announced that he was not training anyone in his division on the new business practices and changes as planned. He declared, "In our division, all we have to do is send out a memo and the reference guide." Without training, the changes would not be accepted by the line organizations, and the project would suffer a major defeat. This change, along with several others made by Mike to his implementation plan, increased the likelihood of organization rejection and misunderstanding of the new practices.

Opportunist Defense Strategies

Sometimes team members have to play nursemaid to prevent saboteur behavior. It was clear to the project team that Mike wanted to impress his new boss with how fast he could move. Personal ambition and an ignorance of implementation complexities were driving Mike's behavior. The project manager first spoke with Mike directly, alerting him that his actions were going to land him and the project in trouble. He promised Mike that, if these actions persisted, the next step would be a visit with Mike's boss to resolve the issues. Mike's behavior improved for about a week. He reinstated the things he had cut from the plan, but then cut back again about a week later. This time, the project manager, with the executive sponsor's agreement, directly contacted Mike's boss to discuss the issue. Mike's behavior changed. The project team now works very closely with Mike to ensure that he carries through with the implementation as originally planned.

The Technocrat

Simon was executive director of the organization. Ann, the executive sponsor for the reengineering project, reported to Simon. Simon was sure that the people in his organization did not have the skills to reengineer the business operation. Having read several journals, he knew exactly what needed to be done. Hadn't he forced the organization to look at multimedia technology when nobody else would? He knew what state of the art was all about. Simon wanted an outside consulting firm to do the job. He was dissuaded by Ann's assurance that a consultant was helping the project team members develop their ideas. Ann participated in the vision workshop, where team members asked whether Simon was committed to change. Ann assured them that he was, but she agreed to ask Simon to join them on the last day to express his commitment to the team directly. At the close of the three-day session, Simon stood in front of the group. Before the first person finished her presentation, he interrupted, "What makes you think you have the right answer?" The room became silent. People felt stunned. Simon proceeded to expound on what a vision should look like. As executive sponsor, Ann had briefed Simon on what he should say, and he had agreed. Now, he was off on a tangent.

Technocrat Defense Strategies

When someone sabotages through what he says, it is often helpful to translate what the person has said. The project facilitator immediately understood what was happening. Simon was very bright, but he was also completely self-centered. His idea of helping was to challenge the group and tell them what he thought they needed to know. The facilitator interrupted Simon as soon as she could, saying, "So, Simon, do you want these people to disband and go home or do you want them to continue their work? From what you have said, every one of your points has been incorporated into their vision." Challenged back, Simon thought for a moment and said, "Well, of course, they should continue. They have my full support. Isn't that perfectly clear?" Rather than debate the point, the project facilitator said, "We are so happy for your commitment." From that moment on, Ann and the project manager worked closely with Simon to limit and control his involvement. They needed him, but only in carefully measured and controlled doses. The project team also received some training on how to handle difficult, intimidating personalities.

The Pretender

Timothy was the project champion for the products division. As a member of the 10-person project team, he attended most of the meetings. In the meetings, he tended to be quiet, not contributing greatly but not creating any opposition either. When asked to perform specific tasks, he willing agreed to do so. But he never met his commitments. At first the rest of the team could function without his full participation. After implementation activities began, however, Timothy's behavior became worse. The deadline for the delivery of division-specific practice cases for the training course passed without any input from Timothy. When called by the project team member in charge, he said he would deliver that day, but it was over three days before the materials arrived. This happened three times. Over 100 of the sales people to be trained were from Timothy's organization. Timothy had jeopardized the project.

Pretender Defense Strategies

Many a project team has been lulled into complacency by a lack of open hostility and resistance. Passive-aggressive behavior is insidious. It's more difficult to deal with than other types of sabotage because it's only after the fact that action can be taken. You need to use persistence and confrontation to handle passive-aggressive saboteurs. After informing Timothy of what he intended to do, the project manager went directly to Timothy's boss. Timothy's problem was simple: He had no interest in the project. He believed that the project would never be implemented, so he did only what his direct boss told him to do. Only at his boss's repeated insistence did Timothy respond to the project team's requests.

Working Effectively with Terrorists and Sabateurs

All these cases demonstrate the fact that, no matter where you work or what your project, there may be a terrorist or saboteur lurking about. They're difficult behavior to handle, but not impossible. You can work with these types of people if you assertively manage the situation. Here are some simple steps for the project team to follow:

• Keep your eyes and ears open. Look for patterns of behavior that indicate a person has a need for control or a secret, self-centered agenda.

• Directly confront the offender privately. Describe the unacceptable behavior and focus on how it affects you and the project team. Reinforce the person's role and the importance of their contribution. Ask the person, "How can we help you?" Jointly develop a plan for proceeding in which the person accepts responsibility for his or her behavior.

• If the behavior persists, do not hesitate to contact the person's boss and your executive sponsor for help. Do not tattle. Position the information as a cry for help. For example, "We are about to launch our business practices training, and we need your help to complete the training materials. We have been unable to obtain the organization-specific materials."

- If the behavior persists, and the person can be moved out of the project, do so. Sometimes appropriate feedback improves behavior; other times it does not.
- If the sabotage continues, but you cannot remove the person from the project team, seek help in improving the team's work, roles, and relationships. Carefully plan the work to minimize terrorist and saboteur activity.
- Don't get too frustrated. Team members and peer pressure can be very effective in changing behavior. Seek out skills training in handling difficult people. It is an essential part of business reengineering projects.

The Plight of Middle Management

The role of middle managers originated from the organization's need to manage growth—the need to collect, manipulate, and transmit information; to approve the work of others; to make decisions; to solve problems; and to maintain control. Too often their role has evolved into bureaucratic information handling, obstacle making, restricting, and fire fighting. Middle managers traditionally do what business reengineering projects set out to change. For example:

- Because of middle managers, inside selling requires more resources than outside selling. A project team can take three months to get approval for a $500,000 budget to redesign a business operation that generates $50,000,000 in nonvalue-adding costs annually.
- In screening information, middle managers reinterpret and translate its real meaning. In a desire to deliver palatable messages to executives, managers resist taking bad news up the line. In one company, for example, executives were told that progress was being made when, in actuality, three projects failed, costing the company millions of dollars and thousands of wasted hours. It took many missed delivery dates and budget overruns before executives began to understand the problems sufficiently to take action.
- Middle managers tend to micro-manage, causing people to attend endless review meetings and to generate nonvalue-adding reports instead of performing productive work. On one project, for

186

example, over 50 percent of the labor hours were spent justifying and reporting project activities.

- Middle managers derive power from territory or head count rather than bottom-line impact. Whether it originates from reluctance or the inability to measure, territory protection is a manager's overriding objective. In one large reengineering project, for example, significant benefits could be achieved only by eliminating a job position held by 100 people, each paid an average of $100,000 year. Doing so could have reduced the process cycle by some 13 weeks (50 percent). Yet both middle managers and executives summarily dismissed the idea.

Organizations can operate with fewer or no traditional middle managers when technology provides direct access to information, allowing people to operate as entrepreneurial groups—decentralized, close to the customer, responsive, and team based. This access includes direct communication and sharing information with those who need it. Technology enables the people who do the work to make the decisions. Physically disbursed people can act as a team, working together instead of competing.

An underlying assumption to the principles of reengineering is that employees are adults, not children. They can be trained to operate in self-managing teams or as independent individuals who assign their own work, create their own feedback systems, accept accountability for clearly defined outcomes, cross job boundaries and organization units, and know when to ask for help. Such employees need managers who say, "Call me when you need help, when you think I need to be involved. Leverage my skills and knowledge in your work. Use my hands and my brain as best fits the work." Therefore the traditional role of middle manager must give way to a new role if middle managers are to survive in our organizations. Peter Drucker said it best in a 1993 *Harvard Business Review* article,

> It is safe to assume that anyone with any knowledge will have to acquire new knowledge every four or five years or become obsolete . . . and the changes that affect a body of knowledge most profoundly do not, as a rule, come out of its own domain . . . [Therefore,] every organization has to build the management of change into its very structure. [This means] the organization must devote itself to continuous improvement of everything it does. [This means] the organization will have to learn to develop the next generation of applications from its own successes. [This means] every

organization will have to learn to innovate . . . a systematic process of introducing chaos which allows us to abandon old ways, to make way for innovation of the new. The managerial job, therefore, is to upset, disorganize and destabilize.

Business reengineering—real business reengineering—dramatically changes how an organization is managed. This fact creates tremendous resistance to change. Implementation will move very slowly unless the executive sponsors and their peers are ready to redevelop many of their managers. Even with that commitment, it takes time and support to embed the new managerial roles and responsibilities into the organization.

Middle management roles, whether staff or line, must be examined and redefined. There are four critical components of the newly reengineered middle manager position:
- Leadership
- Skill and knowledge development in others
- Continuous process improvement
- Planning and visioning

Most essential is leadership—the ability to inspire others to action up, down, and across the organization. Leadership is no longer the sole domain of top executives. Middle managers must exhibit personal mastery, bring passion to their work, and transform themselves and others into integrated, high-performance teams. They must help people unlearn their hard-earned skills, habits of a lifetime, deeply cherished values, and old and treasured relationships. They must help people transform not only their jobs and organizations, but also themselves.

Middle managers must provide the leadership for continued process improvement within the organization. They must learn the skills themselves as well as embed them into the culture through work practices and skill development of others. This cannot be accomplished by a single program, special department, or outside consultant. The middle manager's goal must be to provide fundamental, continuing, and systemic processes that monitor and ensure progress. This is crucial because business reengineering works like a pair of jumper cables—it brings new life but cannot sustain it. Only continuous process improvements can enhance an organization's effectiveness, responsiveness, and profitability so it can flourish in the long term.

Middle managers must be futurists, planning for risk and bringing people together to build shared visions of the future. They must be able to shift from a short-term to a long-term perspective. Their job is to disrupt routine, challenge the status quo, and encourage innovation. Middle managers must be accountable for the creation and proliferation of knowledge across the organization. They must be facilitators, coaches, boundary pushers, and coordinators so that others can inform, analyze, act, decide, fight fires, improve, and innovate. They must stop telling, directing, forcing, obstructing, and making others wait.

Defense Strategies for the Plight of Middle Managers

To change dramatically or eliminate jobs is a serious matter. A business operation redesign that includes such changes probably should be pilot tested before implementation across the organization. It is important to understand fully the consequences and to provide support and training to those affected. Once tested and proven viable, one strategy is to roll out the new approach across the organization all at once. Another, more evolutionary approach, is to cut over to the new business operation one unit at a time, removing people from the organization as they retire or resign. In both cases, change management experts should be involved in both the planning and implementation. The best approach for your organization depends upon many factors.

Another important strategy is for the project team to model the behavior of the new middle managers. The application of facilitation, coaching, boundary pushing, and obstacle removing as basic tactics for project implementation demonstrates the potential of this approach. When people see these new behaviors in action, it becomes easier for them to act out the new role and let go of the old.

Anguish of Cultural Struggle

Transforming an organization is not an easy task. As stated earlier, when you reengineer a business operation, you're asking people to change what they do and how they do it. But, more importantly, you're also asking them to change their values and their beliefs. Giving up a belief system is comparable to giving up an addiction. Consider smoking, for instance. There are many logical reasons to give it up—an important one being that smoking physically injures the smoker and those around him.

Yet few people stop smoking without a struggle because it's not easy and there is real pain in giving up short-term rewards for long-term gain.

An organization is made up of people who collectively create the organization's character. Organizations have a tremendous amount of inertia and resist change much more strongly than any one person within the organization. Not understanding the psychology and sociology of organizations has been the downfall of many reengineering projects. Project teams, we have seen, make three fatal mistakes:

- They believe that implementation is simple.
- They believe the solution is logical.
- They believe the vision is shared by the rest of the organization.

Mistaken Simplicity of Implementation

Most business operation redesigns appear straightforward on paper. The changes to the current organization are described in terms that everyone can understand. For example, in one organization, the project team listed the new business policies, the steps to the process flow, and supporting business practices and methods; described how the technology would support the access, display, and transfer of information among work groups; and identified the specific skills and knowledge training required to embed the new business operations. Changing policy and practices, however, challenged some fundamental assumptions that had been held within the organization for many years. These assumptions included the belief that headquarters must control field organizations, that headquarters control must extend to the product item level, and that sales goals should specify numbers sold rather than profitability of the sale. These fundamental assumptions necessitated hiring many headquarters staff people. To change the assumptions would require training field sales personnel to develop their own plans based on strategic rather than tactical guidance from headquarters. Even more importantly, it would completely redefine the role of headquarters personnel, which could result in downsizing the headquarters staff. Such changes can be achieved only by leadership at the top of the organization. Such leadership would require the executives to let go of control, to realign their own thinking, and to alter the thinking of the headquarters middle managers who controlled the processes. If fundamental business polices were not changed,

190

the new business operation redesign could not be implemented as designed.

Some people mistakenly believe that implementing state-of-the-art technology alone will improve an organization's effectiveness and solve its problems. Technology, even if it can deliver on its promised benefits (which are usually oversold), cannot cure most organizational ills—especially the problems of poor customer relationships and organization leadership. For example, a chronic problem within the computer industry is the inability of IS organizations to deliver quality systems on time to its business customers. Many IS organizations thought they could solve this problem by converting from manual programming to computer-assisted systems engineering (CASE) tools, which generate applications from structured and detailed diagrams. One typical organization installed them in all of its programming groups. However, 12 months later, only 5 percent of the tools were in use and, from a customer perspective, nothing had changed. When the lack of success with the tools was analyzed, there was a consistent pattern of poor or inadequate training in tool use; lack of integration of the tool into the total development process; and a lack of understanding by managers and executives regarding the root causes of systems problems and the ability of technology to solve their organizations' quality problems. Unless business processes are redesigned to work effectively with the technology, benefits will not materialize.

To mistakenly believe that implementation of a business reengineering solution is simple can lead, in our experience, to a focus on quick fixes. A typical response to a business reengineering implementation proposal is, "This all sounds very good, but what can we do to fix the current situation without disrupting everything or making such a large investment?" American executives seem to believe that tweaking a few processes should produce significant improvements and results that can materialize instantly. If this mentality is allowed to dominate, the reengineering team can function only as a process improvement team, focusing on incremental changes that don't create much resistance. As a reengineering team, it will fail to achieve the benefits originally promised.

Logical vs. Political Solutions

Even when they recognize the complexity of the reengineering solution, many people charge ahead without dealing with the centers of

191

power. The assumption that everyone views the organization from a single perspective is an illusion. To consider politics an obstacle to "getting things done" is to misunderstand the nature of organizations. Managing the politics of a project requires practical wisdom, being prudent, and having an expedient plan. Reengineering politics, in the positive sense of the word, is the ability to enlist others in the process of change, capturing their interest and eliciting their ownership of the benefits to come. If a business operation redesign calls for empowering the working level, it means that middle managers must let go of their decision making power. That may be logically feasible, but not easily politically feasible.

Misaligned Visions

There is a natural tendency for people and organizations to focus inward. People sometimes redesign an operation to work effectively with internal people but much less effectively with their customers. Maintaining a customer focus is crucial in all reengineering projects. An organization cannot prosper over time without satisfied customers. By helping customers make decisions that are right for them, you win their long-term trust and give them good reasons to come to you first. A successful business reengineering project aligns the customer with the organizational vision. But what happens when the people within the organization openly distrust their customers? This happened in one business reengineering project. Vice presidents, managers and sales people made negative statements about their customers in both formal meetings and in casual conversation. Because of this, the project facilitator met strong resistance to involving customers in any of the redesign work. As a result, no one was able to gauge what the true acceptance level by customers would be if the redesign was implemented. That left a cloud over the whole project. The fundamental value that customers cannot be trusted prevented the company from making a strategic change in the marketplace. Processes designed by the company to check for cheating by customers could not be eliminated even though the actual data clearly showed that, in 80 percent of the cases, the customer was right. Dramatic change cannot happen when individual and organization values are not aligned with those required of the reengineered vision.

Sometimes the misalignments are between a corporate unit and its divisions or business units. For example, one corporate unit wanted its business units to integrate their operations, thus implementing operational efficiencies throughout the entire business (such as eliminating redundant systems and administrative processing), and to increase their customer focus. However, because rewards to the unit executives were based only on "delivering the numbers" for their units, there was little incentive for the units to cooperate with each other or with the integration project team. In fact, it is senseless to expect an executive to behave in ways that do not reward him and his people.

Another misalignment of vision occurs when the project team or its executive sponsors equate the operation's redesign with its implementation. As previously stated, a business operation redesign can be created in a matter of weeks by the right people in the right circumstances. An implementation is never that simple—implementations take much longer and often cause great anguish in the organization.

Defense Strategies for the Anguish of Cultural Struggle

No magic wand can wave the pain of change away. Like wise physicians, however, street-smart business reengineers can dispense preventative medicine, diagnose early symptoms, and provide therapeutic treatment before the disease becomes terminal. Strategies include the following:

- Educate the project team in the concepts of change and change management. This includes an understanding of:
  —The stages of change and the behaviors that can affect a person's passage through those stages from denial to acceptance
  —The basic tactics for moving an organization through a cultural transformation
  —The associated techniques for managing leaders, helping people cope with ambiguity, and defining roles and meaning in the changed environment
  —The requirements and issues surrounding the principles of business reengineering and the incremental process improvement methodologies
- Learn to listen and ask questions rather than telling everyone what they should do, feel, and expect. Fine-tune project team communication skills, at the heart of which are consulting and selling skills. People up, across, and down the organization must

be taught what the project team knows. A highly skilled communicator helps people make their own, well-informed decisions with a complete understanding of all the consequences.

- If there are implementation problems that cannot be solved, then the project team must help the executives terminate the project or change its direction. Do not allow the project to become another albatross around the organization's neck. If the timing and circumstances necessitate stopping or redirecting the project, this decision must be made openly by the responsible executive sponsors. The project team must provide the climate, process, and structure so that such decisions are viewed as positive actions rather than organizational or project failures.

- To support the cultural change, be realistic about how long it takes to obtain policy change approvals, educate and train operational staff, and provide posttraining support during the first business cycle. At least half of the budget should be allocated for organizational support of this type.

- The project team members should involve everyone they can in the project. They should be willing to "cry for help" when unforeseen problems and issues arise. They should cultivate a partnership with the executive sponsors based on shared goals and responsibilities. The project team is responsible for managing its relationship with the executive sponsors and seeing that the sponsors fulfill agreed-upon responsibilities.

- The project team members should focus on how they work as intently as they focus on what they accomplish, remembering to model the behaviors appropriate for the reengineered environment. They must objectively and critically review their progress and be able to self-correct as the implementation proceeds. Above all, the project team must exemplify determination and patience. When people complain, the team should view their protests as appeals for information and support. Team members should recall their own skepticism when the project began and how they overcame it. The team must help others overcome the anguish of the cultural change.

Project Paralysis

Sometimes the reengineering team can be its own worst enemy. Problem behavior can emerge at any time. If the team has not developed processes for communicating, resolving conflict, and making decisions, then problem behavior can bring progress to a standstill. Problems are likely to originate from a lack of knowledge about the reengineering process and the fundamentals of team process. But even the best business reengineers may run into trouble in these problem areas:

- Perfectionism
- Impatience
- Dizziness of possibilities
- Letting details fall through the cracks

Perfectionism

It's a short step from perfectionism to procrastination. Perfectionists want the reengineering Blueprint and Implementation Plan to be absolutely perfect, which can result in endless refinements and time delays. On one particular project, for example, a project manager wanted the team to run a simulation with five different "what if" scenarios instead of the two originally planned. Her argument was that the additional tests might reveal something new. She wasn't wrong about that, but the additional tests would have added three weeks to an already delayed project timeline. Everyone wants the design to be complete and accurate. But quality and perfection are not the same. A quality design is sufficiently detailed so that the team members can adjust and refine the design as they proceed, not before they proceed, with implementation.

Defense Strategies for Perfectionism

The project team members must openly discuss it if they have tendencies toward being perfectionists. The team must watch for perfectionism early in the project. Talking about *how* things will be implemented before defining *what* needs to be done is a sign of creeping perfectionism. Too much perfectionism can keep the team from progressing, restricting its redesign to fixing the existing environment, not reinventing it. But be careful—a lack of detailed plans can sink an implementation.

Impatience

The reengineering project team must exhibit a patient willingness to make repeated presentations and hold endless discussions to obtain funding for the implementation effort. As the team builds its own ownership of the reengineering Blueprint, it may distrust those who don't see the benefits of what it is proposing. Team members must be careful not to blame their executive sponsors and other managers for every issue or problem that comes up. Doing so can alienate people who should become project allies. In one organization, the project team created an Implementation Plan requesting $20 million for five years. The plan provided detail for one year. The remaining years had no deliverables or time frames. The organizational leadership, suffering (not surprisingly) from sticker shock, denied the request. They would fund only one year of foundation-laying work. Having learned a lesson, the reengineering team revised the Implementation Plan and spent much more time educating senior executives about the risks and consequences of not proceeding with the project.

Defense Strategies for Impatience

The project team must understand that one of its roles is that of evangelist—continually selling the Vision and Blueprint to the organization. Organizational buy-in does not happen without active and persistent leadership from the project team. Project team members must expect others to exhibit skepticism and ask questions, just as they themselves did when the project started. The project director, as the team member connected most closely to senior management, must devote most of his or her time to working with the executives, customers, and key managers on this buy-in. That takes time and practice. It's one skill set for which many people have little or no training. Valuable techniques include formal dialogues with groups, one-on-one meetings, questions and answer sessions, educational seminars, video communications, and formal training.

Dizziness of Possibilities

Too many choices and not enough direction can create paralysis. This dizziness is likely to strike at several points in the process, one of which is during the redesign of the business operation. There may be many ways for a process to operate. Which way is best? Opinions are many, but facts are few. The team can spend hours, days, and weeks comparing the options.

Another stage that can be overwhelming is the time for presentation of the Blueprint and Implementation Plan for approval and funding. Weeks may be spent refining the presentation, deciding how much detail to present, selecting a presentation strategy, and practicing the presentation. Without hard facts, teams can spin around and around.

Another instance of paralyzing dizziness might be at the beginning of implementation. After finally receiving approval to proceed, some teams cannot reorganize themselves for smooth implementation task work. Members may either get bogged down in the endless planning of details or focus on generalities at the expense of specifics.

Defense Strategies for the Dizziness of Possibilities

Shifting from opinions to facts is one of the best ways to overcome mental dizziness. Run a simulation, conduct a walk-through, run a computer test, bring in a subject matter expert, or reexamine benchmark data to determine facts that can help narrow the possibilities. Conduct a pro-and-con analysis to evaluate risks and reassure the group that all implications of the decision have been addressed. Organize thoughts and discuss them systematically. Conduct a forced-paired comparison analysis to determine which of the possibilities is most appealing, given the choice of any two. Conduct a force-field analysis to ensure that all factors required for a successful implementation plan have been uncovered. Compare time estimates for each task to the actual time the task takes. Look for patterns and trends. Does Joe always take three extra days to complete his work? Develop a means of assessing progress and dealing with issues that appear overwhelming.

Letting Detail Fall Through the Cracks

Conceptualism is the reverse of perfectionism. Conceptualists see only the big picture and become frustrated and bored with the perfectionist's focus on details. When designs and plans lack sufficient detail, the team is left floundering, and executive questions go unanswered. A lack of detailed plans can sabotage an implementation. Every team needs a balance. Conceptual creativity is just as important as focus on detail. Typical fall-through-the-cracks problems in reengineering Blueprints include:

- Insufficient definition of business policies and practices needed to support a business process

197

- Lack of definition in a business process to such a degree that people cannot "walk through" a simulation of the process
- Lack of definition of the infrastructure and value components of the Blueprint so that the full impact of the reengineering can be estimated

Typical fall-through-the-cracks problems in an Implementation Plan include:

- Lack of delivery dates and task assignments
- Lack of follow-up to ensure quality delivery
- Lack of communication with managers and other politically sensitive acts
- Inability of team members to create training practice cases and to translate Blueprint designs into the detailed reality of methods, procedures, and reference manuals
- Lack of ability to specify automation requirements in sufficient detail so that accurate applications and databases can be generated and tested

Defense Strategies for Keeping Things from Falling Through the Cracks

Each team member must be aware of all member accountabilities in each phase of the project. They should not assume anything. The team should assign a perfectionist to coordinate task activities. It requires a talent for logistics and the willingness to continually ask the seemingly dumb questions that make people think things through and carry out plans. It requires the team to work as a unit. Studies have shown that successful military teams design and plan their work as partners, drawing on each person's skills and ideas. But when it comes time for action, there is one commander through whom everyone else coordinates and communicates. Every person takes on a specific dedicated assignment and carries it out, trusting that everyone else is doing exactly the same thing. The commander is there to follow up with each individual or subteam.

CHAPTER 8

FORM THE NEIGHBORHOOD WATCH

Business reengineering is a last resort—a strategy to compensate for years of complacency and neglect. Like the neighborhood allowed to decay around us, business operations that need reengineering are beyond repair; they require annihilation and reconstruction. In the future, upheavals of this magnitude can be prevented. In our neighborhoods, concerned citizens are taking responsibility for their own safety and community maintenance. Instead of passively waiting for solutions, they are forming neighborhood watch programs designed to increase awareness, deter crises, and build community activism. Similarly, street-smart business reengineers must form their own "neighborhood watch" to ensure continuous vigilance. Business reengineering will be successful only if the organization commits to total quality. Anything less means another cycle of chaos. Although this book is not about total quality management, step 8 of the reengineering life cycle is about embedding continuous process improvement in the reengineered business operation. We call this process *Critical Reflection* (briefly discussed in chapter 6). Critical Reflection is the savvy business reengineer's neighborhood watch program.

The true purpose of Critical Reflection is to anticipate the future by making preventative, incremental improvements to processes and products before they break or become obsolete. The Critical Reflection process contains four fundamental elements:

- *A set of measures* that provide information about how the process is performed and the quality of its outputs
- *A collection process* that gathers performance and quality information quickly and accurately
- *Analytical techniques* to help people understand what the data means
- An easy-to-use *problem-solving methodology* for generating ideas and implementing the best solutions for improving the process or product

By using the business reengineering life cycle, the reengineering team begins to model the Critical Reflection process. It begins with developing the reengineering Vision, Values, and Goals Statement and Blueprint. These two documents define the excellence criteria and the goals for processes and their products (outputs). These goals are the standards against which implementation success should be measured. They also set the standards against which process performance and product quality should be evaluated on an ongoing basis. The operational benchmark defined in the original business case for the reengineering project provides the baseline against which change is measured. If the organization achieves the excellence criteria by the completion of the reengineering

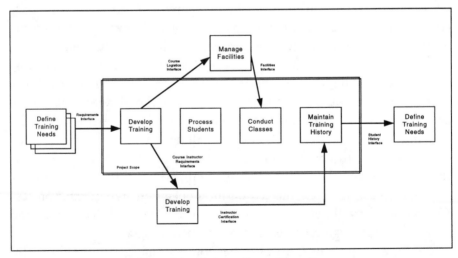

Figure 8.1   Training Center Operation

project, the project is a success. If the organization continues to achieve or exceed the criteria, then it has maintained the benefits of reengineering.

To understand what we mean by excellence criteria, benchmarks, and vision goals, let's look at a training center that wants to reengineer its processes for developing training, processing students, conducting classes, and maintaining training history (Figure 8.1). The vision for the scoped reengineered operation and the current benchmarks might be similar to the seven displayed in Figure 8.2.

Excellence Criteria	Current Benchmark	Vision Goals
Time to respond to training request	Three weeks	Two days
Time to register a student	Two days	Ten minutes
Customer satisfaction with training courses	75%	95%
Cost of training	$1,000/student/day	$250/student/day
Student access to training history	Unavailable	On-line 100% access
Accuracy of training records	50%	100%
Training effectiveness	Unknown	80% achieve increased productivity on the job

Figure 8.2 Training Center Operation Benchmarks

After the excellence criteria and vision standards for achievement have been established, business reengineers can use the Critical Reflection process to measure and improve project results as the project proceeds. This is important for two reasons: First, the project team members must determine if they are achieving their goals; and, second, they need to improve and refine the implementation process as it occurs. They must anticipate potential problems and initiate preventative measures. As modelers of new behavior for the organization, the project team creates, tests, and uses the Critical Reflection process that will be embedded into the reengineered business environment.

Critical Reflection, with its measures, collection process, analytical techniques, and problem-solving methodology, helps people:
- Analyze work in progress to ensure quality and goal achievement
- Anticipate and solve problems with the process
- Ensure customer satisfaction with results

We will now briefly examine each of the four elements of Critical Reflection. Other references, listed at the end of this book, provide further information on continuous process and product improvement techniques and measurements.

Measurement Fundamentals

Critical Reflection requires effective measurements that provide timely and accurate information that can be used periodically to answer the following questions:

- Are our customers pleased with the products and services we produce from this process (or group of processes)?
- If they are dissatisfied, what is the specific cause?
- What part of the process might indicate a potential problem, an opportunity for improvement, or a source of customer dissatisfaction?
- Should we raise our process performance or product/service quality standards?

- External measures should be customer defined.
- Internal process measures help find root causes of customer dissatisfaction.
- Quality can be quantified just like productivity.
- Measures should be based on a common unit. Always compare apples to apples.

Figure 8.3   Measurement Fundamentals

There are four measurement fundamentals (Figure 8.3). One of the basic principles of business process redesign is to get as close to the customer as possible. To put this principle in practice, a Critical Reflection process must be able to measure customer satisfaction. This external view ensures that the organization delivers the "right" products or services to the customer. Internal process measures can easily become estranged from the customer if external customer satisfaction measures are not in place. Let's look at our training center example to see the relationship between the external and internal views and how they affect the definition of measures.

In the vision for our training center, one of the criteria for excellence is the ability to respond to a request for training. To measure excellence from an external view, the standard would be based on the customers' idea of an appropriate response time. From an internal view, the standard might be based on "what the organization thinks is best" for the customer. To measure the organization's ability to respond, an external view might be the elapsed time from the initial customer inquiry to his receipt of the proposed solution. An internal view might measure the elapsed time from log-in of a written request to transmitting the written response. The first measure is customer focused; the second measure is internally focused. In the second case, even if a "quality" standard is attained, the customer could remain dissatisfied. The second measure reflects only part of what the customer experiences in interacting with the training organization. It is essential that all internal measures support the total customer experience. In our example, we use three distinct measures to measure the customer experience:

1. Elapsed time from when the customer initiates an inquiry to when the request is logged
2. Elapsed time from when the request is logged to when its processing is complete
3. Elapsed time from when the request leaves the training center to when it is received by the customer

Customer dissatisfaction with responsiveness to training requests could be sourced to any or all of the three process areas. This external/internal measure relationship is displayed graphically in Figure 8.4 for another excellence criterion, satisfaction with training courses.

Both external and internal measures are critical in measuring processes and products/services. The external perspective keeps the organization customer focused, and the internal perspective helps uncover the root causes of potential and actual problems. Some processes and products are easy to measure; others are more difficult. The degree to which operations are standardized is often a good indicator of measurability. Key outcomes and key events are good starting points.

Another important fundamental of measurements is that quality can be measured. Our belief is that, if you can't measure quality, you don't know if you have quality. The goal should be to find quantitative ways to measure quality. This is difficult in some cases but not impossible. Too

Measure	Quantity	Quality
Customer **(External)**	• % students completing courses/course • % employees (by job category) attending courses/month • Ratio of completed to canceled courses • Ratio of registered to completed course students	• % students rating program as "excellent" or "very good"/course • % of graduated students rate as "improved" or "very improved" in job performance related to training/course • % graduated students passing required job certification test(s)/course on first attempt
Process **(Internal)**	• Number of scheduled courses/month • Students fees paid/course day • Students registrations accepted/day • % classrooms booked/month	• Instructors rating course operations support as "excellent" or "very good"/month • % student materials returned for incompleteness/month • % students complaints/course

Figure 8.4   Training Center Operations
Criteria for Excellence: Satisfaction with Training Courses

often, people think quality is abstract and cannot be measured systematically. However, without concrete measures for quality, obtaining information about the level of quality is a very difficult, time-consuming process. At a minimum, quality should be measured with an overall customer satisfaction measure followed by details on factors to identify what drives that overall quality satisfaction rating. The list below provides a few examples of how the quality measure "customer satisfaction with training courses" can be translated into very specific and measurable factors.

• Percentage of students rating course materials as "usable and very usable" on the job
• Percentage of students rating course instructor helpfulness as "excellent or very good"

- Percentage of graduated students passing the job certification test on the first try (compared to the number passing who had not taken the course before the job certification test)
- Percentage of students who attended more than 90 percent of class hours
- Number of requests for the course from individuals referred by graduated students

No one item fully measures customer satisfaction, and, to provide an external view, you should base measurements on what customers tell you is important to them. For internal measures of process, you can measure quality in the same fashion. For example, you could measure the quality of the process to "develop a training course" by the number of revisions required during testing or the number of corrections required during the first six months of the course presentation. You can use regression analysis, a mathematical technique, to identify which factors (submeasures) are most influential on an overall satisfaction measure.

In summary, you can assure excellence in measurement definition by meeting these criteria:

- The measurement clearly supports what is important to the customer.
- The measurement is easy to understand and is meaningful to those who perform the process.

Meaningful measures are based on a common unit of measure so that people are comparing like items and can assess change over time. For example, the total number of students attending courses may not be meaningful. However, the number attending courses per month, the percentage graduating per course, or the student fees collected per course day can assess specific trends in attendance and customer satisfaction. Time, customers, production volume, and dollars (revenues or costs) are important bases for measurement unit definition.

Collection Fundamentals

The most well-defined measurements are useless if the data cannot be collected in a timely and accurate manner. Old data is not actionable because we need relevant timely data to assess and then correct or improve processes quickly, before damage occurs. For example, a monthly measure is useless for a daily process where day-to-day fluctuations offset profitability. The data collection timing must correlate to the process cycle timing.

In a nonautomated environment, internal process measurements may be difficult to collect without an intrusive process. For example, in a manual order-taking environment, someone must either maintain counts as orders arrive or count orders at the end of the day. Classifying orders would require time-consuming analysis of each order; then the order type would be coded and totals tallied for each type. Manual processes are also subject to errors. With automation, these measurement processes become invisible because they occur as orders are recorded. Classification, coding, and tallying are automatic, and the results can be made available hourly, daily, or instantaneously as requested.

For external customer measurements, written surveys are neither reliable nor timely. Response rates are low and usually too late to enable corrective action. Do you fill out the guest survey in the hotel room when you stay at a hotel? Most of us don't. As a result, completed surveys do not accurately reflect the hotel's guest population. The most effective way to capture customer satisfaction is through well-structured, one- to two-minute telephone surveys conducted within three to five days after the customer contact. The technique, perfected by the telecommunications industry, reliably captures accurate and timely customer feedback. Using statistical, random-sampling techniques prevents survey bias and limits the number of surveys required to obtain an accurate measure.

Another approach to data collection is to employ outsiders to pose as customers. Within 24 hours, you can provide feedback directly to those with whom your "customer" interacted. You can measure all aspects of process performance as well as product delivery quality. The airline industry, restaurateurs, and retailers have used this approach to obtain reliable, accurate, and timely customer-based measurement information for years.

No matter which approach to data collection you use, consider these fundamentals in the development and execution of the collection process.

- Clearly define accountability for data collection and presentation delivery.
- The process should be as transparent as possible and should not interfere with production work.
- The process should not skew or bias the collected data. If

processes are sampled rather than measured 100 percent, a statistically sound, random-sampling process is critical to accuracy.

- The collection process should not introduce inaccuracies or errors into the collected data. A standard, structured, and consistent collection process must be used. In automated data collection, this is fairly easy. In telemarketing survey and outsider observation approaches, people must be specially trained to deliver the survey or observe a process in a consistent, nonbiasing manner.

- The frequency of data collection and presentation must be timely. The definition of timely depends upon the processes being measured. It can vary from minute by minute to monthly.

- The collection process should deliver the measurement results to those who perform the work. When data is delivered first to bosses, the data ages and people fear the measurements will be used to punish them.

- One set of measurement data is not very useful. It is only a snapshot of reality. Therefore, measurement data must be collected systematically over time so that changes and trends can be detected.

Analytical Technique Fundamentals

The measurement data itself tells us little. We need to manipulate the data, translate it into information, so that it tells a story. You can use many statistical analysis techniques effectively. Each technique can tell part of the story. Some key techniques include:

- **Rolling Trend Analysis.** Each measurement period's results are plotted on a graph to show change over time. The term *rolling* indicates that a certain number of measurement periods are always displayed (for example, 13 weeks, 52 weeks). For each analysis, the oldest period is dropped and the newest period is added. You can use this historical trend analysis to predict the future based on the past, if nothing intervenes. The content of the trend analysis can vary. One trend might show the actual numbers or percentage of a total, the average or median for a set of measurement data. Another might show the trend variability by displaying the standard deviation of the data.

- **Trend Toward Goal Achievement.** An overlay on a rolling trend analysis focuses on progress toward achieving a certain set target. It compares the measurement results for each period against the vision goal target (Figure 8.5). For example, if the trend analysis indicates that the percentage of satisfied customers is fairly stable at 90 to 92 percent over time, but the goal is 95 percent, then the team must go into problem-solving mode. If there is no historical data available, a comparison of actual performance against the vision goal is the best place to begin measurement information analysis.

- **Standard Deviation Analysis.** A standard deviation is a statistical measure that enables you to examine the consistency of performance or quality. Over time, the average of a set of data may remain the same (customers are satisfied 95 percent). By using standard deviation analysis, you can determine whether the data variability is increasing or decreasing. The greater the standard deviation for a set of data, the greater the variability of

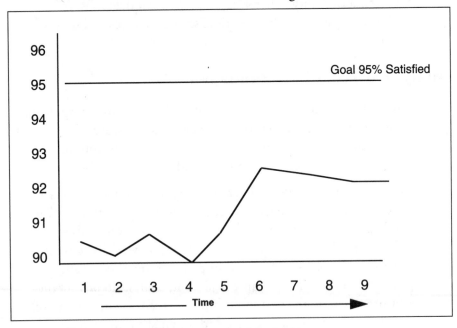

Figure 8.5   Trend Toward Goal Achievement

the data (for example, 95 percent ± 1 standard deviation has less variability than 95 percent ± 2 standard deviations). And, the greater the variability, the less predictable the performance. In other words, some customers are receiving very excellent service and some receiving less than acceptable service. This may indicate a potential problem with a process.

- **Same Time Last Year (or Last Cycle).** Some processes are subject to seasonality or cycle variations that are part of the business itself. In the retail industry, for example, most sales occur between October and the end of December. Trend analysis would be inappropriate because variations in the data are due to customer buying patterns rather than the process of selling or the quality of the product. Therefore, a snapshot comparison of one set of measurement data to a set from a similar period in the previous cycle is the best way to measure performance or quality change accurately. Seasonality, once known, can be factored out of measurement data using other mathematical techniques.

- **Regression Analysis.** Regression analysis is used to identify specific factors that may be influencing an overall measurement result. It compares the parts to the whole and each other. This provides insights for possible improvement targets. For example, regression analysis was used by a large automobile dealership with a chain of six dealers when its overall customer satisfaction rating dropped from 95 to 90 percent. The objective was to identify which aspect of the servicing experience was at fault—the service order writing, quality of repairs, timeliness, courtesy. The analysis revealed that repairs were driving the customer satisfaction decline more than any of the other service components. A recent turnover in mechanics was identified as the possible root cause of the problem.

These are but a few of the analytical techniques that can help you interpret measurement data and transform it into useful information. There are many computerized software packages to assist in the analysis. What's important is to design and use techniques that make sense for your business, your processes and products, as well as your people. People can learn to read analytical results if they are displayed in an easy-to-understand graphic format. Someone trained in statistical analysis and measurement practices can help a project team select the right measurements and analytical tools.

Problem-Solving Fundamentals

Critical Reflection problem-solving should take place on a regular basis. The team leader should call a meeting as soon as the analysis of measurement information is complete. The results should be "hot off the press." A process facilitator, who may be a team member or an outsider, should lead the meeting. This will ensure full participation of all team members as well as an efficiently conducted meeting. Critical Reflections should also be built into the redesign of the business operation to provide for it within the normal operation of the business unit. Follow the methodology outlined below. This may require from one to four hours depending upon the extent and depth of the measurement data available.

A note of caution: Early measurement of a newly installed process will be affected by the learning curve of those performing the process and the start-up problems common to a new operation. Therefore, it is important that people not become discouraged by early measurement results. Over time, with focus and effort, significant increases in quality and productivity should appear. The better the training and support at installation, the less the learning curve should affect overall results.

- **Step 1: Share the Measurement Results**
  Display the measurement results that quantify what has been happening. Summarize the interpretations of the data. Find the answer to this question: "What has happened since the last measurement period?" This may include a discussion about progress (or lack of it) toward a goal, indications of continuing trends, spikes in results, and so on. Stick to facts. Do not speculate about causes of the problems or make judgments. Write the facts on an easel board so everyone can see them.

- **Step 2: Define Accomplishments and Positive Behaviors**
  Explore what has happened since the last measurement period that could be contributing to the positive results. Give recognition to members, the team as a whole, and any others for their accomplishments and for modeling desired behaviors. Post the accomplishments and positive behaviors next to the facts so everyone can see them.

- **Step 3: Define What Has Not Worked and Inhibiting Behaviors**
  Explore what has happened since the last measurement period
  that could be contributing to negative results or that indicates a
  potential problem. Do not attempt to develop solutions. Don't
  blame people. Avoid generalizations. Give specific and clear
  examples of each incident. Post what did not go well next to the
  accomplishments.

- **Step 4: Define Inhibiting Assumptions**
  Identify the assumptions that were operational during the last
  measurement period that could have affected the measurement
  results negatively. Explore the attitudes, belief systems, and
  possible hidden agendas that could have influenced the situation.
  Post the assumptions.

- **Step 5: Uncover Potential Systemic Causes**
  Identify factors within the structural design of the process or
  product that may be contributing to the negative measurement
  results. In other words, what in the process or product itself
  contributes to the situation?

- **Step 6: Generate Ideas for Alternative Assumptions**
  With the situation fully defined, now generate a list of alternative
  assumptions people could have made that would have resulted in
  better measurement results. Focus on the people who are involved
  in the process. Do not blame others for their bad attitudes,
  behaviors, or belief systems. Post these alternative assumptions.

  If the previous steps showed that not only were the vision goals
  achieved, but there was opportunity to exceed those goals, the team
  may decide to increase the performance or product goal targets.
  The assumption alternative is that the goal targets are too low.

- **Step 7: Generate Ideas for Alternative Process Performance or
  Product Production**
  Define alternatives that could have been taken before, during, or
  after the measurement period that could have affected the
  measurement results. Generate as many ideas as possible, building
  on each other's comments. Do not dismiss an idea because it
  seems off-the-wall or impossible. Ask clarifying questions. Post all
  ideas.

- **Step 8: Construct Improvement Solution(s)**

  Create a solution to prevent negative results from recurring and to improve future results. The solution may be to tackle all or only a few aspects of the process or product—policies, procedures, tools, techniques, relationships, and so on. Then develop an action plan for implementing the solution. Be sure each team member understands and accepts his or her role. The solution should have a champion to ensure its implementation. Determine when information should be available to measure the success of the solution. Set a Critical Reflection meeting date for review of those results.

CHAPTER 9

CHARACTERISTICS OF THE SUCCESSFUL JOURNEY

As we read through the literature published on business reengineering over the past several years, we counted over 50 companies that were cited by name as business reengineering success stories. A survey of several hundred chief information officers revealed that 30 percent of the companies say they are presently using business reengineering, and 65 percent say they are going to embark on such projects within the next year. Yet, other surveys and writers consistently report that 75 to 85 percent of all business reengineering efforts do not survive or fail to meet their objectives. Another report was even more pessimistic, saying that only 1 in 10 succeed. What is the seduction of business reengineering when it is very clear that success is not easy? Is American business once again in search of the "silver bullet," the final solution? Part of the problem may be that the label, *business reengineering,* is being inappropriately applied to any kind of improvement project. Furthermore, the ability to create a radical design *quickly* is being confused within the *complexity of change* and the *prolonged time* required for implementation of such designs. Not one reported success story saw implementation succeed in less than two years from the time funding for implementation was obtained.

It is clear from our experience and the experience of others that business reengineering is fraught with obstacles. It is the nature of business reengineering to have obstacles—big, tough, challenging obstacles. If your reengineering effort is not facing strong resistance, then you have either died and gone to heaven or you do not *have* a business reengineering project. As we discussed earlier, there are other solutions to business problems besides business reengineering. On the continuum of change (Figure 9.1), business reengineering is the most extreme. That is, it has the greatest potential for disruption and anguish within the organization. Therefore, if you recommend that your organization undertake a business reengineering project, you must realize the kind of journey that you are embarking upon.

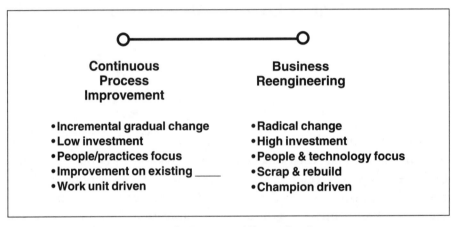

Continuous Process Improvement

- Incremental gradual change
- Low investment
- People/practices focus
- Improvement on existing ____
- Work unit driven

Business Reengineering

- Radical change
- High investment
- People & technology focus
- Scrap & rebuild
- Champion driven

Figure 9.1 The Disruption/Change Continuum

Radical change requires that the organization's track record of both successes and mistakes be challenged. It demands that people to let go of old ways (the successful reliable ways); leave the comfortable and the familiar; open themselves up to the potential of growth; and become learners, not blamers. This does not happen overnight. It takes patience, many consistent messages, lots of education, and sometimes some very hard-nosed direction to people at many different levels within the organization. When people do start letting go, they begin to listen instead of defending the status quo and attacking the messengers. Only then can people create a vision based on the future rather than the past, commit to the development and enrichment of people in the organization, make the required infrastructure changes to support the new environment, and invest in the technology that lets people make decisions and act on those decisions.

Few people are going to welcome you and your message of radical change. Knowing this will prepare you for the initial rejection. You are promoting unpopular ideas and rocking the boat. You have to turn the objections into opportunities and fulfill people's need for more information, for more understanding. The resistance you will encounter comes from legitimate as well as unfounded fear—many people will be scared of what the change means to them individually. It is estimated that 25 percent of the 90 million job losses over the next decade will result from business reengineering. Of that total, 18–22 percent will be white-collar middle managers. That amounts to over 4.5 million jobs of a work group that makes up only 5–8 percent of the total work force. Given this scenario, it is only natural that people would react negatively to business reengineering.

Those who wish to survive must commit to lifelong learning and develop the ability to work in a state of constant change and ambiguity. Predictability is replaced with flexibility. As you begin working on your business reengineering project, you must realize that an organization that undertakes business reengineering has a responsibility to help its people make this kind of change. Business reengineering is more about people than technology and finances.

Survival Characteristics for Business Reengineers

There is no cookbook solution for business reengineering, no "winning formula" that, if applied, will guarantee success. This book can be your guide, a road map. But, as with all road maps, there are many paths from one location to another. It is up to each traveler to pick the roads that work best for him or her. As experienced street-smart business reengineers, we can provide some of the important signposts along the way—the essential characteristics of success. The rest is up to the executives who sponsor the project and the team that drives it.

Success Characteristic #1: Customers Matter Most

Whether your customers are external or internal to your organization, without customers you have no business, no reason for existing. Listen to them. What matters to them is what should matter to you. Therefore,

215

those business processes that support the customer relationship should be the focus of your reengineering efforts. Those operations include product/service design and development, manufacturing, distribution and delivery, marketing and sales, customer support and postsales service. How you work with your customers may be the only thing that distinguishes you from your competitors. Start your business reengineering project with what your customers agree is broken. Your employees and managers can provide the confirmation. With those insights, you can get "the vision thing" straight. With vision alignment across, up, and down the organization, it's easier to unleash people's creativity and mobilize them to construct a solution that is customer driven. From there, you can find the key drivers to revenues and costs. Design from the outside in— start with the customer and work backward.

Success Characteristic #2: Create and Keep Only What Is Value Adding

Most people expect a 15- to 40-percent improvement in productivity from business reengineering. That means you have to get rid of any work that does not significantly increase product or service value. Don't rely on information technology alone to do this for you. Information technology may be the cornerstone of business reengineering, but it is not the whole building. It's the people and how they use that technology that count. Are they empowered to make decisions, to work with the customer, to take accountability for both quality and quantity, and to act to resolve problems? If they aren't, you are just automating the existing mess. If you are redesigning the right processes, then you can find ways to do the work right and define the performance that is needed.

Success Characteristic #3: Lead from the Top; Work the Detail from the Bottom

An axiom in the business of selling, as we have mentioned, is that "people do not buy until they own." The same applies to business reengineering. Ownership in the solution design is required for successful implementation. Executives must target the vision with strategic direction. They must provide reality boundaries if there are any (investment dollars available, and so on), and they must be able to say "thank you" to the team that delivers the results. Professionals, whether they are managers or workers from the production line, need to define the Blueprint, which details how the whole thing will function. They are close enough to the business and the customers to know what is needed on a day-to-day basis. Create a project team made up of people from across the organization and from different levels; sprinkle this team lightly with experts in systems, facilitation, and business reengineering; and the result will be process ownership and knowledge where it is most needed. Co-opt the established interest groups. Make them part of the solution, not just part of the problem. Everyone on the team, both executives and professionals, has to be ready to make hard trade-offs among conflicting goals, keep from becoming elitists, manage internal project workings, run political interference, and be able to challenge each other without shedding blood. Reengineering should not cause a fractious organizational war. It should, however, create a crusade that forces people to look beyond their noses. Those who can't see beyond their noses must eventually leave or be asked to leave.

Success Characteristic #4: Design the Whole; Implement in Pieces

The business reengineering design is like a blueprint for a house. It defines all the details. If you're building a large and sprawling house, you can lay the foundation and then build each section, one or two at a time. In fact, many people live in the first section while the rest is being built. The blueprint ensures that the end result matches the original vision. The same applies to business reengineering. The foundation should be laid in first. That may include a new common language, a new technology infrastructure, and a simplification of past practices. Then, as each new radical change is implemented, it can be phased in as resources become available and the organization is ready to accept the change. Each phase should deliver results, providing an increasing stream of the benefits throughout the implementation until all benefits are achieved. Each phase should ready the organization for more learning and more change. Having the Blueprint keeps you from losing focus. Success is at hand when people demand to track their own performance, make their own improvements, and create an environment for continuous process improvement. This ongoing renewal is preventative health care for the organization—it prevents new disease and keeps it healthy.

Success Characteristic #5: Be Disciplined and Stick to It

There are at least six or seven "proven" diagramming techniques for business process redesign in the marketplace today. Which one you choose really doesn't matter as long as it works for you and provides the structure and discipline needed for both documentation and education. You must be systematic in your work. If you aren't, a lot is going to fall through the cracks. The methodology provided in this book will support any of the business process redesign techniques. The steps and outcomes of our methodology provide the framework for assessing, designing, and implementing business reengineering. Without a methodology, you are sure to get lost during the journey, even with a set of sound diagramming techniques, or never complete it.

Success Characteristic #6: Don't Let Consultants Do It for You or to You

As we speak, hundreds of consultants are preparing themselves to help you reengineer your business. The problem is that they may not know what they are doing. Those with an information technology expertise may want to sell you automation as a solution. Some management consultants will want you to focus on only the people issues. Others believe they have the solution for you—because they've done the same thing in an organization just like yours. These are not the consultants you want. They descend upon your organization like locusts, telling your people what to do and how to do it. Then, after piles of money and years of frustration, they slink out of the organization leaving your people to clean up the mess. But outsiders can help you where you cannot help yourself because of limited expertise and resources. The consultants you want to hire for business reengineering projects are those that act like "safari guides." They know the territory of reengineering, where to camp, how to make a gourmet meal on an open fire, how to approach beasts without being attacked, and how to survive the trip. But they know this is *your* trip, that *you* have to live with the results, and that only you can make the final decisions. This kind of consultant provides the process and structure for a reengineering project, facilitating meetings where you break with the past, and helping you challenge the resistors and create strategies that make breakthroughs. After you have your Vision and Blueprint, then, during implementation, you can contract consultants to complete specific implementation tasks—testing through simulation, building systems, developing training, writing business practices, and so on. But the delivery and installation of these products should be done by your own people. People learn more when they are asked to teach other. The message must come from within at all times.

Is There an Ideal Reengineered World?

Several authors, including us, have suggested what an ideal reengineered environment should look like. These perspectives are helpful, but should not be taken as gospel of what your organization must do to be positioned for the future. They are beacons by which your team can navigate the uncharted waters of business reengineering. These ideas should stimulate your thinking, not dictate your solution. We have summarized some of these beacons below.

Beacon: Business Strategy

Our economy, the growth of the global marketplace, and other factors indicate more volatility than stability for most businesses as they move into the future. Therefore, the past becomes less a predictor of success than the future. Historical quarterly and annual results are less important than marketplace and economic trends. Furthermore, because customers are critical to your survival, business strategy must focus on value-adding service more than cost efficiencies.

Beacon: Business Processes and Work Flows

Functional boundaries must give way to cross-functional processes and integrated, shared systems to support end-to-end processes. Even the boundaries between your customers and your suppliers and you must be redefined. If they are involved in your business (and they most certainly are), then they are now part of your organization.

Beacon: Jobs and Organization Structure

When handoffs are eliminated, jobs get bigger and have clearer accountability and more authority. Generalists replace specialists. Teamwork replaces individual work. The need for supervision (watching and controlling the work) disappears when isolated tasks are combined into a complete process that a team or individual can own. Thus managers become coaches, and organizations can eliminate hierarchy.

219

Organization boundaries disappear as people work directly with each other, not through intermediaries.

Beacon: Information Technology

Systems should be designed for thriving in uncertainty. They must be able to use a variety of technologies for their implementation. Information technology should be a shared corporate resource and not owned by one person or organization. These systems should allow the expertise of a few to be used effectively by many. They should deliver accurate, timely, portable information in meaningful formats to anyone who needs it, including suppliers and customers.

Beacon: Reward Systems

Incentive systems and rewards should support the job and organization structure. When an organization creates teams, the individual reward system should be replaced with a team-based collective reward system. Careers are made by moving across the organization, not necessarily up the organization. Rewards are based upon business results and innovation, not technical proficiency.

Beacon: Management Strategies

Employees do not need to be supervised; they need to be coached, not controlled and audited. They are adults who are willing to take accountability for their work products. Process ownership is critical, and, because processes integrate so many different functional pieces, process ownership belongs to the teams who run the process. Employees have the capability for continual growth and performance mastery if provided with the right support and developmental environment. What is good for them is also good for the business. People are most productive when they enjoy their work and relish doing it.

Beacon: Values and Culture

In the new reengineered environment, people are capable of working cooperatively, without competing with each other, because they share common goals. Customers and suppliers are members of the team. People seek out risk rather than shun it. They thrive on change and are uncomfortable with the status quo. Managers and professionals share the same values, the same ethics, and the same concerns for the organization and its people.

The Ideal Business Reengineer

Street-smart business reengineers take up the call for action. Not only do they know *what* needs to be done, they know *how* to do it. They are equipped with an insatiable curiosity for everything that has never been. They balance theoretical purity with practical realism. They know how to help people make the right decisions at the right time. They are politically astute and as persistent as commissioned salespeople. Above all, they want to create environments where employees can work to their fullest potential, so that both the organization and all who work there can reap the profits of success.

Bibliography

Anderson, Richard E. "HRD's Role in Concurrent Engineering."
  Training & Development (June 1993): 49–54.

Andrews, Dorine C., and Susan K. Stalick. "Business
  Reengineering." *American Programmer* (May 1992): 10–19.

Andrews, Dorine C., and Naomi S. Leventhal. *Fusion—Integrating
  IE, Case, and JAD: A Handbook for Reengineering the Systems
  Organization.* Englewood Cliffs, N.J.: Yourdon Press, 1993.

Bailey, George, and Richard A. Moran. "Window of Opportunity."
  Perspectives 4, no. 1: 50–57.

Barthel, Matt. "As Technology Marches, Can Banks Stay in Step?"
  American Banker (November 29, 1992): 2–3.

Brenner, Aaron. "1. Automate Your Information Flow with
  Workflow Software. 2. Re-engineer, Too." *Imaging Magazine*
  (June 1993): 23–29.

Bridges, William. *Surviving Corporate Transitions.* New York:
  Doubleday, 1988.

Broadhead, James. "The Post-Deming Diet: Dismantling a Quality
  Bureaucracy." *Training* (February 1991): 41–43.

"Business Reengineering." *Insights* 1, no. 2 (Fall 1989): 2–8.

Cafasso, Rosemary. "Rethinking Reengineering." *Computerworld*
  (March 15, 1993): 102–5.

Cafasso, Rosemary. "Re-Engineering Projects: Up, Up and Away."
  Computerworld (March 29, 1993): 92.

Carroll, Lewis. *Alice's Adventures in Wonderland.* New York:
  William Morrow, 1992.

Corbin, Lisa. "Reengineering: The Nest Management Revolution."
  Government Executive (September 1993): 26–30.

Corrid, Charyl. "Everyone's Reengineering Except the Computer
  Companies." *Computerworld* (August 30, 1993): 62.

Davenport, Thomas H. *Process Innovation: Reengineering Work
  Through Information Technology.* Cambridge: Harvard Business
  School Press, 1993.

Deal, Terrence E., and Allen A. Kennedy. *Corporate Cultures: The Rites and Rituals of Corporation Life.* Reading, Mass.: Addison-Wesley Publishing Company, Inc., 1982.

Demming, W. Edwards. *Out of the Crisis.* Cambridge, Mass.: Massachusetts Institute of Technology, 1988.

Dixon, George, and Julie Wiler (compilers). *Total Quality Management Handbook.* Minneapolis, Minn.: Lakewood Books, 1990.

Drucker, Peter F. "The New Society of Organizations." *Harvard Business Review* (September–October 1992): 95–104.

Drucker, Peter F. "The New Productivity Challenge." *Harvard Business Review* (November–December 1991): 69–79.

Ehrbar, Al. "Re-Engineering Gives Firms New Efficiency, Workers the Pink Slip." *The Wall Street Journal* (Tuesday, March 16, 1993).

Errico, Stephen G., and Anthony D. Sullivan. "Redevelop in Pieces." *Software Magazine* (December 1992): 6.

Errico, Stephen G., and Anthony D. Sullivan. "Radical IS Change: Can We Get There from Here?" *CASE Trends* (March 1993): 16–20.

Fitzpatrick, Edmund W., Ph. D. "Information Management." *Journal of the American Society of CLU and ChFC* (September 1992): 34–35.

Fraser, Bruce. "Michigan National Takes Lead in Electronic Overall." *American Banker's Management Strategies* (February 1, 1993): 12A.

Freiser, Theodore J. "The Right Start for Business Reengineering." *Information Strategy: The Executives Journal* (Fall, 1992): 26–30.

Gleckman, Howard, "The Technology Payoff." *Business Week* (June 14, 1993): 57–68.

Hall, Edward T. *The Dance of Life.* New York: Doubleday, 1983.

Hall, Edward T. *The Silent Language.* New York: Doubleday, 1981.

Hammer, Michael. "Reengineering Work: Don't Automate, Obliterate." *Harvard Business Review* (July–August 1990): 104–112.

Hammer, Michael, and James Champy. *Reengineering the Corporation: A Manifesto for Business Revolution.* New York: HarperBusiness, 1993.

Hayley, Kathryn, Jeffrey Plewa, and Michael Watts. "Reengineering Tops CIO Menu." *Datamation* (April 15, 1993): 73–74.

Hemp, Paul. "Preaching the Gospel." *The Boston Globe* (June 30, 1992): 39–40.

Hirschhorn, Larry, and Thomas Gilmore. "The New Boundaries of the 'Boundaryless' Company." *Harvard Business Review* (May–June 1992): 104–115.

Howard, Robert. "The CEO as Organizational Architect: An Interview with Xerox's Paul Allaire." *Harvard Business Review* (September–October 1992): 107–121.

Impoco, Jim. "Working for Mr. Clean Jeans." *U.S. News & World Report* (August 2, 1993): 49–50.

James, Philip N. "Cyrus F. Gibson on IS Reengineering." *Information Systems Management* (Winter 1993): 83–86.

Karlgaard, Rich. "ASAP Interview: Mike Hammer." *Forbes* (1993): 69–75.

King, Julia. "Re-engineering Repercussions." *Computerworld* (June 28, 1993): 149–51.

Kinlaw, Dennis. *Continuous Improvement and Measurement for Total Quality: A Team Based Approach.* San Diego: Pfeiffer & Company, 1992.

Korzeniowski, Paul. "Workflow Software Automates Processes." *Software Magazine* (February 1993): 73–76.

Krauss, Peter. "A Delicate Balance." *Information Week* (May 1993): 26–30.

Kunda, Gideon. *Engineering Culture: Control and Commitment in a High-Tech Corporation.* Philadelphia: Temple University Press, 1992.

Lee, Chris. "The Vision Thing." *Training* (February 1993): 25–34.

Margolis, Nell. "Re-Engineering Gets Real." *Computerworld* (January 18, 1993): 69.

Martin, James. "Reskilling the IT Professional." *Software Magazine* (October 1992): 140–141.

Marshall, Bob, and Larry Kelleber. "A Test of Restructuring Success." *HR Magazine* (August 1993): 82–85.

McDoniel, Tom. "Business Reengineering: Blind Alley or Opportunity?" Paper published by Performance Development Corporation (1991): 1–9.

McPartlin, John P. "Just Chasing Rainbows?" *Information Week* (February 1, 1993): 55.

Mehler, Mark. "Mobile Net Exec Preaches Patience." *Computerworld* (February 1, 1993): 72.

Moad, Jeff. "Does Reengineering Really Work?" *Datamation* (August 1, 1993): 22–28.

Moskal, Brian. "Born to Be Real." *Industry Week* (August 2, 1993): 14–18.

"Motorola's Great Galvin on Motorola's Magic." *Boardroom Reports* (September 1, 1993): 3–5.

Nadler, David A., Marc S. Gerstein, Robert B. Shaw, et al. *Organizational Architecture: Designs for Changing Organizations.* San Francisco: Jossey-Bass, 1992.

Nonaka, Ikujiro. "The Knowledge-Creating Company." *Harvard Business Review* (November–December 1991): 96–104.

Nopper, Norman S. "Reinventing the Factor with Lifelong Learning." *Training* (May 1993): 55–58.

Pearlstein, Steven. "A Rage to Reengineer." *The Washington Post* (July 25, 1993).

Pearlstein, Steven. "Industry's Productivity-Led Recovery Shows Promise." *The Washington Post* (July 5, 1993).

Pfrenzinger, Steven. "Reengineering Goals Shift Toward Analysis, Transition." *Software Magazine* (October 1992): 44–57.

"Picking Apart Warehouse Processes at Ford Motor Company." *Insights* (Fall 1989): 9–12.

"The Promise of Reengineering." *Fortune Magazine* (May 3, 1993): 94–95.

Ray, Garry. "Just How Do You Spell 'Re-engineering?'" *Computerworld* (March 15, 1993): 98.

Robson, George D. *Continuous Process Improvement: Simplifying Work Flow Systems.* New York: The Free Press, 1991.

Rifkin, Glenn. "Reengineering Aetna." *Forbes ASAP* (1993): 78–86.

Rubin, Robert M. "Combating Complexity." *CIO* (May 1992): 20–21.

Ryan, Kathleen D. "All About Workplace Fear—The Quality Killer." *Boardroom Reports* (August 15, 1993): 13–14.

Scholtes, Peter R. *The Team Handbook,* Madison, Wisc.: Joiner Associates, 1988.

Senge, Peter M. "The Leader's New Work: Building Learning Organizations." *Sloan Management Review* (Fall 1990).

Senge, Peter M. *The Fifth Discipline: The Art & Practice of the Learning Organization.* New York: Doubleday, 1990.

Short, James E., and N. Venkatraman. "Beyond Business Process Redesign: Redesigning Baxter's Business Network." *Sloan Management Review* (Fall 1992): 7–21.

Sisco, Rebecca. "What to Teach Team Leaders." *Training* (February 1993): 62–67.

Sobkowiak, Roger T. "Reengineering HRS to Meet Future Challenges." *The Human Resources Professional* (Winter 1991): 65–71.

Sterne, Aimee L. "Managing by Team Is Not Always as Easy as It Looks." *The New York Times* (July 25, 1993).

Stewart, Thomas A. "Reengineering: The Hot New Management Tool." *Fortune* (August 23, 1993): 41–49.

Tapscott, Don, and Art Caston. *Paradigm Shift: The New Promise of Information Technology.* New York: McGraw-Hill, 1993.

Tereske, John. "Be Customer-Driven Not Function Driven." *Industry Week* (August 2, 1993): 20–25.

Tsang, Edward. "Business Process Re-Engineering and Why It Requires Business Event Analysis." *CASE Trends* (March 1993): 8–14.

Woolfe, Roger. "The Path to Strategic Alignment." *Information Strategy: The Executives Journal* (Winter 1993): 13–22.

Wendel, Charles. "Reengineering Is a Working Tool, Not Just Another Business Buzzword." *American Banker* (June 7, 1993): 4–5.

CURRENT SITUATION ANALYSIS DIAGNOSTIC

We have created the following questions to help identify reengineering opportunities and assess whether radical change is necessary. The questions can be answered in one-on-one interviews, in focus groups of four to eight people, and through on-site observation and work counts. It is important to collect hard data as well as anecdotal evidence. You can also use these questions to benchmark competitors and best-in-class performers outside your own industry who operate similar processes.

1. What, in the business processes you perform, prevents you from satisfying your customers and creating quality products and services?

   Probe: *How much/many?   What frequency?   What trends?*

   ☐ Time delays
   ☐ Handoffs
   ☐ Transaction error
   ☐ Lack of controls
   ☐ Rigid procedures
   ☐ Exception processing
   ☐ Facility problems
   ☐ Paperwork problems

- ☐ Approval layers
- ☐ Review cycles
- ☐ Duplication of work
- ☐ Lack of standards
- ☐ Documentation errors
- ☐ Transaction volatility
- ☐ Fragmentation of work
- ☐ Inconsistent inputs to work
- ☐ Inaccurate inputs to work
- ☐ Unclear work outputs
- ☐ Incomplete work outputs
- ☐ Policy problems
- ☐ Procedure problems
- ☐ Content complexities

2. What does technology (automation, computers, communications, and so on) or lack of it do to enhance or inhibit effective process performance?
   Probe: *With customers?   With internal people?*
   - ☐ Communication
   - ☐ Information access
   - ☐ Data creation, updating, deleting
   - ☐ Decision support
   - ☐ Transaction processing
   - ☐ Outcome production
   - ☐ Information timeliness
   - ☐ Information availability
   - ☐ Performance monitoring
   - ☐ Work flow handling

3. What does the organization structure do to enhance or inhibit effective process performance?
   Probe: *How much/many?   What frequency?   What trends?*
   - ☐ Job position structure
   - ☐ Job reporting relationships
   - ☐ Job content
   - ☐ Job skill/knowledge requirements

- ☐ Job accountabilities
- ☐ Job complexity
- ☐ Organization structure
- ☐ Job groupings
- ☐ Work group relationships
- ☐ Organization type (militaristic, consensus, team based, and so on)

4. What do the reward structures (financial, nonfinancial, formal, and informal) do to enhance or inhibit effective process performance?
   Probe: *How often? What kind?*
   - ☐ Alignment/nonalignment with process performance objectives
   - ☐ Consistency of application
   - ☐ Clarity of definition/understandability
   - ☐ Relationship with actual process performance
   - ☐ Discrepancies

5. What do the measurement systems or lack of them do to enhance or inhibit process performance?
   Probe: *How much/many? What frequency? What trends?*
   - ☐ Customer satisfaction
   - ☐ Quality of process outcomes
     —Dates met
     —Consistency
     —Appropriateness
     —Accuracy
     —Completeness
     —Requested changes
     —Volumes produced
   - ☐ Process performance
     —Efficiency
     —Cost
     —Profitability
     —Accuracy
     —Errors

6. What do the management methods or lack of them do to enhance or inhibit process performance?
   Probe: *How often?   What trends?   What consistency across managers?*
   - ☐ Leadership capabilities
   - ☐ Leadership style
   - ☐ Control of decision making
   - ☐ Management style (hands-on, distant, coaching, directive, and so on)
   - ☐ Performance development support
   - ☐ Performance management guidance
   - ☐ Qualification of managers
   - ☐ Managerial experience
   - ☐ Decision style (proactive/anticipatory, cautionary, slow/fast, reactive, and so on)
   - ☐ Predictability of rule enforcement
   - ☐ Degree of subordinate involvement in decision making
   - ☐ Praise from managers
   - ☐ Punishment from managers

7. What does the culture do to enhance or inhibit process performance?
   Probe: *What kind?   To what degree of severity?*
   - ☐ Rituals, symbols and myths
   - ☐ Language
   - ☐ Attention/focus (internal, external, solution, problem, and so on)
   - ☐ What is important (people, customers, things, tools, and so on)
   - ☐ Position in industry
   - ☐ Position to customers

8. What does the political power within the organization do to enhance or inhibit process performance?
   Probe: *Key players?   How often?   To what degree?*
   - ☐ Coercive/punishment power used
   - ☐ Influencers

- ☐ Legitimate power sources
- ☐ Personal power sources
- ☐ Power styles (confrontational, subversive, and so on)
- ☐ Empowerment of subordinates
- ☐ Focus of power (for organization, personal use, and so on)

9. What do the belief systems of individuals do to enhance or inhibit process performance?
   Probe: *Key individuals?   How extreme?*
   About . . .
   - ☐ Customers
   - ☐ How things work (get done)
   - ☐ Change
   - ☐ Accountability
   - ☐ Competency of others
   - ☐ Trust in leaders
   - ☐ Products and services
   - ☐ Organization mission
   - ☐ Organization culture
   - ☐ Themselves
   - ☐ Work environment
   - ☐ Ability to influence others

INSTRUCTIONS AND PROCEDURES FOR FOCUS GROUP INTERVIEWS

You should normally set aside two to five days for focus group interviews and business operation walk-throughs during a current situation analysis. If more than one site will be affected by the reengineering project, then you may require additional time. Allow one to two hours for each interview or walk-through. Most reengineering projects require 6 to 12 focus group interviews to detect patterns in the data. Conduct additional interviews only if organizational politics dictate the necessity of touching base with additional groups to establish positive rapport or reduce hostilities.

The steps for using focus group interviews and business operation walk-throughs for current situation analysis are:

1. Construct the interview and walk-through questionnaires. For the focus group and individual interviews, select 10 to 12 questions from the Diagnosis Questionnaire in appendix A. For the walk-through, develop 10 to 12 questions on operational work flow based on your current knowledge of the business processes. You should also write an opening script introducing the project

facilitator and the purpose of the interview, assuring anonymity, and defining rules for the interview.

2. With the project team, the reengineering project facilitator selects organization groups and individuals to participate. A group should consist of peers (people at the same level in the organization or who perform the same type of work). Do not mix subordinates and superiors in the same focus groups. For walk-throughs, a mixed group may be more appropriate to get an overview of the operational process from beginning to end. For example, in a sales operation, you may hold separate focus group interviews with salespeople, sales managers, customers, and administrative support personnel. The walk-through may consist of a team that includes one salesperson, one administrator, and one sales manager to get a complete overview of the operation. Invitations to participate should come from the project director, a champion, and/or the executive sponsor.

3. Arrange for interview facilities at the site of the interview or walk-through. Find a pleasant and quiet room. For walk-throughs, use the room to preview what you will see during the operation walk-through.

4. The project team should schedule the interviews, allowing enough time between interviews to review notes and prepare for the next one. Do not schedule more than three to four interviews and walk-throughs per day.

5. Decide if a project team member will observe the interview. If so, review that member's role as observer and remind him or her that there will be time at the end of the interview to ask questions. In some cases, it is more appropriate for the facilitator to meet with the group alone. In one government agency, the internal customers of the organization being reengineered were so angry and hostile that no one from that organization could accompany the facilitator on the focus group interviews.

6. Prepare a project team member to take notes (if possible). Using a separate page for each question or observation event captures responses from each interview or step of the walk-through in one place. This makes analysis much easier.

7. The focus group leader must keep the group on track. Consensus

is not necessary. Differences in opinions should be encouraged to get all perspectives. Examples are important. Don't judge responses and welcome all contributions. During walk-throughs, let the people talk you through the operation. Ask questions when you need to. Don't try to fix a situation or offer solutions.

8. In documenting results, maintain anonymity. Identify patterns and key issues. Use examples and quotes to give definition to more general comments. Integrate walk-through data to support perceptions.

9. The project team should send formal thank-you notes to all participants. Each participant should receive a copy of the deliverable (report) documenting the interview and walk-through results.

DESIGNING AND USING FACILITATED MEETINGS

To prepare for a facilitated meeting, the project facilitator works with the project team to define specific outcomes, design an agenda, and assemble supporting materials. During the meeting, the facilitator leads discussions, keeps the meeting on track, brings the group to decision when necessary, and closes the meeting on time. The procedures for planning for and conducting facilitated meetings include five distinct steps as displayed in Figure C.1.

Plan: Making Meeting Objectives Concrete

Planning for a facilitated meeting translates the desired objectives for this meeting into a detailed agenda. For example, a reengineering project team that is preparing to ask for implementation approval may want to hold a meeting to *identify and resolve all potential problems in getting approval and funding*.

Planning consists of eight tasks (Figure C.2). To accomplish these tasks, the reengineering project facilitator asks the project team or subset of the team these questions:

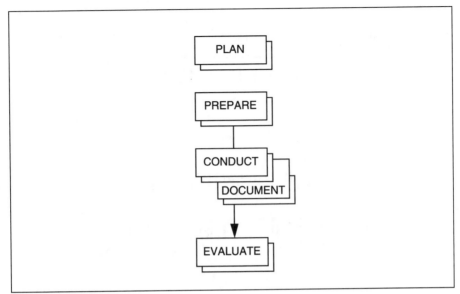

Figure C.1 Steps to Succeeding with Facilitated Meetings

- *What decisions and actions do you want to take as a result of this meeting?* The facilitator documents these questions and decisions so everyone can see them. Continuing with our example, the decisions and actions made by the end of the reengineering team meeting might include:
  1. We want to assign people to research and propose problem resolutions.
  2. We want to be able to create an executive briefing presentation that will address all potential objections.
  3. We will be able to finalize our resource and funding plan so that it is attractive to our executive decision makers.
- *What information do you need in order to make the decisions and take the actions?* The facilitator documents this information under each decision and action. For example, the data needed for the three decisions/actions in our example include:
  1. Problem description, problem type, potential solution sources and key players, problem priority, problem dependencies, date by which the problem needs to be resolved, and available people to be assigned to research and resolution process
  2. Executive perceptions and expectations regarding the project, questions executives are likely to ask, type of presentation that

will elicit and sustain executive attention, other concerns and issues competing with the reengineering effort for resources

3. Weaknesses in current plan; examples of plans that were previously approved by the same executives; possible alternatives for resources and funding; key benefits to the plan; key points in the plan to emphasize; and format, level of detail, and media for the plan document

- *Do you want a formal document from this meeting, and, if so, what should it look like?* Many meetings generate good discussions and decisions, but few produce solid documentation that people can use for follow-up. If a formal document is needed, the facilitator works with the team to identify format, level of detail, and media for the document. In our example, the facilitator and team decide that a formal document is required for only the problems. They need the following:

1. A problem book in which all relevant problem information appears, providing a basis for research and an effective

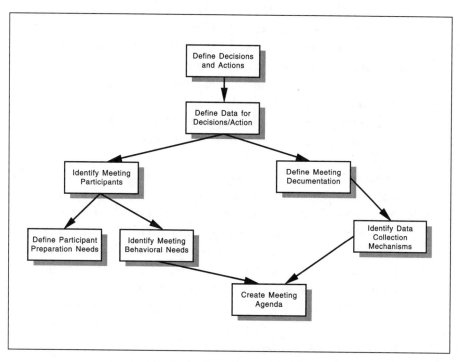

Figure C.2   The Eight Tasks for Effective Facilitated Meeting Planning

mechanism for tracking and updating efforts to resolve problems.

2. For presentation information, the information can be generated during the meeting and given directly to the people assigned to develop the presentation.

3. For the resource and funding plan, the information can be generated during the meeting and given directly to the people who will develop and finalize the plan.

- *What data collection mechanisms are needed for the meeting?* The facilitator must decide whether data collection worksheets are required, whether data can be captured on easel sheets, and whether documentation support is needed. Traditional notes taken by a secretary are meaningless in a highly structured and disciplined reengineering environment. The axiom, "If it is not written down, it does not exist" applies. Worksheets are forms that can be filled out by the meeting participants or a documentation support person. They are useful when large amounts of detailed information must be collected. Use room displays, such as easel boards and electronic white boards, when everyone needs to see what is being discussed and when the discussion does not generate so much data that the facilitator spends all his or her time writing. In our example, the facilitator decides that, because of the level of detail and probable number of problems, the problem-book information requires a worksheet for each problem. The rest of the information will be captured in room displays.

- *Who should attend the meeting?* Knowing what the meeting should accomplish tells you who should attend. If the people you need to produce the desired result(s) can't attend, cancel the meeting. One of the biggest mistakes people make with meetings is not controlling participation. If the people who can make decisions don't attend, you must repeat the meeting later. The reengineering project facilitator with the people for whom he or she is designing the meeting must take the time to identify the right attendees. Here are some guidelines. You know you have the right participants when they:

1. Have the expertise and information you need.

2. Have the authority to make decisions.
3. Can influence the rest of the organization.
4. Have busy schedules because they are critical players in the organization.
5. Are eager to attend because they recognize the importance of the meeting and their contribution.
6. Represent the right hierarchical levels and disciplines.

A facilitated meeting can have anywhere from 5 to 30 participants. The facilitator in our example decides that project team members would attend (12 people). The team and facilitator also decide to invite a manager who has recently completed a very successful project, a presentation expert from the public relations department, and two assistants to the vice president who prepare documents for his approval.

- *How should the participants prepare for the meeting?* For an important meeting, participants may need to spend considerable time (up to four hours) preparing. When you ask people to prepare, be specific. Otherwise, they are likely to misinterpret what you want or "blow it off." In our example situation, project team members must bring the latest draft of the Implementation Plan and a list of potential problems. Other attendees don't need to bring anything other than their expertise and ideas.

- *Are there any personality conflicts, behavioral problems, biases, hidden agendas, or political issues that may influence meeting success?* Knowing about the participants and the organization's politics helps the facilitator design an agenda that ensures a productive meeting. Politics and personality issues always exist and should be planned for. In our example situation, the project facilitator learns that the team includes a "griper" and a "naysayer." A political issue involves previous conflicts between the successful project manager who has been invited to participate and one of the team members.

The reengineering project facilitator is now ready to define a meeting agenda, which defines the work of the meeting. The agenda must fit into the specified time limit. If that can't be done, the facilitator must work to identify priorities. The agenda may be written out or diagrammed. The key to a successful agenda is a logical flow of topics that enables partici-

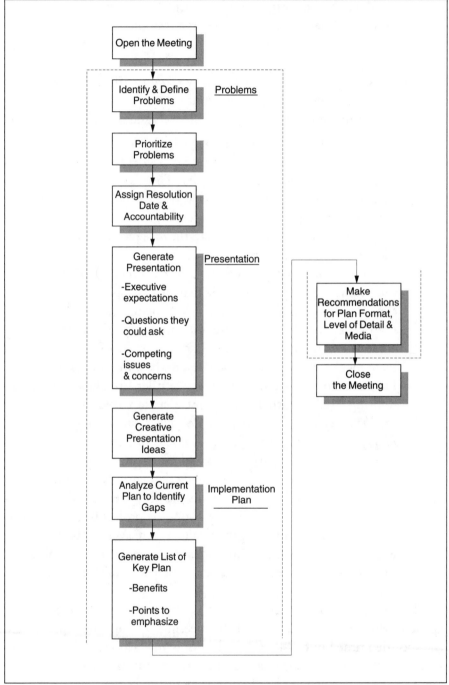

Figure C.3 Sample Facilitated Meeting Agenda

pants to meet all objectives. Every agenda also includes opening and closing topics, which are appended to the agenda's technical content. The agenda for our example situation is outlined in Figure C.3.

Prepare: Orchestrating the Meeting

You must accomplish these tasks before a meeting can begin:
- Ensure participants attend as planned.
- Create worksheets.
- Complete logistical arrangements.
- Write the meeting script.

Ensure Meeting Attendance

Here are three steps for encouraging people to attend your meetings:
1. Explain the reason for and benefits of their attendance. Help them clear their calendars. Follow up with a note thanking attendees, reminding them their attendance is critical and conveying all logistical information.
2. The day before the meeting, call to reconfirm their attendance and the meeting time. Ask if there is anything you can do to ensure their on-time participation.
3. Within five days after the meeting, send a note thanking each participant along with the meeting documentation.

To do less is to say, "Come if you like; we don't really care."

Create Worksheets

Worksheets are an effective means of collecting large amounts of detailed information. To create a worksheet, identify the data you need, lay out the data fields in the most logical order, and then test the worksheet by trying to fill it out. Leave plenty of space for people to write, and be sure to define each field clearly. In our example situation, the reengineering project facilitator designed a worksheet (Figure C.4) for documenting all problem-related information.

Complete Meeting Logistics

Logistics for the meeting involve the following items:
- Room location and size: Make sure the room is convenient, comfortable, and well ventilated.

Project Problem/Issue #: _____   Date Identified: __/__/__

Needed Resolution Date: __/__/__

Problem Name: _____
   (short name used to reference problem)

Problem Description:

Problem Type: ❏ Organization/Political

❏ Business practices

❏ Technical

❏ Other _____

Problem Priority: ❏ Resolve ASAP (critical path)

❏ Dependent on other problems #_____

#_____

❏ Eventually needs resolution (not critical path)

Problem Sources:

Key Players/Organizations Needed for Resolution:

         Name   Organization

1. _____   _____

2. _____   _____

3. _____   _____

4. _____   _____

Assign to: _____   _____ (phone)

Date for Follow-up Report: __/__/__

Figure C.4   Problem Data Collection Worksheet

246

- Room furniture: For six or fewer attendees, a rectangular table is sufficient. For more than six, a U-shaped table is required so attendees can see each other and the facilitator is close to everyone.
- Room equipment: Keep it simple. Use easel boards for room displays and an overhead projector and screen for presentation materials. Stay away from anything that requires darkening the room. You can also use computers and other related technologies, but make sure you know how to use them before the meeting.
- Refreshments: If the meeting runs over two hours, provide a coffee break. Keep coffee and water in the room so attendees can help themselves any time.
- Supplies: Supply 3 × 5 Post-Its®, water-based color markers, write-over tape, and masking tape for easel-board room displays. Use water-based pens and clear transparencies for overheads. Use a different color for each worksheet and have extra copies on hand.

Write the Meeting Script

Working from the agenda, the reengineering project facilitator must create a meeting script. Each agenda item must be expanded into a script segment containing the following information:

- Start and stop time for working on the topic
- Transition or introduction to the agenda topic
- Instructions and procedures for the work
- Documentation techniques and equipment
- Opening remarks and activities
- Closing activities

Some facilitators create their own custom worksheets for writing agendas. The worksheet in Figure C.5 provides an example of the script segment for identifying problems in our example situation.

Developing a script from the agenda generally requires the knowledge, techniques, and creativity of a trained facilitator. An amateur who unexpectedly lands the role of facilitator is not without hope, however, if he or she follows these guidelines.

- *Total group vs. subteams.* You can increase meeting productivity by initiating subteam work groups. But total group sessions are

Page _3_ of _10_

Script Segment Name: ___*Problems*___

Start Time: *11:00*
End Time: *12:00*

Worksheets:

*Problem Data
Collection
Worksheet*

Easel Displays:

1. *Forced Paired
Charts (see #3)*
2. *Grouped
Problems
(see #2)*

Materials:

☐ Sample on
Transparency

☐ Worksheet
copies for teams

☑ ___*Post-Its*___

☑ ___*Easel Sheets*___

☑ ___*Forced-Paired
Charts*___

☐ _____

Introduction/Transition:

*Tell group, "Now that the problems have been
identified, defined, and discussed, we need to
prioritize them. We will first classify them into
three priority categories, then rank those
within each category."*

Exercise/Worksheet Instructions:

*1. Divide group into subteams. Distribute
numbered problem worksheets among the three
teams. Each team should have an equal amount.
Each team must assign a problem priority and
document it on the worksheet.*

*2. After teams complete work, each team
presents the results of their prioritization. Each
problem (annotated on a Post-It) is placed on
one of 3 easel sheets marked:*
 "Resolve ASAP - Critical Path"
 "Dependent on Other Problem"
 "Eventually needs resolution"
*Other teams have opportunity to comment before
placement.*

*3. For each category conduct forced-paired
comparison exercise with total group to rank
problems within the priority group.*

Figure C.5   **Scripting Worksheet**

essential also. Total group discussions are excellent for the
following work:

—Making final decisions and setting priorities

—Generating an initial set of ideas without judgment

—Hearing different perspectives or recommendations

—Developing criteria or other lists of items

—Reviewing or validating a subteam's work

To create subteams, divide attendees into groups of four to six
people. Subteams are an excellent way for people to:

—Analyze ideas or options in detail

—Generate recommendations from which the entire group may
select

—Review or validate the work of the total group or another
subteam

—Work simultaneously on different ideas, options, problems,
and so on

When working with the entire group, the facilitator will probably
use room displays such as easel boards or assign a documentation
support person to complete worksheets as the discussion
proceeds. When working in subteams, each group should
document its discussions on worksheets as well as easel sheets.
Easel sheets and transparencies are used for presentations to the
entire group.

- *Round-robin data collection and decision making.* This basic
  technique ensures that everyone has an equal opportunity to be
  heard, influence a decision, or share an idea. The facilitator polls
  each person in the group or each subteam, asking them to present
  one of the recommendations or ideas. The rest of the group must
  listen without comment or judgment. When all the ideas are out,
  judgmental analysis and evaluation begins. This technique forces
  people to listen to each other.

- *Conducting discussions that stay on track.* The facilitator should
  establish rules of operation at the beginning of each meeting,
  create an open issue list, and conduct a bias-management exercise.
  These devices enable the facilitator to remain on the topic, while
  allowing people to comment or ask questions at any time.
  Another important technique that promotes productive

discussions is for the facilitator to help the group distinguish among generating ideas without judgment, analyzing and evaluating ideas, and implementing ideas. Too often discussions degenerate because people:

—Judge an idea without enough information

—Allow biases and assumptions to prejudice their analysis and evaluation

—Worry about how to implement a plan of action before deciding which plan is best

The facilitator needs to prevent premature judgments, confront biases, and document implementation concerns as open issues to be resolved at another time.

- *Control information overload.* Too many options, priorities, or possibilities can overwhelm a group. The facilitator should use structured techniques like pro-and-con analysis, force-field analysis, and forced-paired comparisons to focus people on priorities and evaluate the possibilities.

Conduct: Providing Facilitation Leadership

The project facilitator must accomplish four goals to guide the group:

- Unite the group
- Target the group
- Mobilize the group to consensus
- Confront problem behaviors

Unite the Group

When people walk into the meeting, they bring along baggage and biases. The skilled facilitator enables attendees to vent any concerns or issues quickly, so they can focus on the tasks at hand. The facilitator should not make value judgments or disregard the attendees' concerns. It is better to elicit comments from other participants by asking questions such as "Let's see. What's the situation in your unit, Jack?" or "Can anyone else shed some light on this issue?" What's important is to remain focused on facts rather than on judgments or emotions. In all cases, document the facts on an easel sheet as they emerge so that everyone can see them. Before proceeding, check to ensure there are no other undercover problems or concerns on people's minds.

Target Group Discussions

In nonfacilitated meetings, discussions tend to wander. Even in facilitated meetings, the project facilitator must remain alert and make a conscious effort to keep people on track. Use an open issue list to keep people focused. The facilitator also must ask simple questions to verify comprehension. This may be difficult for the facilitator with content knowledge, but it is crucial to make sure everyone understands what is being said. Paraphrasing, such as "So what you mean is . . . " works well. And always use the round-robin technique to ensure that everything is out on the table before moving on.

Mobilize the Group to Consensus

In the heat of the moment, people may become contentious, aggressively promoting their own ideas and attacking those advanced by others. The facilitator must ensure that everyone has an opportunity to be heard, building on participants' ideas and suggestions. Summarizing what people have said helps; for example, "So, if we can find a way to get Tom back into the office by next week, and Jane can get the production of the plan completed, we could get John to a meeting for final decision making. Is that what we're saying here?" The facilitator must be patient, allowing ideas and solutions to emerge spontaneously. Too often, leaders make statements such as "What we need to do is . . . " rather than asking questions that empower attendees to reach the solution themselves. Finally, when the facilitator thinks agreement has been reached, he or she must ensure consensus by asking, "Can we all live with this?" If the answer is no, then discussions should continue until consensus is reached.

Confront Problem Behaviors

Some people act in ways that create problems for the rest of the group. The facilitator must address the behavior. Depending on the circumstances, the facilitator may confront the offender in front of the group or during a break. An experienced facilitator will probably want to address the situation as it occurs. Skillful facilitators use simple, straightforward and effective techniques to confront problem behavior.

Document: Making Meeting Results Concrete

The information gathered during the facilitated meeting must be transformed to a meeting document, which should be distributed to all participants within one to five days after the meeting. As in our example situation, some information can be forwarded directly to work groups. Other times, however, it is necessary to issue a formal document. The facilitator or documentation support person must transform data from the room displays and worksheets into a readable document, easily understood by all (even nonparticipants). Some basic guidelines for documents include:

- Keep it as short and simple as possible.
- Provide a summary and table of contents at the beginning.
- Highlight follow-up requirements, noting who, what, and when.
- Use diagrams and bullet lists as well as narrative.
- Number and date every page.
- Make it professional, but keep the work "value added."

Evaluate: Learning from Experience

After more formal meetings and those that generate key decisions, the facilitator and project team should evaluate the meeting. It is very important to improve continuously the facilitated meeting approach.

DESIGNING AND USING FACILITATED WORKSHOPS

The Need for Workshops

As discussed earlier in chapter 6, the objectives for a reengineering workshop are always the following:

- Building a team
- Building consensus and common perspectives among participants
- Creating a reengineering process deliverable (such as a Vision, Values, and Goals Statement; Blueprint; or Implementation Plan)

Although a workshop is similar to a facilitated meeting, the complexity and structure of its goals and deliverables require a more sophisticated and complex design. Workshops normally run two to five days. It may not be possible to meet all objectives in less time, especially if there are over 10 participants. A successful workshop creates fundamental commitment to the reengineering project. The key to success is the synergy created between the work of becoming a team and the work of reengineering. Neither is as powerful alone.

We can use workshops to create many of the reengineering deliverables. Because of the difficulty in taking people from their jobs for two to five days at a time, however, it is best to use the workshop format judiciously. We recommend using workshops to create core deliverables: the Vision, Values, and Goals Statement; the Blueprint; and the Implementation Plan. You can use facilitated meetings and out-of-session techniques discussed in this book to supplement the workshops. The number of workshops required to produce the core deliverables can vary dramatically (from two to eight) based upon the scope of the reengineering effort and the complexity of the deliverable.

Designing a Workshop or Series of Workshops

Designing a workshop requires the same procedures used to design a facilitated meeting. The reengineering project facilitator, in concert with the project team, follows the five steps: *plan, prepare, conduct, document, and evaluate.* Preparations require additional attention, however, because the deliverables are more complex and the workshop has additional behavioral objectives. The relationship of the different pieces that go into designing a workshop or series of workshops is diagrammed in Figure D.1. The procedures for designing a workshop or series of workshops are as follows.
- Design deliverable and worksheets
- Develop the technical agenda
- Develop the workshop number, length, and content structure
- Write the workshop script

The definition of a deliverable (or set of deliverables) determines the necessary worksheets and diagrams. The deliverable also forms the basis of the technical agenda, which specifies when diagrams are built and worksheets are used. The technical agenda defines what the workshops will accomplish and what will be done out of session through other means.

Design the Deliverable Worksheets

Select the Project Deliverable Set

Facilitated workshops should be used to create three deliverables: the Vision, Values, and Goals Statement; the Blueprint; and the Implementation Plan. Two deliverables may be combined into a deliverable set. In a small project, for example, the project team may combine the Vision,

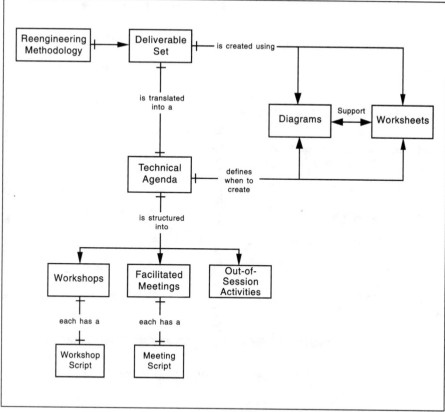

Figure D.1   Working Design Relationship Chart

Values, and Goals Statement and the Blueprint into one deliverable set, leaving the Implementation Plan as the second deliverable set.

After identifying deliverable(s) for the deliverable set, the project facilitator and the project team use the business reengineering methodology information in chapter 5 for that deliverable (Figure D.2).

Select Diagrams for the Deliverables

After the deliverable requirements have been identified through the outlining process, the project facilitator and project team select the diagrams to support the outline information. Diagram selection should be based on what works best for the project, prevailing organizational standards, and the creativity of the project team. Figure D.3 suggests some uses of diagrams based upon our experience.

Blueprint Summary Outline

I.   Physical/Technical Component

    A. Process Model
    B. Information Model
    C. Organization Model
    D. Technology Model

II.   Infrastructure Component

    A. Management Strategy
    B: Measurement System
    C. Rewards Programs

III.   Value Component

    A. Culture Precedent
    B. Power Utilization
    C. Belief Systems

Vision, Values & Goal Statement Summanry Outline

I.   Vision Statement

II.   Supporting Values

III.   Behaviors that Demonstrate Values

IV.   Goals

    A. Outcomes
    B. Excellence Criteria

Implementation Plan Summary Outline

I.   Plan Phases

    A. Team structure and roles
    B. Phase stategy, purpose and scope
    C. Objectives and measureable expected
       accomplishments for each phase
    D. Risk factors
    E. Total resource requirements and costs
    F. Expected return on investment (ROI)
    G. Schedule and timeline

(By Phase)

II.   Project Team Maintenance

III.   Communications Program

IV.   Culture Change Management Program

V.   Education and Training Program

VI.   Technology Development Program

Figure D.2   Business Reengineering Deliverables

256

Select and Customize Worksheets

Diagrams alone do not make a deliverable. Some parts of a deliverable may be in narrative form. For both, the project team and reengineering

Deliverable	Diagram Options
VISION, VALUES & GOALS STATEMENT	Matrix Diagram Decomposition Diagram
BLUEPRINT	
I. Physical/Technical Component Process Model	Matrix Diagram Decomposition Diagram Dependency Diagram Data Flow Diagram State Transition Diagram Decision Table
Information Model	Entitiy Relationship Diagram Entity Table
Organization Model	Matrix Diagram Decomposition Diagram
Technology Model	Graphical Pictures Matrix Diagram
II. Infrastructure Component	Matrix Diagram
III. Value Component	None
IMPLEMENTATION PLAN	Matrix Diagram Decomposition Diagram Dependency Diagram

Figure D.3   Suggested Diagrams for Business Reengineering Deliverables

project facilitator need to define the data required and create worksheets to capture the data. All information for the deliverable must be defined and have a capture point. Worksheets help people record exactly the information they need, whether it's from a workshop discussion or an out-of-session phone call.

Select Standards and Tools for Deliverable Production

Large projects may involve more than one person in deliverable production. For the Blueprint, for example, different subteams may complete different portions. When different people produce different parts of one document, standards and conventions become very important. The project team must develop standards for:

- Type fonts and sizes
- Page margins, headers, and footers
- Use of boldface, italics, and so on
- Symbology for diagrams (boxes, circles, arrows, labeling)
- Graphics and diagram sizing
- Printing (laser, dot matrix)

Automated tools can be used before, during, and after workshops to create and maintain the deliverable. Automated tools can range from simple word processing and graphics software to more sophisticated technology such as computer-assisted systems engineering (CASE), which can support the modeling diagrams and data collection. Automated project management tools can support the Implementation Plan. Most projects will require a combination of automated tools, so it is important that the project team be able to make informed decisions. Skillful application is important, and the learning curve is quite steep for some of the more sophisticated technology. If the team decides to use a tool that none of the members is experienced with, build learning time into the production schedule.

Technical Agenda Development

The technical agenda translates the deliverable set into a project itinerary for the reengineering project facilitator. The technical agenda defines what will be done in workshops, in facilitated meetings, and in out-of-session activities. It is not an agenda for a single workshop. There are five topics that a technical agenda may cover (Figure D.4). Each topic creates a logical grouping of content and a natural break point for the work. Since a technical agenda can be created to support almost any project deliverable, these topic areas are a useful way to classify deliverable content information.

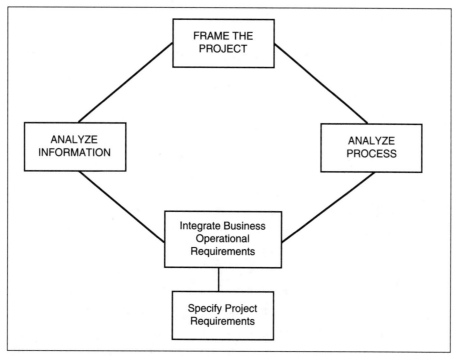

Figure D.4 Technical Agenda Areas

For the topic area *Frame the Project*, the purpose of the agenda work may be to:

- Generate or validate the project scope, boundaries, and size
- Define problems, opportunities, impacts, or issues
- Identify relationships among existing systems, processes, geographic locations, business units, problems, opportunities, impacts, or issues
- Create business mission and vision statement, goals, criteria for measuring goal achievement, and/or statements of policy and strategic directions
- Recommend directions for business change, technological improvement, planning needs, and so on
- Prioritize any of the above

For the topic area *Analyze Information*, the purpose of the agenda work may be to generate, validate, and/or define details about:

- Current and/or future business information needs

- Current and/or future business rules to drive the use of the information
- Access needs for information maintenance, manipulation, retrieval, or transformation
- Technology needs for effectively using information

For the topic area *Analyze Process,* the purpose of the agenda work may be to generate, validate, and/or define details about:

- Current and/or future business processes required to operate the business
- Dependencies and relationships of the processes based upon time, work flow, information flow, or event triggers
- Resources (technology, job positions, equipment, and facilities) for efficient process operations
- Business practices needed for efficient process operations
- Measuring the effectiveness of the process production
- Data transformed and manipulated in the process operation

For the topic area *Integrate Business Operational Requirements,* the purpose of the agenda work may be to generate, validate, and/or define details about:

- Organization structure and job configurations
- Technology requirements
- Infrastructure requirements
- Value requirements

For the topic area *Specify Project Requirements,* the purpose of the work may be to generate, validate, and/or define details about:

- Implementation strategies and requirements
- Problems, opportunities, impacts, and so on

Task 1: Select the Topic Areas Needed to Produce Project Deliverable Set

The first step in creating the technical agenda is to select the topic areas required to produce the deliverable set. Some technical agendas include only one topic area; some include all of them. Figure D.5 shows how the three reengineering core deliverables map into the technical agenda topic areas.

	Vision, Values & Goals Statement	Blueprint	Implementation Plan
Frame the Project	✓	✓	✓
Analyze Information		✓	
Analyze Process		✓	
Integrate Business Operational Requirements		✓	
Specify Project Requirements			✓

Figure D.5   Deliverable Topic Area Relationship

Task 2: Sequence the Topic Areas

The second step in creating the technical agenda is to sequence the topic areas. Figure D.6 shows the two most probable sequencing paths for the Blueprint work. To determine whether to choose to analyze information before or after process analysis, use the following factors:

• Orientation of the participants: People who think in terms of linear steps and transactions may find it difficult to examine their information needs before knowing the processes they will perform in the reengineered environment.

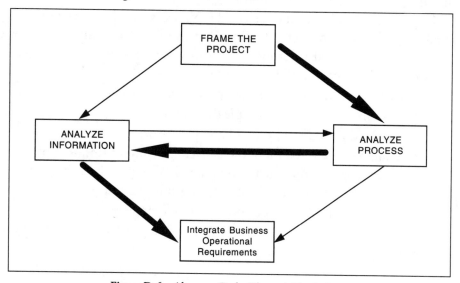

Figure D.6   Alternate Paths Through Topic Areas

- Type of business functions subject to the reengineering: Some business operations are focused on information access and use. Others are very transaction oriented.
- The need to break people away from their current process environment: Performing information analysis first may assist in accomplishing that break.

It is important to address the business operational requirements after both process and information needs have been identified. For example, you should design the Blueprint infrastructure component of management style, measurements, and reward programs after the redesign of the business operation, not the other way around. Or, for example, do not restructure the organization before redesigning the processes and defining technology requirements. Changing the boxes on the organization chart may feel like an accomplishment, but nothing can change until the processes themselves are redesigned.

Task 3: Identify Workshop, Meeting, and Out-of-Session Activities

All, part, or a combination of the reengineering deliverables (Vision, Values, and Goals Statement, Blueprint, and Implementation Plan) may be developed from one technical agenda. In most cases, the technical agenda is delivered through a combination of workshops, facilitated meetings, and out-of-session activities.

Review the technical agenda selected topic areas and the previously created project deliverable set. Identify what should be accomplished in a workshop, a facilitated meeting, or out-of-session activity. For example, the workshop sessions should be used for:

- Discussion and consensus making among participants
- Decision making with multiple decision makers
- Examination and resolution of complex issues
- Building the foundation of the deliverable content (for example, the Blueprint, Implementation Plan, or Vision, Values, and Goals Statement) to which individuals and subteams can add detail
- Integration of differing perspectives into a single solution
- Detail development by multiple people and groups simultaneously
- Speedy definition and development

- Creating ownership and buy-in from the people who must supply the information or live with the solutions

Use facilitated meetings for:

- Validating and finalizing work done in workshops
- Follow-up on issue resolution

Work that is best done out of session by the reengineering core support group or subteams of workshop participants includes such activities as:

- Preparing a first draft to focus discussions in a workshop session
- Completing diagrams or worksheets started in a workshop session
- Developing draft diagrams based on workshop outcomes that will be validated in subsequent workshop sessions or facilitated meetings
- Reviewing workshop outcomes to identify issues that must be resolved in workshop or facilitated meetings

The time between workshops and facilitated meetings can be anywhere from two to three days to several weeks. The interval should allow the project facilitator and project team to bring closure to the previous workshop or facilitated meeting, prepare for the next workshop or facilitated meeting, and perform out-of-session activities. Some of the activities that typically occur between workshops, in addition to those previously listed, include:

- Documenting workshop outcomes and communicating them to the session participants
- Researching open issues
- Creating the script for the next workshop or facilitated meeting
- Constructing a prototype, model, or simulation from the workshop outcomes
- Preparing materials for the next workshop or facilitated meeting
- Briefing the executive sponsor(s) and other key managers
- Making a decision to change the schedule or stop the sessions

Task 4: Detail the Technical Agenda

The work of the first three tasks results in a technical agenda such as this:

Vision, Values, Behaviors, and Goals
Technical Agenda

Introduction to visioning

Facilitator defines what a vision is and why it is important, the characteristics of a vision, and how to develop a vision.

Materials: Overheads, easel preboards, and handouts.

Develop vision statement

Subteams generate draft vision statements. Each team presents their draft vision statement; then facilitator works with the total group to develop a single vision statement integrating the best of each statement.

Materials: Easel sheets.

Define vision behavior

Facilitator presents examples and divides the group into subteams to identify the vision behaviors their team(s) should be exhibiting. Each team shares results with total group. Total group reviews the behaviors for final agreement.

Materials: Easel sheets and Post-Its®.

Roles/accountabilities definitions

Facilitator introduces need for specific role accountabilities and provides examples. Subteams develop top five to seven accountabilities for each possible work unit. Each team presents to the total group and the total group reaches consensus on these accountabilities.

Materials: Preboard easel sheet and easel sheets.

Practicing the vision behaviors

Facilitator sets up the "future drama," reviews the feedback guidelines for the process interrupts that can occur during the drama, and then begins the drama. After 60 minutes, the facilitator debriefs the experience with the total group and shows how the vision behaviors can be applied immediately in today's environment.

Materials: Handouts, 4 x 6 colored index cards.

Future drama is based upon a situation that could arise in the organization. The background description should not be more than two pages. Each role personality should be defined in a paragraph.

Goal setting	Facilitator defines what goals are, how to set them and provides examples. Total group divides into subteams to develop three to five goals. Each team presents its goals. Facilitator assists group to develop a composite list of top-priority goals. Then, subteams take one or more goals to flush out the excellence criteria. Total group reviews each goal and its excellence criteria. Facilitator assists in getting group to reach consensus. Materials: Overheads, handouts, preboard easel sheets.
Finalize Vision, Values, and Goals Statement	Project team assembles materials into a readable, draft document. Each participant reviews the draft. Group comes together under the direction of the facilitator to make revisions and final changes.

The technical agenda should specify the following:

- How information will be collected (room display or worksheet)
- Whether the work will be done as a total group or in subteams
- What exercise structure and/or diagrams will be used to complete the work
- What process decisions may be needed before, during, or after the work

For the out-of-session activities, the technical agenda should indicate:

- Who is responsible for the work.
- Exercise options for completing the work.

Task 5: Calculate Workshop Number, Length, and Content Structure

The technical agenda identifies what needs to be accomplished in workshops, meetings, or out-of-session activities. However, it does not usually indicate the number of workshops required, workshop length, or workshop content. To answer these questions, conduct an analysis using the insights and information from Figure D.7.

A number of factors affect workshop length. The earlier in the project the workshop is conducted, the more time people need to learn how to work as a team, build a common language, and create a common set of agreements for the deliverable content. For example, it may take a group three days to agree on a vision statement of one or two paragraphs. The

---

The *length of workshops* (in days) is influenced by these factors:
- Time of workshop in relation to total project timeline
- Risk-aversion nature of organization culture
- Elapsed time available for project
- Number of distinct organization units impacted by project

The *number of workshops* is influenced by these project complexity factors:
- Number of business processes within project scope
- Diversity of those business processes
- Relationship of organization units to business processes
- Project deliverable extent and level of detail

Figure D.7   Workshop Calculation Factors

same group, later in the project, may be able to redesign an entire set of processes for their business in the same time frame.

The more intense the organizational politics, the more likely you will encounter mistrust, hostilities, and territorial behaviors. People will need more time and support so that they can change their behavior and begin working as a team. In a systems organization being reengineered, for example, at the beginning of project work, the six unit supervisors did not speak to one another except when their manager was present—it was a competitive battleground.

The more risk adverse the culture, the more time and support will be required to make people feel comfortable making decisions outside the bounds of "the ways things are done today." You must reassure session participants that they will have a role in the reengineered organization and that their ideas are important to its future. Organization policies and practices often don't encourage or reward innovative or "out-of-the-box" thinking or actions. For example, in a government agency project, participants were so cynical about change that the first half-day of each session was set aside for venting and creative thinking exercises. This added extra days to the reengineering sessions.

The less time there is for workshops because of project deadlines, the longer each workshop should run and the less time there should be between sessions. An initial workshop should last three to five days. You can add subsequent facilitated meetings of one or two days or additional workshops of three or more days. Approximately three hours are required at the start of each subsequent session before content-sensitive decisions can be made. Workshops minimally require one hour at the beginning and end of the technical work for opening and closing activities. Facilitated meetings normally require 15 minutes for opening activities and one hour for closing activities.

The greater the number of distinct organization units impacted by the project, the more participants there will be. More participants means more time required for total group discussions and consensus making. It takes 25 people longer to reach consensus than it does six. But limiting participation to reduce session length violates the critical success factor of *involving those directly affected in the decision making.*

The complexity of the project largely determines the number of workshops and facilitated meetings required to complete a technical agenda. The more complex the organization and deliverable, the more sessions required to complete the work.

The average business has 10 to 15 major business processes, each consisting of three to five supporting processes or subfunctions. If the project addresses over three to five of the major processes, multiple workshops will be required to develop the Blueprint. If all the project processes are within a supporting process, but there are over five smaller processes within the scope, there may also be a need for multiple workshops for the Blueprint. For example, if the project includes 30 distinct subprocesses within the major process of filling customer orders, project complexity is high.

The more diverse the principal business processes, the more complex the project. More time will be required for workshop participants to develop a common language and understand each other's business needs and issues. If integration of business processes is not required, then you can use separate workshop sessions to address each major process. If all the project processes are within a single major business process, then the project will be less complex. For example, if all the processes within a project scope relate to planning, designing, and developing computer systems, then diversity complexity is fairly low. But, if the processes within the project include order processing, account management, and customer support, diversity complexity is high.

The relationship of the organization units to the business processes is also a measure of complexity. The more organizations involved in executing a single business process, the more time it will take to simplify relationships and processing and resolve power and control issues. A matrix of the organization units to business processes illustrates this complexity. For example, if the customer service process is supported by 15 different divisions, then organization relationship complexity is high.

Of the three reengineering deliverables recommended for development through workshops, the Vision, Values, and Goals Statement is the least complex or detailed. One-, two-, or three-day workshops or two days at the start of a longer workshop that also begins work on the Blueprint should be sufficient. On the other hand, developing the Blueprint requires considerable detail and the completion of nine distinct work segments. Anywhere from two to six workshops may be needed, depending on other complexity factors. The Implementation Plan requires detail, but its level of detail tends to be the same regardless of the specifics of the project business redesign. One to two workshops are normally required for its development, depending on other complexity factors.

After analyzing project complexity, the reengineering project facilitator and project team can estimate how many workshops and facilitated meetings are required to produce their project deliverable set and how long each session will take. The next issue is which session should address which item on the technical agenda. This multiple workshop session structuring and sequencing are most often necessary for the Blueprint work. Production of the other two deliverables is more straightforward—one session creates the draft document; the second finalizes the deliverable.

There are two basic approaches for multiple workshop content sequencing and structuring: the waterfall approach (Figure D.8) and the umbrella approach (Figure D.9). They can be used separately or together. The waterfall approach is used to produce an integrated solution for a large project. The project processes can be divided into separate process redesign modules, and there is a core process (or set of processes) which, when completed, provides the essential project solution. The umbrella structure is intended for large projects with diverse business processes that do not require extensive integration but use much of the same information. Customer organizations do not overlap extensively, and no single process dominates or is more critical than the others. In this case, resources must be available to provide inter-session communication. Because the workshops and facilitated meetings accelerate the design process, either approach is appropriate for short time frames; however, the umbrella may be the quicker of the two.

Workshop Script Writing

After defining the number, sequence, and content of each workshop, the reengineering project facilitator can write the scripts for each workshop and facilitated meeting. Don't write all the scripts before the first workshop. Write the first script, conduct the workshop, evaluate the results, and then write the next script. This prevents a lot of nonvalue-adding rework.

Writing a script for a workshop is very similar to writing a script for a facilitated meeting. Timing, pacing of events, participant interaction, team building, and behavior support exercises are added to the technical agenda. Script writing is a visualization process. Like an athlete in training, the reengineering project facilitator envisions an ideal workshop and then documents the vision in a script. The workshop script provides a detailed road map against which the facilitator can measure accomplishments and self-correct in the real-time environment. The script should be sufficiently detailed so that any trained facilitator could take over if necessary. See chapter 6 for an example of a workshop script to support the development of a Vision, Values, and Goals Statement.

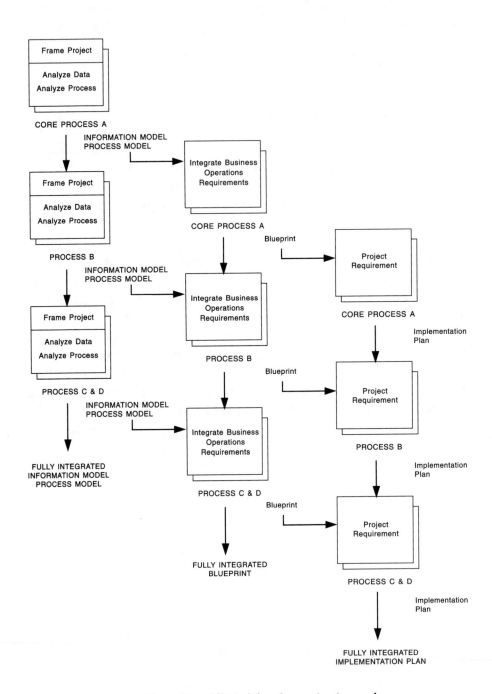

Figure D.8   Waterfall Workshop Sequencing Approach

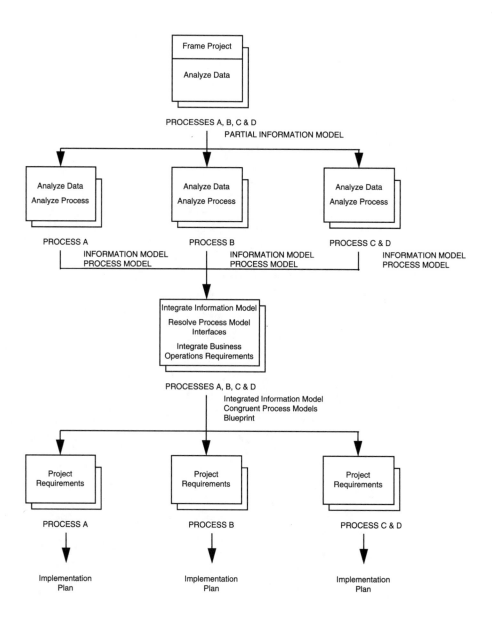

Figure D.9   Umbrella Workshop Sequencing Approach

THE JEFFERSON COMPANY DESIGN DEPARTMENT VISION WORKSHOP SCRIPT

Topic	Instructions
DAY 1	
Create the Workshop Environment 8:30–9:45	**Executive Sponsor:** Opens the workshop with welcoming remarks. Thanks the customers for taking the time to participate in this workshop with the team. Also states that this is one of the steps the organization is taking to create a partnership relationship with the other business departments. Talks briefly with everyone on what brought everyone to this workshop, that the group is here today to look to the future, not the past. Turns the meeting over to the facilitator.

Topic	Instructions

Facilitator:
Introduction

Introduces self and explains how the group will be working as a whole part of the time and how it will be working in subteams part of the time. Tells the group, *I'll have you introduce yourselves by subteam. Since you know each other, we need to make this more interesting and "loosen up" a little before we get started. As I give you your place card, which is annotated with your subteam designation, tell us what you do and what one thing you would take with you if you were marooned on a desert island and why. I'll start with myself. My name is Diana Smith, my job is facilitator and business reengineering project designer. I would want my mobile telephone with me so I could talk with people and call for help.* Facilitator conducts introductions.

Review Meeting Objectives　　(Easel)

Review the project objectives and the objectives for this workshop. The project technical objectives are:

- ☐ Create a vision for what the organization wants to become over the next three to five years.
- ☐ Define the role of the organization within the company.
- ☐ Identify the values and behaviors that will be supported and rewarded.
- ☐ Define our customers' role in planning for, developing, and managing our design and drafting products.

Topic	Instructions

☐ Define roles and accountabilities for these groups:
—Customers (exec. committee, dept. heads, managers, professionals)
—Executive team (VP and direct staff)
—Group managers
—Professionals

☐ Define measurable goals for achieving the vision, including the identification of process redesign efforts.

☐ Develop an action plan strategy and plan for transitioning the organization to the new vision.

☐ Identify and resolve organizational issues.

The latter two objectives will be covered in following workshop.

There are also behavioral objectives to be achieved as we work. These include the following:

☐ Change from event to process orientation.

☐ Develop inclusion, anticipatory, and active commitment behaviors.

☐ Develop self-correction behavior.

Discusses need for:

• "I" behavior instead of blaming behavior.
• Recognizing that if we want things to happen we have to be ready to "pick up" for others that don't follow through (that's helping each other as a team).

Topic	Instructions

- Not making assumptions; we need to ask questions.
- Recognition of the importance of selling skills in our work as design specialists.

Workshop Agenda (Easel)

Reviews overall two-day agenda.

Housekeeping

Reviews start and end times, breaks, and luncheon arrangements.

Rules for Operations (Easel)

Reviews how meeting will be run and the guidelines the group will follow:

- ❑ One conversation at a time
- ❑ Everyone is equal (the ability to influence the final decision)
- ❑ Be specific, give examples
- ❑ Five-minute rule
- ❑ Manage your biases

Open Issues (Easel)

Discusses how open issues will be boarded and reviewed at the end of the workshop.

Participant Roles

Reviews with the participants each of these roles and why they are important.

- ❑ Facilitator
- ❑ Decision maker

Topic	Instructions

☐ Subject-matter expert
☐ Advisor

Reminds the group that no one should play devil's advocate. *There are plenty of perspectives here. If you have a doubt or a question, express it directly. If you need clarification, ask a discovery question like, "Tell me why you say that."*

Bias Management Exercise

Has teams complete the bias management exercise, "Different People, Different Thoughts."

Introduction
Visioning
9:45–10:15

Facilitator: (Handouts) (Overheads)

Tells the group, *Regardless of your current capabilities or lack of capabilities, your ability to lead can be enhanced only by the strength and clarity of your vision for the organization. It is your vision that engenders trust, that allows you to take risks, that empowers you and others, that is the message you communicate, that keeps your focus on the future and shapes the culture of your organization. Without a vision, you can only manage. With a vision, you can lead no matter where you sit in the organizational hierarchy.*

By projecting yourself in the future and imagining outcomes that you want—that you really want—and sharing them with others, you are "articulating a vision." We all have expectations of the future, either positive or negative. For too many of us, these expectations are unconscious and are the results of our beliefs and past experiences. We have allowed our minds to go into a

Topic	Instructions

"rinse" cycle and we become reactive. This is why the results we get so often are the same results we always get, whether or not they are desirable. There is much truth in the axiom "you get what you want."

We can, however, harness this natural tool. We can create the outcomes and results we want by intentionally visualizing or picturing specific goals that we want to accomplish as individuals and as members of a team. While seeming quite simple, this process of purposefully picturing the outcome or results that we want, if done with regularity, has a powerful impact on what happens. Good athletes use this technique frequently.

The Wallenda Effect is the term coined to describe what happens when we visualize what we don't want. Karl Wallenda was one of the greatest tightrope walkers of all time. Although he usually concentrated on making it across the wire, the night before he fell to his death he expressed concern about falling. By focusing on what he did not want to happen, it is assumed he made it happen.

When we intentionally create a vision of the outcomes and results we want, the way to get there seems to announce itself. We find ourselves reprogramming our thinking so that we are "sorting" for helpful ways to bring about the desired results. We focus on the tightrope, not the fall. Provides group a personal example of visioning and asks the group to contribute their own experiences.

Vision is very different from goals and objectives. Goals and objectives are predictions of what we are going to do in the next week or month or

Topic	Instructions

quarter to get to our vision. The vision must come first. It provides the foundation for goal setting that is based in the future and not the past.

A vision is a dream created in our waking hours of how we would like the work to be.

Reviews with the group **"Characteristics of a Vision."** (Easel)

Visions, like leaders, come in all shapes, forms, and sizes. But those that are most effective generally meet these criteria.

(Handout)

Hands out copies of sample visions and asks people to read through them. Asks the group if these visions meet the criteria. Discusses the responses.

This is just the beginning for you. As you develop your visions, don't constrain yourselves. Be as creative as you can. As Tom Peters has said, "Developing a vision and values is a messy, artistic process . . . The process of discovery is personal and the essence of the art of managing and leading in chaotic times . . ."

Provides instructions for creating the vision. (Easel)

❏ Each subteam will construct a vision statement and set of values that support the vision statement (60–90 minutes).

❏ As a total group, share all the visions and integrate them into a single vision.

As you work, remember this: (Easel)

❏ Forget about being number one.
The wish to be on top reflects a myopic self-interest to get ahead. It does not belong

Topic	Instructions
	in your vision statement. Your vision expresses the contribution you want to make, not what the external world is going to bestow on you.
	❏ Don't be practical.
	We live in a pragmatic culture in which we have been taught to set specific measurable objectives and to have a work plan that shows how we are going to meet those objectives. Our desire to be practical works against the creation of a vision.
	❏ Begin with customers.
	Your long-term survival depends on how well you stay in touch with and serve your internal and external customers.
	❏ Talk about how you treat and work with each other.
	There is nothing wrong with the golden rule.
	❏ Don't be afraid to be embarrassing.
	Provides each subteam with easel sheets and markers for documenting its statements on easel sheets. Reminds people to reference any materials they think appropriate, including old vision statements, work from earlier sessions, and the handouts.
Develop Draft Visions 10:15–11:15	Subteams work. Facilitator monitors groups.
Develop Single Vision 11:15–12:00	**Facilitator:** **Vision Readouts** Each team presents its vision statement and set of values to support the vision.

Topic	Instructions

Integration into Single Vision

Manages the discussion and development of a single vision statement and set of values.

Lunch
12:00–1:00

Defining Vision
Behavior
1:00–3:00

Facilitator: (Worksheet) (Overhead)

Tells the group, *The next step in our visioning work is to define the behaviors we want to see in this future environment. These behaviors will show us that the vision has become a reality. To do this we need to reorganize our subteams.*

Has the participants regroup into these sub-teams:

   (1) Customers and executive team
   (2) Group managers
   (3) Professionals (may be two teams of five
        or six)

Tells the group using the overhead, *As was defined in the current analysis, your organization has three business processes that it performs. The task of each team is to define the behaviors we should see for each team (group of people) as they perform these processes.*

Walks group through an example using the overhead. For example, for group managers a vision behavior might be—when pressured with too much work, the manager calls the other group managers to a team meeting to discuss priorities and resource alignments.

Tells the group, *Each team will work on some-one else's behaviors; then the affected subteam will have an opportunity to enhance them. The assignments are:*

Topic	Instructions
	• (1) defines professional behavior • (2) defines customer and executive behavior • (3) defines group manager behavior Teams can use the worksheets. Posts final results on an easel sheet. Provides 60 minutes to work. **Behavior Readouts Round 1** Each team shares its results with the total group. **Team Enhancements** Each team now gets to review its own "defined" vision behavior. Makes additions, changes, deletions. Provides 15 minutes for this. **Behavior Readouts Round 2** Each team now shares the updated results with the total group and gains consensus on final list of behaviors.
Role/Accountabilities Definition 3:00–4:30	**Facilitator:** Tells the group, *Now that you have vision, values, and expected behaviors, it is time to define the specific accountabilities we want people to commit to in each of the process areas. By accountable, I mean that a person or team of people will publicly commit to and have their performance measured by the ability to carry out the accountabilities. Let's go through several examples:*

Topic	Instructions

Provides these examples using an overhead:

(Overhead)

☐ The executive team is accountable for strategic planning and priority setting with the customer departments.
☐ Professionals are accountable for ensuring that all customer requests for changes to existing products or the development of new products are managed and quickly put into the change management process.
☐ Group managers are accountable for resolving all intra-organization issues.

Each team develops three to five top priority accountabilities for each appropriate functional area. They work with Post-Its®—one accountability to a Post-It®. Post-Its® are placed on the overall easel chart (that looks like the supporting worksheet) at the front of the room. Provides 45 minutes to do this.

Accountability Finalization

Conducts discussion to integrate the responses into a single, agreed-to accountability list.

Closure for Day
4:30–5:00

Facilitator:

Day's Accomplishments

Reviews accomplishments of day.

Evaluation

Has each person complete the end-of-day eval-

Topic	Instructions

uation. *On separate index cards write the answers to these questions:*

- ☐ *What is it that you really appreciated about today?*
- ☐ *What is it you want me to focus on tomorrow?*

DAY 2
Start-Up
8:30–8:45

Facilitator: (Easel)

Agenda Review

Reviews today's agenda.

Feedback on Evaluation Comments

On easel, displays and reviews evaluation comments of the first day.

Practicing the
New Vision Behaviors
8:45–10:00

Facilitator: (Handout) (Easel)

Tells the group, *I believe it is important for everyone to understand how to apply the vision to their daily lives. I am going to provide you this opportunity through a 'Future Drama.' Some of you will have a role in the drama; others will be part of the Greek chorus. Through this drama we can see how the vision works in real life and provide examples to use on the job.*

Tells the group about the drama, the players, and the roles they will play. The roles are:

- ☐ The Marketing Vice President
- ☐ Customer Service Rep, who receives an emergency call from a department manager
- ☐ The group manager who has one problem

Topic	Instructions

☐ The operations manager
☐ The group manager who has another problem
☐ A professional who reports to a group manger

Distributes the situation background and role descriptions to everyone. Tells everyone, *The goal is to act out the drama using the new vision behaviors and role accountabilities you defined yesterday. Each player should do whatever he or she thinks is best. The rest of you, the Greek chorus, can hold up a sign for me to interrupt the action if you think a nonvision behavior is occurring. If I interrupt, the Greek chorus must redirect the actor's behavior so that it is visionary. Then, given that guidance, we'll resume the action.*

Feedback Guidelines   (Easel)

Discusses basic feedback techniques:

☐ Use "I" statements, not "you" statements.
I couldn't understand what you said; **not** *You aren't making any sense.*
I'm worried about meeting the deadline; not *You haven't given me the information I need.*

☐ Avoid these traps.
—*Acting like a "parent" and lecturing*
—*Should ... ought*
—*Always ... never*
—*The imperial "we"*

☐ Tell people the behavior you see; don't make assumptions.

285

Topic	Instructions

I have observed that you have missed the last two meetings we have scheduled; not You don't care about what we are doing.

❐ Ask questions instead of making statements.
What do you see as the key factors to solving this problem? **not** *These are the factors we must consider in solving this problem.*

❐ Explain the consequences of actions or nonactions instead of threatening.
The impact of not testing with your staff this week is a two-week delay in installation; **not** *If you don't give us your staff to test this week, we won't deliver for two weeks.*

The role-play drama should take about 60 minutes.

Facilitator:

Leads the debriefing discussion asking these questions:

❐ What did it feel like to act out an unfamiliar role? For those of you who do play those roles in real life, what was it like to watch?

❐ What did you see occurring as the play progressed?

❐ What skills and actions were taken to help solve the problem?

❐ What vision behaviors were difficult? Which were easy?

❐ What are the implications of the drama for implementing your vision?

❐ What are the implications of the drama

286

Topic	Instructions

for your work in the current environment?

Goal Setting
10:00–12:00

Facilitator: (Overheads)

Tells the group, *Goals and objectives are the links between vision and the new environment. Goals clarify expectations about what needs to be done to help the organization make the transition into the vision environment. Goals give direction to individuals and teams for planning and executing change. Goals tell us what we need to do. As such, goals must be measurable.*

Without goals we are like Alice in Wonderland: "Cheshire Puss, would you please tell me, please, which way I ought to go from here?" "That depends a good deal on where you want to get to," said the Cat. "I don't much care where," said Alice. "Then it doesn't matter which way you go," said the Cat. "So long as I get somewhere," Alice added as an explanation. "Oh, you're sure to do that," said the Cat, "If you only walk long enough."

Reviews the overheads with the group:

- ☐ Why goals?
- ☐ Purpose of goal setting
- ☐ Components of a goal
- ☐ How to write a goal
- ☐ Pitfalls of goal setting

Provides several easel board examples: (Easel)

Topic	Instructions
	Output: Budget
	Excellence Criteria: — Approved by end of year — Requires no more than two revisions — Uses the correct format — Costs are 95 percent of preceding year
	Output: Change management process for operational systems
	Excellence Criteria: — Each release contains six months of changes — Every change request classified/costed within 72 hours of receipt and customer notified — Content of release negotiated at facilitated meeting with customers — Release costs less than current operation — Customer agrees that no changes processed until next release date
	Output: Facilitators
	Excellence Criteria: — All group mangers trained in facilitation techniques by end of year

Topic	Instructions

— Four professionals formally trained in Joint Application Development (JAD) techniques
— JAD process used for three major products for requirements, logical design, test planning, or implementation planning by end of year.
— Facilitation performance goals in each manager's performance plan.

Board for Excellence Criteria: (Easel)

Those things that make goal quality measurable:

• What standards must be met?
• Who needs to be involved?
• What relationships must be maintained?
• What quantities must be achieved?
• What schedule must be met?
• How accurate must the work be?
• Who must be satisfied? (Give approval)
• Within what budget must the work be accomplished?

Reminds group that they are setting goals for vision implementation. These goals may include current technical or project work or may stand alone (e.g., enhance our design methodology, develop a customer orientation program).

Topic	Instructions
	Develop Goals Has subteams work 60 minutes to develop three goals to share with the total group. **Reach Consensus on Goals** Manages goal readouts and integration of goals into a single agreed-to set. Teams may have to reconvene to finish or enhance goals before the session can end.
Lunch 12:00–1:00	
Critical Reflection 1:00–2:00	**Facilitator:** Tells the group, *High-performing teams and organizations have the ability to self-correct as they work. They continually improve the process of their work. Today, you will learn how to conduct a Critical Reflection session. You can then go back to the job and begin to use it immediately. Your assignment is to use it at least twice before the Implementation Plan workshop next month and report what happened and what improvements you were able to make.* Reviews Critical Reflection steps. (Handout) (Overhead) **Team Critical Reflection Work** Subteams conduct Critical Reflection for 45 minutes. **Critical Reflection Feedback** Each subteam reports "what we are going to do next time."
Workshop Closure 2:00–2:30	**Facilitator:** Reviews and assigns open issues.

Topic	Instructions

Boards next steps and dates:

☐ Document production and distribution.
☐ Implementation Plan meeting.

Executive Sponsor:

Thanks everyone for coming. Makes closing remarks. Ends the workshop.

INDEX

benefits statement, 131-32
key activities, 132-34
pilot tests, 130-31
simulations, 128-30
statement of purpose, 127-31
tips and techniques, 134

R

Reengineer, ideal, 221
Reengineering
  benefits of, 8-9
  dimensions of, 2-8
  ideal environment for, 219-21
  infrastructure dimensions, 3, 5-6
  physical/technical dimensions,
    3-5
  signs of need for, 9-12
  situations found during
    diagnosis, 12-13
  successful, 169-72
  survival characteristics for,
    215-19
  value dimensions, 3, 6-8
  when appropriate, 8-13
Reengineering principles
  continuous process-
    improvement, 35-40
  process redesign, 20-27
  transformation, 27-34
Reengineering teams, essential
  nature of, 72-75
Reengineering team structures,
  77-84
  advisory members, 82-83
  business specialist, 85
  core coordination and support
    members, 80-81

executive sponsorship, 77-79
financial specialist, 86
implementation SWAT groups,
  83-84
IS/IT specialist, 85-86
knowledge coordinator, 86
project champions, 81-82
project director, 80
project facilitator, 84-85
project operations manager, 84
Regression analysis, 209
Resources for projects, 57-58
Reward programs, operation
  redesign, 112-13
Reward structures, 5-6
  diagnostic for, 231
Reward systems, 220
Risk-aversion nature of culture,
  59-61
Robson, George D., 61, 62
Rolling trend analysis, 207-8
Root cause analysis, 60, 69

S

Saboteurs, 179-86
  defense strategies for, 185-86
Scatter diagram, 68
Schotes, Peter, 61
Scoping projects, 50-54
  common culture and, 52
  criteria for, 51-53
  inputs and outputs, 53-54
  vision and, 52
Scripts
  meeting, 247-50
  writing, 269
Senge, Peter, 28, 29, 40, 49

modeling behavior, 29-30
reengineering principles, 27-34
time needed for change, 32-33
Tunnel vision, 47-48

U

Umbrella workshop sequencing,
   271
Unbiased facilitation, 154

V

Value-adding, 216
Value dimensions, 3, 6-8, 113-17
Values and culture, 220-21
Vision, creating, 41-43
Vision, values, goals statement
   key activities, 100-102
   outcome, 100
   statement of purpose, 99
   tips and techniques, 102-3
Vision and scoping project, 52
Vision idolatry, 46-47
Vision session, 100

W

Waterfall workshop sequencing,
   270
Work-flow diagram, 63
Work flows, 219
Worksheets, 245, 254-58
Workshops. *see* Facilitated
   meetings;
Facilitated workshops